The Fiction of Postmodernity

The Fiction of Postmodernity

Stephen Baker

EDINBURGH UNIVERSITY PRESS

This book is dedicated, with love,
to my parents,
Kenneth and Nancy Baker.

© Stephen Baker, 2000
Edinburgh University Press Ltd
22 George Square, Edinburgh

Typeset in Monotype Apollo
by J&L Composition Ltd, Filey, North Yorkshire and
printed and bound in Great Britain by
Creative Print and Design, Ebbw Vale, Wales

A CIP Record for this book is available
from the British Library

ISBN 0 7486 1088 X

Contents

Acknowledgements

Thanks are due, primarily, to the supervisor of my Ph.D. thesis in the English Literature Department of Edinburgh University, Randall Stevenson. Without his advice and generously tempered criticism, my thesis and this book would never have been completed. I would also like to thank the staff of those libraries in which much of the research involved was carried out: Edinburgh University Library, Edinburgh Central Library, the Andersonian Library, and the National Library of Scotland. A version of the section on Alasdair Gray's *Something Leather* was previously published in *The Glasgow Review*, 3 (1995).

Friends and colleagues at the Departments of English in both Strathclyde and Edinburgh Universities, at the Scottish Universities' International Summer School and more recently in the English division at South Bank University have contributed much needed, much appreciated encouragement and advice. Particular debts are owed to the following: Donald Fraser, David Goldie, M. J. Kidnie, Vassiliki Kolocotroni, Andrew Noble and Geraldine Stoneham.

And, of course, thanks to Nicola Baker, who has been a source of continuing inspiration and motivation.

Introduction

My inclination here and throughout is to insist on an
approach which would try to work out the affirmative and
the critical moments of the postmodern, or, for that matter,
the avantgarde, rather than either celebrating it uncritically or
condemning it *in toto*. If such an approach were to be called
dialectical, it would neither be the Hegelian dialectic with its
move toward sublation and telos, nor would it be the Adornean
negative dialectic at a standstill. But, clearly, I do not believe
that a cultural criticism indebted to the tradition of Western
Marxism is bankrupt or obsolete today any more than I would
concede to the false dichotomy between postmodern cynicism
and the strong defense of modernist seriousness. Neither postmodern pastiche nor the neoconservative restoration of high
culture has won the day, and only time will tell who the true
cynics are.

Andreas Huyssen, *After the Great Divide*

This book shares the same critical impulse described above by
Andreas Huyssen. Though indebted to a large extent to Adornean
analyses of the culture industry and of the fate of commodified
art, it is nonetheless motivated by a belief that such theoretical
accounts remain incomplete, inadequate both in terms of their
theoretical self-understanding and their ability to grasp the complexities of those literary and cultural texts to which they are
applied. Unlike Huyssen, though, I am less interested in the
postmodern than in postmodern fiction. Subsequent chapters
will look closely at examples of that fiction – novels by Don
DeLillo, Toni Morrison, Thomas Pynchon, Salman Rushdie, Alasdair
Gray and Martin Amis – in the attempt to identify the coexistence
in these texts of precisely those affirmative and critical moments
to which Huyssen refers.

In fact, I will argue in the course of this book for a necessary

acknowledgement of the limitations and inadequacy of any conceptual or theoretical understanding of literary works. The mode
of reading postmodern fiction that I am suggesting is one that is
informed by theoretical writings on the postmodern, but searches
for those moments when art breaks free of all categorical boundaries, inflicting upon us a form of experience for which armfuls of
Jameson, Lyotard and Baudrillard have left us less than fully
prepared.

The opening chapter offers a largely theoretical account of the
Western Marxist model of transition from modernism to postmodernism. It establishes a set of critical and theoretical parameters which later chapters explore in relation to examples of
postmodern fiction. The concluding chapter returns to those
explicitly theoretical concerns, readdressing Fredric Jameson's
writings on the postmodern in light of the preceding literary
analyses and the theoretical texts of postmarxists such as Jean-
François Lyotard and Jean Baudrillard. Chapter 2 outlines the
major features of the postmarxist critique of Marxist theory,
demonstrating some of those features through fairly extended readings of Toni Morrison's and Don DeLillo's fiction.

Chapters 3 and 4 address the representation of history in
postmodern fiction and that fiction's engagement with postmodern political perspectives. Chapter 3 offers readings of
Thomas Pynchon's *Mason & Dixon* and Martin Amis's *Time's Arrow,*
exploring how both of these texts represent postmodern historical
narratives, and analysing the effects of their self-consciously contemporary reworkings of history. Alasdair Gray's *Something
Leather* and Salman Rushdie's *The Satanic Verses* are discussed in
the fourth chapter. The chapter examines, in relation to both these
texts, the attempt to develop a politically radical fiction in the
context of postmodernity. In addressing this aspect of the novels,
the chapter also engages with both Western Marxist and postmarxist explanations of the consequences of a postmodern politics.
As the book progresses, the focus is more and more on the fiction
itself rather than the theory. Those theoretical formulations remain
important aspects of the book's argument, but after the first two
chapters there are few sections that are exclusively theoretical;
instead, the fiction is shown to produce reflections on those
theoretical ideas rather than having them either imposed on it,
or applied to it.

The following literary studies also engage – albeit sometimes
implicitly – with the major literary-critical categorisations of
postmodern fiction's stylistic characteristics offered in the work

of two of the most influential critics of postmodern fiction: Linda
Hutcheon and Brian McHale.[1] The next few pages summarise what
I see as the limitations and contradictions of these literary-critical
models, reinforcing the need for those theoretical descriptions of a
cultural condition of postmodernity that we find in Western
Marxist and postmarxist critical theory. A number of the issues
raised in the context of this discussion of Hutcheon and McHale
will therefore return in the studies of postmodern fiction to follow,
though sometimes with rather different interpretative results.

Hutcheon has categorised postmodern fiction as almost a genre
unto itself: historiographic metafiction. As her term suggests,
Hutcheon emphatically does not agree with those who identify
postmodern texts with a loss of history: 'Despite its detractors,'
she writes, 'the postmodern is not ahistorical or dehistoricized,
though it does question our (perhaps unacknowledged) assumptions about what constitutes historical knowledge.'[2] The canon of
Hutcheon's postmodern fiction is, as Brian McHale notes,[3] particularly circumscribed by her definition of such fiction as '*co-
extensive with* the category "historiographic metafiction"'.[4]
Novels such as Robert Coover's *The Public Burning*, E. L. Doctorow's
Ragtime, and Salman Rushdie's *Midnight's Children* are quite
obviously grist to Hutcheon's mill, focusing as they do on the
instability and ideological construction of historical knowledge.
Hutcheon insists on the role which historiographic metafiction
plays as an intervention in our understanding of social relations
through discourse. It is in this explicit engagement with the status
of historical knowledge that Hutcheon situates the distinction
between her form of postmodern fiction and the more radically
self-reflexive texts of American 'surfiction' which she identifies as
late modernist.[5] Postmodern fiction (or historiographic metafiction), she suggests, involves a self-conscious and simultaneous
absorption and subversion of realist narrative conventions. Avoid-
ing the outright rejection of such conventions to be found in what
Hutcheon calls late modernist texts, postmodern fiction thus
attempts to engage us in a process of self-critical rereading:

> In challenging the seamless quality of the history/fiction (or
> world/art) join implied by realist narrative, postmodern fiction
> does not, however, disconnect itself from history or the world.
> It foregrounds and thus contests the conventionality and un-
> acknowledged ideology of the assumption of seamlessness and
> asks its readers to question the process by which we represent
> our selves and our world to ourselves and to become aware of

the means by which we *make* sense of and *construct* order out of
experience in our particular culture. We cannot avoid representation. We *can* try to avoid fixing our notion of it and
assuming it to be transhistorical and transcultural. We can
also study how representation legitimises and privileges certain
kinds of knowledge – including certain kinds of historical
knowledge.[6]

Much of what Hutcheon argues seems to me correct and will be
echoed throughout the literary studies to follow. For example, an
appreciation of the extent to which *Midnight's Children* both
internalises and critiques the nineteenth-century 'historical novel'
(whose contours were described by Lukács[7]) is invaluable to any
reading of Rushdie's novel. However, for the purposes of this
book, Hutcheon's categorisation is inadequate in two principal
(and related) respects: first, the identification of postmodern fiction as 'historiographic metafiction' is too exclusive – it would
seem unhelpful to allow Don DeLillo's *Libra* into this canon while
disqualifying the same author's *White Noise* (a variation on the
campus novel); and secondly, Hutcheon insists on postmodern
fiction's interrogation of history and historical discourses, without
ever really offering a historicised analysis of the forms that interrogation might take. In other words, while asserting that postmodern fiction 'contests the conventionality and unacknowledged
ideology' of realist forms of historical representation, Hutcheon
neglects to study in any depth the ideology of that very critique
beyond acknowledging the often contradictory stance which postmodern cultural texts adopt in relation to the societies in which
they are produced.[8]
    In what might superficially appear a far more exclusively form-
alist model of postmodernist fiction, Brian McHale asserts more
explicitly than Hutcheon ever does (despite entitling a chapter
'Historicizing the Postmodern') the possibility of a mimetic relation of the forms of postmodernist fiction to advanced, late capitalist societies:[9]

Postmodernist fiction at its most mimetic holds the mirror up to
everyday life in advanced industrial societies, where reality is
pervaded by the 'miniature escape fantasies' of television and
the movies. The plural ontology of television-dominated everyday life appears, for instance, in Robert Coover's 'The Baby-
sitter' (from *Pricksongs and Descants*, 1969) and Walter Abish's
'Ardor/Awe/Atrocity' (from *In the Future Perfect*, 1977); here

the ubiquitous television set, a world within the world, further destabilizes an already fluid and unstable fictional reality.[10]

Whilst Hutcheon describes postmodern fiction as an identifiable genre of writing which can be contextualised by comparing it to other forms of contemporaneous discourse (such as the sceptical historiography of Hayden White), McHale is here attempting to ground his postmodernist fiction in a particular social and historical experience. It is, then, perhaps not surprising that, despite McHale's own general reluctance to pursue questions of the cultural and social significance of postmodernist texts, his categories have been found at times useful for more materialist-inclined critics.

McHale's central thesis is that the difference between modernist and postmodernist texts is most easily grasped as a difference in their dominant.[11] 'I will formulate it as a general thesis about modernist fiction,' he writes,

> the dominant of modernist fiction is *epistemological*. That is, modernist fiction deploys strategies which engage and foreground questions such as those mentioned by Dick Higgins in my epigraph: 'How can I interpret this world of which I am a part? And what am I in it?' Other typical modernist questions might be added: What is there to be known?; Who knows it?; How do they know it, and with what degree of certainty?[12]

Novels such as Ford Madox Ford's *The Good Soldier*, which relies to a large extent on the convention of the unreliable narrator, or Kafka's *The Trial*, whose depiction of the individual's persecution withholds any apparent motive for the Court's actions, would clearly fit in well with McHale's categorisation. He subsequently argues that 'the dominant of postmodernist fiction is *ontological*':

> That is, postmodernist fiction deploys strategies which engage and foreground questions like the ones Dick Higgins calls 'post-cognitive': 'Which world is this? What is to be done in it? Which of my selves is to do it?' Other typical postmodernist questions bear either on the ontology of the literary text itself or on the ontology of the world it projects, for instance: What is a world?; What kinds of world are there, how are they constituted, and how do they differ?[13]

Again it is not difficult to provide suitable examples for McHale's thesis: David Lynch's film *Blue Velvet* and Alasdair Gray's *Lanark* are two which spring readily to mind. The coexistence of different worlds in these texts is not something to be resolved according to the conventions of narrative (un)reliability or by recourse to characters' construction of fantasy worlds. Instead, it is evocative of an ontological instability to which both readers and characters are subject.

David Harvey, in *The Condition of Postmodernity*, uses elements of McHale's argument to show the mimetic relation of postmodernist fiction's ontological concerns to a cultural and social condition of postmodernity:

> Our postmodern ontological landscape, suggests McHale, 'is unprecedented in human history – at least in the degree of its pluralism.' Spaces of very different worlds seem to collapse upon each other, much as the world's commodities are assembled in the supermarket and all manner of subcultures get juxtaposed in the contemporary city. Disruptive spatiality triumphs over the coherence of perspective and narrative in postmodern fiction, in exactly the same way that imported beers coexist with local brews, local employment collapses under the weight of foreign competition, and all the divergent spaces of the world are assembled nightly as a collage of images upon the television screen.[14]

Harvey is clearly engaging here with what Terry Eagleton has called 'Lyotard's jet-setters', those typically postmodern subjects who take full advantage of contemporary cultural eclecticism: 'you listen to reggae, you watch a western, you eat McDonald's at midday and local cuisine at night',[15] etc. Missing from Lyotard's formulation, according to Eagleton, is an acknowledgement of how this eclecticism might be experienced in terms of labour relations and employment practices: the globalisation of consumption has also entailed the globalisation of production, accompanied by a widening of the gap between the rich and poor of Western, late capitalist economies since the end of the 1960s.[16] Harvey's exploitation of McHale's thesis is, in one sense, little more than an extension of the latter's own identification of the mimetic function of postmodernist fiction. McHale, after all, writes the following on Jameson's definition of postmodernism as late capitalism's cultural logic:

> I do not see that this higher-level, motivating metanarrative is incompatible with the story I have chosen to tell; but I have preferred to remain at a lower level of narrative motivation, in

hopes that any loss in scope and explanatory power will have been compensated for by a closer, finer-grained engagement with the mechanisms of postmodernist texts themselves.[17]

In another sense, though, the stress which Harvey places on this mimetic function raises the issue of the historical periodisation of the postmodern. Here McHale has muddied the waters somewhat by suggesting that both Jameson and Harvey posit a model of the development from modernism to postmodernism

> according to which modernism and postmodernism are not period styles at all, one of them current and the other outdated, but more like alternative stylistic options between which contemporary writers are free to choose without that choice necessarily identifying them as either 'avant-garde' or 'arrière-garde'.[18]

Although it is true that Jameson does not define postmodernism as a period *style*, McHale's interpretation seems difficult to comprehend in light of Jameson's forthright repudiation of such practices:

> what follows is not to be read as stylistic description, as the account of one cultural style or movement among others. I have rather meant to offer a periodizing hypothesis, and that at a moment in which the very conception of historical periodization has come to seem most problematical indeed.[19]

Instead, McHale seems to be rehearsing the revision which he later offers of his own *Postmodernist Fiction*. He now suspects, he writes in *Constructing Postmodernism*, that the earlier book had offered a misleading account whereby 'a modernist poetics of fiction gave way to a postmodernist poetics'. 'What is missing from *Postmodernist Fiction*', he adds,

> is the counter-story according to which modernism and postmodernism are not successive stages in some inevitable evolution from less advanced to more advanced aesthetic forms, but rather alternative contemporary practices, equally 'advanced' or 'progressive,' equally available, between which writers are free to choose.[20]

Contrary to McHale's argument, there is in fact little common ground to be shared here by his thesis and the theoretical constructs of Jameson and Harvey.[21] Postmodern cultural texts are, for Jameson, necessarily engagements with something like Harvey's 'condition of postmodernity', the cultural and socio-economic formations of late capitalism. Furthermore, Jameson argues that it is in the 'force field' of a postmodern condition that all Western, contemporary cultural production takes place. The distinction between modernism and postmodernism is not, therefore, defined by Jameson in primarily stylistic terms, but with reference to the role of the whole sphere of culture in distinct moments of capitalist history. '[E]ven if all the constitutive features of postmodernism were identical with and continuous to those of an older modernism,' he writes,

> the two phenomena would still remain utterly distinct in their meaning and social function, owing to the very different positioning of postmodernism in the economic system of late capital and, beyond that, to the transformation of the very sphere of culture in contemporary society.[22]

The continuation of a modernist poetics and/or aesthetic would not, for Jameson, constitute anything like a continuation of modernism proper. This is not to say that all contemporary cultural production is postmodern, but that the postmodern is 'the force field in which very different kinds of cultural impulses . . . must make their way'.[23] In a more recent book (*The Seeds of Time*), Jameson describes the postmodern, as it relates to architecture, as 'the situation or dilemma to which the individual architects and their specific and unique projects all have to respond in some way or other'.[24] By extension, it would be fair to say that, although the cultural dominant of postmodernism does not determine the form a novelist's writing may take, it provides the parameters to which that writing is a response and by which its 'meaning and social function' are necessarily informed. Thus the novels of Saul Bellow cannot helpfully be described as postmodern; but they can be seen as engaged in a meaningful response to precisely the social and aesthetic situation which Jameson and Harvey describe as the postmodern, a response in which the novel's reliance on ostensibly realist narrative conventions plays a significant part.

Postmodernism, then, for Jameson, is not a period style but is to be grasped as a cultural dominant through a process of historical periodisation. This, as Jameson acknowledges, involves the adoption of what Jean-François Lyotard would call a metanarrative, a Marxist understanding of the historical development of the capitalist mode of production. Breaking what McHale calls the 'Prime Directive' implicit in Lyotard's definition of the post-modern condition – 'incredulity toward metanarratives'[25] – Jameson attempts to offer an explanation for that very condition, a historicised account of the cultural logic by which such incredulity is asserted. Opposing the prevalent Marxist definition of postmodernism as a culture of assent, a culture generally emptied of political radicalism and a sense of history, the following literary studies are undertaken with the intention of identifying post-modern fiction's own historicised and critical self-understanding.

Notes

1. See Linda Hutcheon, *A Poetics of Postmodernism*; Linda Hutcheon, *The Politics of Postmodernism*; Brian McHale, *Postmodernist Fiction*; Brian McHale, *Constructing Postmodernism*.
2. Hutcheon, *A Poetics of Postmodernism*, p. xii.
3. Brian McHale, 'Postmodernism, or the Anxiety of Master Narratives', pp. 20–1.
4. Ibid., p. 20.
5. 'Surfiction' is a term associated with Raymond Federman and cited by McHale in *Postmodernist Fiction*, p. 4.
6. Hutcheon, *The Politics of Postmodernism*, pp. 53–4.
7. Georg Lukács, *The Historical Novel*.
8. See Hutcheon, *A Poetics of Postmodernism*, pp. 201–21. The critique which Jameson offers in *Postmodernism* (pp. 22–5) of Hutcheon's analysis of *Ragtime* is, in this respect, instructive, and is summarised in the next chapter.
9. McHale avoids the phrase 'postmodern' when dealing with fiction and instead stresses the suffix of 'postmodernist' to underline the extent to which it is a response to modern*ist* concerns and techniques. When summarising McHale's argument, I shall follow his usage even though it is not my usual practice.
10. McHale, *Postmodernist Fiction*, p. 128.
11. McHale borrows this term from Roman Jakobson, citing Jakobson's 'The Dominant', in Ladislav Matejka and Krystyna Pomorska (eds), *Readings in Russian Poetics: Formalist and Structuralist Views* (Cambridge, Mass., and London: MIT, 1971), pp. 105–10. See McHale, *Postmodernist Fiction*, pp. 6–11.
12. McHale, *Postmodernist Fiction*, p. 9.
13. Ibid. p. 10.
14. David Harvey, *The Condition of Postmodernity*, pp. 301–2.
15. Jean-François Lyotard, 'Answer to the Question: What is the Post-modern?', in *The Postmodern Explained to Children*, p. 17.

16. The source of the following statistics is B. Harrison and B. Bluestone (1988), *The Great U-Turn: Capital Restructuring and the Polarizing of America*, New York: Basic Books (see Harvey, *The Condition of Postmodernity*, p. 193).

> A rising tide of social inequality engulfed the United States in the Reagan years, reaching a post-war high in 1986; by then the poorest fifth of the population, which had gradually improved its share of national income to a high point of nearly 7 per cent in the early 1970s, found itself with only 4.6 per cent. Between 1979 and 1986, the number of poor families with children increased by 35 per cent, and in some large metropolitan areas, such as New York, Chicago, Baltimore, and New Orleans, more than half the children were living in families with incomes below the poverty line. (Harvey, *The Condition of Postmodernity*, pp. 330–1)

17. McHale, *Constructing Postmodernism*, pp. 8–9.
18. Ibid., p. 9.
19. Jameson, *Postmodernism*, p. 3.
20. McHale, *Constructing Postmodernism*, p. 207.
21. In *Constructing Postmodernism* (p.301), McHale cites Jameson's identification of Claude Simon's 'alternation between a Faulknerian evocation of perception and a neo-novelistic practice of textualization' (*Postmodernism*, p. 135). However, Jameson prefaces this point by defining Simon's relationship to both the Faulknerian style and the *nouveau roman* in terms which identify it as a *post*modern stance:

> I will suggest, therefore, that his relationship to *both* is pastiche, a bravura imitation so exact as to include the well-nigh undetectable reproduction of stylistic authenticity itself, of a thoroughgoing commitment of the authorial subject to the phenomenological preconditions of the stylistic practices in question. This is, then, in the largest sense what is postmodern about Simon: the evident emptiness of that subject beyond all phenomenology, its capacity to embrace another style as though it were another world. (Jameson, *Postmodernism*, p. 133)

This is a point which McHale concedes in 'Postmodernism, or the Anxiety of Master Narratives', p. 24: 'Thus the fiction of Claude Simon can be seen as postmodernist, according to Jameson's account, for the way it pastiches both Faulknerian modernism and the poetics of the *nouveau roman*.'

Harvey's position is rather more complicated. Although his history of the development from modernism to postmodernism is less linear than that of Jameson, he does not allow for the free, individual agency which McHale presupposes. Instead, he suggests that rather than hold fast to a notion of postmodernism superseding modernism it would be more useful to think of stages in the development of the cultural history of capitalism. 'Put more concretely,' he writes, 'the degree of Fordism and modernism, or of flexibility and postmodernism, is bound to vary from time to time and from place to place, depending on which configuration is profitable and which is not' (Harvey, *The Condition of Postmodernity,* p. 344). Thus it is possible, he suggests, that the social and cultural features of modernism might, in certain circumstances, be found useful economically and re-employed. Both terms, though, remain crucially tied to a metanarrative of historical development – in this case, that of the capitalist mode of production.

22. Jameson, *Postmodernism*, p. 5.
23. Ibid., p. 6.
24. Fredric Jameson, *The Seeds of Time*, p. xv.
25. Jean-François Lyotard, *The Postmodern Condition*, p. xxiv.

I

The Broken Promise: Ideology and the Ageing of the New

The principal issue for twentieth-century Marxist aesthetics has been that of cultural or aesthetic autonomy. It is precisely the nature of the relation between various aspects of what we shall see Georg Lukács call the social 'totality' (such as the distinct but interdependent spheres of the aesthetic and the economic) that has been the main focus of analysis and interpretation. That this should be so ought to come as little surprise. The aesthetic necessarily occupies an ambiguous and ambivalent position in Marxist thought. As we shall see, Marxist aesthetics in the twentieth century have been preoccupied with the precarious nature and very survival of art and of the aesthetic in the face of the ever more stringent demands of a market economy. On the one hand, there is a deep unease with regard to an aesthetic sphere whose claim to autonomy is clearly at odds with perceived Marxist orthodoxy concerning the ultimately determining role of the economic; equally, though, that autonomy is to be prized as it offers a window onto the non-existent, the possible vision of a possible alternative. To say this, though, is to do little more than to paraphrase the opening sentences of Theodor Adorno's *Aesthetic Theory*: 'Today it goes without saying that nothing concerning art goes without saying, much less without thinking. Everything about art has become problematic: its inner life, its relation to society, even its right to exist.'[1]

The following description of a Marxist model of transition from modernism to postmodernism will posit three precise stages in that development. These will be shown to relate dialectically – both to each other as distinct but related historico-cultural moments, and to the historical situations which engender them. From aesthetic high modernism, then, represented by Faulkner's *The Sound and the Fury*, we shall move to a later modernism of the 1930s and 1940s, preoccupied by its inability to sustain the modernist claim to autonomy and acting out the disintegration of those very assumptions on which modernism itself was based; finally, we turn to postmodernism to analyse the form of its relation to late capitalism and to its modernist progenitors. Of crucial significance is the establishment of a relation between aesthetic form and historical or social forces. For that reason, it is important to begin with a consideration of the early work of Georg Lukács, whose *The Theory of the Novel* and *History and Class Consciousness* represent a breakthrough in the study of formal and historical development in art and philosophy.

Georg Lukács and the Reification of Consciousness

The key category in *History and Class Consciousness* is that of reification, as it is with the essay 'Reification and the Consciousness of the Proletariat' that Lukács first attempts to demonstrate what was later to be taken as the cornerstone of cultural critique by members of the Frankfurt School such as Adorno and Max Horkheimer, and by contemporary Marxist literary critics like Fredric Jameson and Terry Eagleton: namely, that 'the problem of commodities must not be considered in isolation or even regarded as the central problem in economics, but as the central, structural problem of capitalist society in all its aspects'.[2] For the Marx of *Capital* this was already self-evident. In the opening chapter of volume 1, 'The Commodity', Marx writes of the magical fetishism of commodities using the analogy of religion: 'There,' he writes,

> the products of the human brain appear as autonomous figures endowed with a life of their own, which enter into relations both with each other and with the human race. So it is in the world of commodities with the products of men's hands. I call this the fetishism which attaches itself to the products of labour as soon as they are produced as commodities, and is therefore inseparable from the production of commodities.[3]

That the commodity does not appear as the product of actual labour allows it to transcend (in ideology) the mundane world of class and labour relations – that is, to transcend history.[4] In effect, though, this process is dialectical; for if the economic commodity has escaped its moment of historical particularity, then the relations of production too that have gone into its making

have also been wiped clean of their historical markings and appear
– now reified or fetishised themselves – as autonomous, independent, natural:

> The mysterious character of the commodity-form consists . . .
> simply in the fact that the commodity reflects the social char-
> acteristics of men's own labour as objective characteristics of
> the products of labour themselves, as the socio-natural proper-
> ties of these things.[5]

For Lukács, this suggests that the essence of the commodity
structure can best be understood in terms of the reification of
human relations. Thus, he emphasises the expression of that
structure in human consciousness probably more than economic
formations themselves:

> Just as the capitalist system continuously produces and repro-
> duces itself economically on higher and higher levels, the
> structure of reification progressively sinks more deeply, more
> fatefully and more definitively into the consciousness of
> man.[6]

Lukács writes that Marxist thought must combat this fetishism or
reification by insisting on the inter-relation of consciousness and
the economic. But the reification of consciousness is also wonder-
fully ideologically efficient, for one of its principal effects is the
incapacity of bourgeois consciousness to comprehend that structural inter-relatedness of which its reified form is a feature and
consequence; in other words, reified consciousness is unable to
grasp itself as reified consciousness and can only think of itself as
a given, as *natural*.

   This is the argument that Lukács applies in part 2 of 'Reification
and the Consciousness of the Proletariat' – 'The Antinomies of
Bourgeois Thought' – to German idealistic philosophy (and particularly to the philosophy of Kant): 'Modern critical philosophy',
he writes, 'springs from the reified structure of consciousness.'[7]
Kantian philosophy, to Lukács, represents the most advanced form
of bourgeois thought. As Jay Bernstein, in an important book on
Lukács called *The Philosophy of the Novel: Lukács, Marxism and the
Dialectics of Form*, writes:

> In HCC [*History and Class Consciousness*] Lukács identifies
> Kant's critical philosophy as the philosophy of our age, as the

theory which most completely articulates our experience of ourselves and the world now. Kant's philosophy, for Lukács, is the philosophy of the bourgeois world; it philosophically consecrates the world of capital. Thus, from a Marxist point of view, the Kantian system harbours the essential antinomies (contradictions) of bourgeois thought. The antinomies of Kant's philosophy are the antinomies of bourgeois thought.[8]

Lukács argues that the very form of Kant's philosophy expresses and gives ideological justification to the commodified world of capital. It is worth paying close attention to how this argument is made.

It is, for Lukács, Kant's refusal to extend his critique of ethical facts beyond those to be found in the individual consciousness which epitomises the limits beyond which his thought cannot go. This, he writes, has 'a number of consequences'. First of all, the constructedness of these facts is veiled by a mystificatory appearance of naturalness; in Kant they were 'transformed', writes Lukács, 'into something merely there and could not be conceived of as having been "created"'.[9] Secondly, the external world of suffering and exchange is itself depicted as immune to ethical activity (an activity which is the province only of the free-thinking individual): 'in nature and in the "external world" laws still operate with inexorable necessity, while freedom and the autonomy that is supposed to result from the discovery of the ethical world are reduced to a mere *point of view from which to judge internal events'*.[10]

That the 'inexorable necessity' with which the world continues its uninterrupted business is, in Kant's formulation, a particular effect of subjective reason is neatly noted in Bernstein's summary of Kant on causality:

Oversimplifying, Kant's thesis is that the world's appearance of being a causally determined domain is to be explained by the *imposition* of the category of causality on it by human beings in their cognitive activities. Thus, the objective world's being causally constituted is, in part at least, a result or product of human activity. Because the objective, spatially and temporally extended world confronting human beings is causally constituted, then human freedom and spontaneity can gain no purchase on it; human freedom remains exiled within human subjectivity, unable to determine or shape the objective world in terms appropriate to it. For Kant our spontaneity, freedom and rationality are what define us as human beings; yet, in the simplest expression of those powers in the act of knowing we construct a world in which there is no room for freedom or reason. What 'is' is determined by relations of cause and effect; human rationality hence becomes an 'ought' forever transcending the objective world.[11]

This then, for Lukács, is the essential antinomy to be found in Kant's philosophy: 'The "eternal, iron" regularity of the processes of nature and the purely inward freedom of individual moral practice', he writes, 'appear at the end of the *Critique of Practical Reason* as wholly irreconcilable and at the same time as the unalterable foundations of human existence.'[12] The contradictoriness is not a flaw, however; rather, it is an expression of what Adorno would call the work's 'truth content', its formal disclosure of the essential untruth of society and of itself. Lukács attributes Kant's 'greatness' to the fact that he 'made no attempt to conceal the intractability of the problem by means of an arbitrary dogmatic resolution of any sort, but that he bluntly elaborated the contradiction and presented it in an undiluted form'.[13] The inability of Kantian philosophy, for Lukács exemplary of bourgeois thought as a whole, to construct a meaningful set of dialectical relations between individual consciousness and dominant social forces is a mark both of its honesty and of its saturation by the structure of reification.

It would be wrong, though, to limit Lukács's discussion of modern, bourgeois philosophy and reification to the formal contradictions found in the former as an expression of the latter's structure. It is also important to look at the construction of the sphere of philosophy itself in capitalist society. In 'What is Orthodox Marxism?', the opening essay in *History and Class Consciousness*, Lukács writes of the emergence of avowedly *autonomous* disciplines and spheres of study.[14] This too he identifies as an expression of reification and of the fetishistic commodity structure:

The fetishistic character of economic forms, the reification of all human relations, the constant expansion and extension of the division of labour which subjects the process of production to an abstract, rational analysis, without regard to the human potentialities and abilities of the immediate producers, all these things transform the phenomena of society and with them the way in which they are perceived. In this way arise the 'isolated' facts, 'isolated' complexes of facts, separate, specialist disciplines (economics, law, etc.).[15]

Bourgeois philosophy is another of these specialist disciplines, whose autonomy in capitalist society is an ideological effect of the reification of consciousness.

Lukács's important insight is that capitalist society necessarily encourages the perception of its various elements (such as economics, law, philosophy, art, etc.) as isolated, independent and not meaningfully related. It is not Lukács's intention to substitute for such autonomy the uniform reflection throughout the social totality of some form of social *essence*; rather, he suggests a theory of semi-autonomy:

> The apparent independence and autonomy which they [the various elements of the social totality] possess in the capitalist system of production is an illusion only in so far as they are involved in a dynamic dialectical relationship with one another and can be thought of as the dynamic dialectical aspects of an equally dynamic and dialectical whole.[16]

He goes on to add that 'the objective forms of all social phenomena change constantly in the course of their ceaseless dialectical interactions with each other'[17] It is not enough, then, to analyse the formal features of, say, Kantian philosophy or modernist artworks with reference only to the texts themselves; rather, it is necessary also to trace the specific features of the construction of the spheres of philosophy and of aesthetics themselves in which these texts are produced and take their place. What we might infer from these two essays by Lukács is that the contradictions (or 'antinomies') of capitalist society are reflected both in the relation of philosophy and art to other social spheres and in the formal characteristics of individual philosophical systems or, as we shall see, works of art. The 'antinomies of bourgeois thought', exemplified so fully in Kant, are a further reflection, then, of the ideological lie of transcendence in which philosophy *as an institution* (or as a separate, specialist discipline) is forced to indulge itself in capitalist societies. It is only with an appreciation of how this might be reduplicated in the aesthetic or cultural sphere that we can come to a proper understanding of the significance for Marxist theory of modernist artworks and, consequently, of their relation to contemporary postmodernist texts.

Lukács and the Novel

Lukács's *The Theory of the Novel*, according to Jay Bernstein, proposes that 'the novel is essentially antinomic, an impossible or contradictory practice'.[18] Bernstein's thesis is that, though preceding *History and Class Consciousness* and generally regarded as a mish-mash of neo-Kantian and Hegelian idealism, *The Theory of the Novel* is in fact Marxist. A brief summary of the case Bernstein makes should illuminate to some degree the analysis of modernism that is to follow, and will also make it easier to see Theodor Adorno, rather than the later Lukács, as the true heir to these two seminal texts of Western Marxism.

In a passage also cited by Bernstein, Lukács asserts the following:

> A totality that can be accepted is no longer given to the forms of art: therefore they must either narrow down and volatilise whatever has to be given form to the point where they can encompass it, or else they must show polemically the impossibility of achieving their necessary object and the inner nullity of their own means. And in this case they carry the fragmentary nature of the world's structure into the world of forms.[19]

The novel here, as a genre, is defined in terms of its historical function. That function, as Lukács understands it, is to subject a disordered world to the order of artistic form; moreover, it does this while acknowledging the intrinsic deceit upon which such an act – the aesthetic act – is based. While it may be argued that Lukács's definition applies to some degree to all artistic forms, Lukács writes that the novel may be distinguished as the conscious descendent of epic literature in modern times: 'The novel', he writes, 'is the epic of a world abandoned by God.'[20] The distinction becomes clearer: 'The epic gives form to a totality of life that is rounded from within; the novel seeks, by giving form, to uncover and construct the concealed totality of life.'[21] The epic, in creating the semblance of totality through artistic form, is also, for Lukács, carrying out its mimetic function. In the novel, however, these two artistic duties have become contradictory:

> The epic and the novel, these two major forms of great epic literature, differ from one another not by their authors' fundamental intentions but by the given historico-philosophical realities with which the authors were confronted. The novel

is the epic of an age in which the extensive totality of life has become a problem, yet which still thinks of itself in terms of totality.

Thus, as Bernstein argues, Lukács's novel 'is to modern society what the epic was to the integrated world of the Greeks. The difference between epic and novel is analogous *and internally related to* the differences between the societies of which they are a part'.[23] The absence of an integrated society means that the novel, for Lukács, becomes a constant dialectic of 'form-giving and mimesis'; thus the novel is continually denying, for mimetic reasons, the validity of a form-giving aestheticisation which nonetheless remains its own *raison d'être*. This is the antinomy of bourgeois art, a form of contradiction which, as Bernstein notes, modernism inherits from realism 'now exacerbated and deepened rather than diminished'.[24]

The exacerbation of this inner-contradiction is, suggests Bernstein, largely a product of modernist literature's more highly developed social autonomy. Bernstein's argument seems at times a little confused: he writes, for example, that the expanding commercialisation in 'the conditions of production, distribution and consumption of literature' were illustrative of its increasing social autonomy in the nineteenth century, as literature became associated with 'non-practicality, uselessness, amusement, pleasure', etc.[25] This, of course, runs counter to that strand of literary-historical analysis – whose advocates have included Andreas Huyssen[26] and John Carey[27] – which argues that modernism could be characterised as precisely a reaction to literature's gradual loss of autonomy during the nineteenth century, its developing usefulness as a mass-market commodity. As the discussion to follow of Adorno on the 'culture industry' will make clear, I am much more persuaded by this latter argument. However, Bernstein seems to me correct to point to modernism's eschewal of both realist conventions and the 'sustained employment of experiential discourse' as a marker of its assertion of social autonomy.[28]

In this sense, then, the modernist novel can be seen to enact, in an almost exaggerated form, those antinomies with which Lukács identifies the genre as a whole, reasserting its distance from social actuality while offering visions of aesthetic beauty which claim an essential truth more valid than the reality that is lived. Adorno's defence of modernist writing as capturing a historical truth of both a social and an aesthetic situation seems ironically consistent with the thought of the early Lukács while taking the form of an explicit response to the latter's *The Meaning of Contemporary Realism*: 'Art', he writes, 'is the negative knowledge of the actual world.'[29] It is with an appreciation of how these complexities might contribute to the significance of the modernist novel that we shall now look at one of its foremost examples, William Faulkner's *The Sound and the Fury*, in the attempt to extend this analysis of modernist literature and to show how such an analysis might add to our understanding of an individual work.

Realism, Modernism, Totality and Faulkner's *The Sound and the Fury*

The whole is the false.

(T. W. Adorno, *Minima Moralia*)

The suggestion that Faulkner's *The Sound and the Fury* ought to be interpreted as a modernist novel is hardly original. However, it is useful to ponder the sorts of dialectical relations that such an association suggests between the novel and that which modernism appears to disavow; namely, certain aspects of literary realism.

For Lukács, that great partisan of bourgeois realism (and one of modernism's most hostile critics), realism can achieve 'a comprehensive description of the totality of society'.[30] Likewise, for Erich Auerbach – author of *Mimesis: The Representation of Reality in Western Literature* – modern contemporaneous realism (which covers the work of writers such as Stendhal, Balzac and Flaubert) developed first in France because of the political and cultural unity which followed the Revolution. 'French reality,' writes Auerbach, 'in all its multifariousness, could be comprehended as a whole.'[31] The chief characteristic of realism is, then, for these critics, its capacity for representing authoritatively the totality and wholeness of lived experience. Thus Fredric Jameson, in an essay called 'Beyond the Cave: Demystifying the Ideology of Modernism', writes that in the work of Lukács and Auerbach 'realism is shown to have epistemological truth, as a privileged mode of knowing the world we live in and the lives we lead in it'.[32]

But in what way is modernism different? First we shall look at the descriptions and critiques of modernism offered by Auerbach and Lukács, while bearing in mind that Lukács in particular is writing from a consciously pro-realist position. Distinguishing the modernists from their realist predecessors, Auerbach writes of those modern writers who prefer the exploitation of random, everyday events, contained within a few hours and days, to the complete and chronological representation of a total exterior continuum – they. . . are guided by the consideration that it is a hopeless venture to try to be really complete within the total exterior continuum and yet to make what is essential stand out. . . . [T]hey hesitate to impose upon life, which is their subject, an order which it does not possess in itself.[33]

Instead, claims Auerbach, these writers

have invented their own methods – or at least have experimented in the direction – of making the reality which they adopt as their subject appear in changing lights and changing strata, or of abandoning the specific angle of observation of either a seemingly objective or purely subjective representation in favor of a more varied perspective.[34]

It is clear how relevant this is in the case of Faulkner's *The Sound and the Fury.* There we have four narrative perspectives, reflecting an unwillingness on the part of Faulkner to provide that surface representation of totality that we have seen both Lukács and Auerbach associate with the realist novel. It is on the implications of such a refusal that Lukács concentrates. For him, this unwillingness to offer a representation of objective events, the portrayal of an objectively *knowable* reality, is effectively a 'negation of outward reality', a negation which, he claims, 'is present in almost all modernist literature'[35]

Totality and wholeness thus appear to give way to fragmentation and disjunction. It is this fragmentation and the neglect of 'objective' experience in favour of the subjective (and often perspectively unstable) refraction of sensations or experiences – to which we, as readers, are offered no avowedly direct access – that Lukács condemns as an outright dismissal of the objective world and, therefore, of historical reality itself. The difference between Auerbach and Lukács is significant: for Auerbach, modernism negates the very essence of *realism*; for Lukács, it is reality itself which is negated. For the latter in particular a key factor here is the use of stream-of-consciousness narration.

Lukács claims that modernism attempts to represent the objective world only as it can be absorbed by the alienated individual subject. Stream-of-consciousness narration is, then, the paradigmatic example of such a process. There the narrative offers a representation of the thoughts of a particular character without the mediating presence of a narrator or narrative authority, save that inevitably indicated in the narrative's status as written representation (about which I shall say more with regard to *The Sound and the Fury* later). Lukács, then, associates the 'attenuation of reality' with Joyce's stream of consciousness in *Ulysses* and claims that this neglect of reality 'is carried *ad absurdum* where the stream of consciousness is that of an abnormal subject or of an idiot — consider the first part of Faulkner's *Sound and Fury* or, a still more extreme case, Beckett's *Molloy*'.[36]

While Lukács admits to some measure of critique in modernist writing — 'the obsession with psychopathology in modernist literature', he writes, 'expresses a desire to escape from the reality of capitalism' — this remains nonetheless an impotent critique, falsely asserting 'the unalterability of outward reality'.[37] From this perspective, modernist texts are seen as escapist. Their avoidance of objective reality is interpreted as an angst-ridden cry (Lukács specifically cites Kafka) but it also leads to 'the reduction of reality to a nightmare'[38] Modernism, for Lukács, doesn't take objective reality seriously enough. As a consequence, 'the protest is an empty gesture, expressing nausea, or discomfort, or longing. Its content — or rather lack of content — derives from the fact that such a view of life cannot impart a sense of direction'.[39] For Lukács, Stephen Dedalus's complaint that 'History is a nightmare from which I am trying to awake' contains the essence of almost all modernist literature, which escapes from a nightmarish historical reality to the subjective consciousness of the individual — whether Molly Bloom or Benjy Compson. There is no attempt, though, to suggest that historical reality might be anything other than a nightmare. Thus might we paraphrase the case for the prosecution.

Those who see something other than self-indulgent escapism in modernism also stress its intrinsic opposition to realism and to the attempt to represent objective social totality. Adorno writes that

> Even the suggestion that the world is unknowable, which Lukács so indefatigably castigates in writers like Eliot or Joyce, can become a moment of knowledge. This can happen where a gulf opens up between the overwhelming and unassimilable world of things, on the one hand, and a human experience impotently striving to gain a firm hold on it, on the other.[40]

The critical impotence that Lukács castigates in modernism, portraying it as passive escapism, is itself seen here as a form of critique. Modernist texts, according to Adorno, criticise society by depicting a mind or minds often unable even to grasp the complex workings and interrelations of society, much less analyse them. This inability of the mind to grasp, and of the literary text to represent, social totality is itself a sign of the damage done to the psyche by dominant social forces. In this way, the inability to offer critique *is* a form of critique. 'It is this alone', writes Adorno, 'which gives the work of Joyce, Beckett and modern composers their power. The voice of the age echoes through their monologues: this is why they excite us so much more than works that simply depict the world in narrative form'.[41] Adorno's defence of modernism is, then, a *historical* defence. The impotence of modernist writing expresses an artistic and historical truth, and that truth encompasses the very denial of objective truth as a plausible artistic goal.

So we move to the central critique of realism that modernism embodies. Here it is summarised by Fredric Jameson:

> [T]he target of their [the modernists'] attack becomes the very concept of reality itself which is implied by the realist aesthetic as Lukács or Auerbach outline it, the new position suggesting that what is intolerable for us today, aesthetically, about the so-called old-fashioned realism is to be accounted for by the inadmissible philosophical and metaphysical view of the world which underlies it and which it in its turn reinforces. The objection is thus, clearly, a critique of something like an *ideology of realism*, and charges that realism, by suggesting that representation is possible, and by encouraging an aesthetic of mimesis or imitation, tends to perpetuate a preconceived notion of some external reality to be imitated, and indeed, to foster a belief in the existence of some such common-sense everyday ordinary shared secular reality in the first place.[42]

Realism, then, in its representation of social totality, implies an external reality which is objective, knowable and representable. Jameson then cites developments in modern science (for example, the theory of relativity), modern philosophy (for example, post-structuralism) and the great mass of modern art from the cubists and Joyce to Beckett and Andy Warhol. Jameson comes to the following conclusion:

> [A]ll these things tend to confirm the idea that there is some-thing quite naive, in a sense quite profoundly *un*realistic . . .

about the notion that reality is out there simply, quite objective and independent of us, and that knowing it involves the relatively unproblematical process of getting an adequate picture of it into our own heads.[43]

The highest achievement of realism – the representation of an objective social totality – is here interpreted as 'profoundly *unrealistic*'. Thus, characteristic features of realist narrative such as totality, objectivity and strict temporal chronology are negated for the sake of historical truthfulness. 'The whole', writes Adorno, 'is the false.'

However, the distinction remains rather more complicated than that. For Jameson, 'all modernistic works are essentially simply cancelled realistic ones'.[44] According to Jameson, realism is a decoding of allegory. The meaning of allegory is drawn from an external or transcendent authority: for example, lamb = Christ; we needn't be told this in the text because it's allegory and we know to look for a meaning in another code system, in this case Christianity. This is discarded by realism, which depicts events which are meaningful *in themselves*. There is no need to look for meaning in another code system, as in allegory; meaning is already there. This is realism as a decoding of allegory. Modernism recodes. The significance or meaning of modernist texts does not exist simply in the representation of particular incidents, as we might find in realism. Instead we find a return to symbolic meaning in the appeal to other coding systems such as myth or to earlier, often Classical, literature. This is very different, though, from allegory or myth itself. Modernism cannot appeal directly to symbolic meaning; so instead, according to Jameson, it rewrites or 'stylizes' a realist narrative *as though* it were a mythic one full of symbolic meanings. Essentially, then, modernism is here viewed not simply as the negation of realism, but as its conscious repression.

What the text represses we, as readers, reveal. Jameson writes:

when you make sense of something like Kafka's *Castle*, your process of doing so involves the substitution for that recoded flux [which is the modernist text] of a realistic narrative of your own devising. . . . I think it's axiomatic that the reading of such work is always a two-stage affair, first, substituting a realistic hypothesis – in narrative form – then interpreting that secondary and invented or projected core narrative according to the procedures we reserved for the older realistic novel in general.[45]

So the modernist writer writes a 'stylization' of a realist narrative and then we, as readers of modernist texts, take that stylisation and turn it back into a realist narrative. It is worth looking at this in relation to Faulkner's *The Sound and the Fury.*

Explaining the basic narrative that underlies his novel, Faulkner writes the following:

> I saw that they [the children] had been sent to the pasture to spend the afternoon to get them away from the house during the grandmother's funeral in order that the three brothers and the nigger children could look up at the muddy seat of Caddy's drawers as she climbed the tree to look in the window at the funeral, without then realising the symbology of the soiled drawers, for here again hers was the courage which was to face later with honor the shame which she was to engender, which Quentin and Jason could not face: the one taking refuge in suicide, the other in vindictive rage which drove him to rob his bastard niece of the meager sums which Caddy could send her.[46]

This, then, is the story. Reading the novel, it all seems rather more complicated. It is told from four different perspectives; chronological order is disrupted (instead, we get a narrative representation of the flux of psychological time). The plot itself, as summarised by Faulkner, is available only in an estranged form, mediated both by the consciousnesses of different characters and by the juxtaposition of their narratives. But if Jameson is right, it is that realist plot that we mentally juxtapose with *The Sound and the Fury* itself. We try to spot the temporal shifts in part 1, ordering the haphazard temporal flux of Benjy's narrative into its proper, realist chronology: A and then B and then C. We redo precisely what the text, by focalising the narrative through Benjy's consciousness, has undone.

Jameson cites Alain Robbe-Grillet's *La Jalousie* (*Jealousy*). He refers to the common belief that in Robbe-Grillet's novel chronology is abolished. He points out (quoting Gerald Prince) that one event — the crushing of a centipede — takes place *before* a trip taken by two characters, *during* it, and *after* it. The very same incident takes place at three different points in time. This, then, is the abolition of chronology. Jameson disagrees. 'On the contrary,' he writes,

> as every reader of Robbe-Grillet knows, this kind of narrative exasperates our obsession with chronology to a veritable fever

pitch. . . . So it is quite wrong to say that Robbe-Grillet has abolished the story; on the contrary, we read *La Jalousie* by substituting for it a realistic version of one of the oldest stories in the world, and its force and value come from the paradoxical fact that by cancelling it, the new novel tells this realistic story more forcefully than any genuinely realistic, old-fashioned, decoded narrative could.[47]

In its negation and repression of realism, totality and chronology, modernism ends up provoking in the reader its own rewriting in terms of realism, totality and chronology. And yet it is also doing something else. For while it may provoke in the reader the desire to substitute for it a realist text or narrative, its own aesthetic appearance, its surface disjunction, continues to deny the validity of that rewriting. What this contradiction – on the one hand provoking a desire in the reader for all that the realist aesthetic satisfies, and on the other unmasking the realist representation of objective social totality as a deceitful and comforting illusion – expresses is, I think, neither totality nor fragmentation, but the process of attempting to construct a totality from fragmentation and alienation. This is a process of utopian wish-fulfilment, which texts such as Faulkner's both inscribe and repress.

The representation of totality and wholeness is a lie as long as experience remains that of alienation and suffering. We need only bear in mind the Compsons or Kafka's protagonists. But it can also be seen as the figure of a desire for, and belief in the possibility of, a better life. It is this dialectic that modernist fiction expresses. Moreover, it confronts us with the need to *construct* some form of order, indicating the constructedness, or manufacturedness, of all ordering systems. The modernist slogan 'Make it New' places as much emphasis on the first word as on the last. And yet the negation, the insistence that the whole is the false, remains necessary. The artistic truth of modernist fiction lies in neither side of this contradiction, but in that contradictoriness itself.

In Ernest Hemingway's *The Sun also Rises*, the narrator – Jake Barnes – is impotent. He is in love with Brett Ashley, but can never have sex with her. He stands by while she sleeps with the other male characters. At the very end of the novel, they are together in a taxi; a policeman holds up a baton to stop the traffic (the symbolism is a bit obvious); they fall against one another on the back seat. Brett turns and says, 'Oh Jake . . . we could have had such a damned good time together.' Here is the nostalgic possibility of wholeness and reconciliation. But for the impotent

Jake that possibility exists only as a pleasing but false illusion. He replies, 'Isn't it pretty to think so.' This is the dialogue that modernist fiction is acting out all the time.

Caddy and Faulkner's *promesse du bonheur* in *The Sound and the Fury*

So I, who had never had a sister and was fated to lose my daughter in infancy, set out to make myself a beautiful and tragic little girl.

(William Faulkner, 'Introduction' to *The Sound and the Fury*)

In order to see how the preceding discussion of modernism might contribute to our understanding of *The Sound and the Fury*, it is necessary to stress the importance of the relationships which Faulkner establishes between his characters – the Compsons – and the social locale in which they are situated: Yoknapatawpha Co., Mississippi. For here Adorno's rebuke of Lukács is particularly telling:

The great works of modernist literature shatter [the] appearance of subjectivity by setting the individual in his frailty into context. . . . Lukács evidently believes that when the Habsburg monarchy in Kafka or Musil, or Dublin in Joyce make themselves felt as a sort of 'atmospheric backcloth for the action', it somehow goes against the programme but nonetheless remains of secondary importance. But in arguing thus for the sake of his thesis, he clearly reduces something very substantial, a growing epic plenitude with all its negative potential, to the status of a mere accessory.[48]

Faulkner's novels construct a social environment with both attentiveness to detail and ambition of scale comparable to that of Balzac's *Comédie humaine*. Yet, the town of Jefferson and the county of Yoknapatawpha are here available to the reader, in all their 'epic plenitude', principally as refracted through the consciousnesses of the various characters. Lukács's suspicions, therefore, may appear to some extent validated: it is, for the most part, only through the inner space of the individual consciousness that the external space of social relations can be all-too-momentarily glimpsed.

What we find in *The Sound and the Fury*, then, is the uneasy coalescence of an outright preoccupation with characters' psycho-pathology (as Lukács suggests) and an unrelenting sense of the need to re-establish a picture, in all its totality, of the society in which these consciousnesses were formed. Richard H. Brodhead points astutely to a further complicating factor, the aestheticising function of the novel itself: 'The writing does not fail, eventually, to project a world that has been radically recomposed. And recomposed, the writing tells us, *by* the writing: the world not as it is, but as an act of style has made it.'[49] We shall return to Brodhead later; for the moment, however, it is necessary merely to note the extent to which his point renders problematic the whole assumption of direct mimesis underlying Lukács's critique of modernist narrative: Yoknapatawpha is not available to us merely via the consciousnesses of individual characters but ultimately through the stylised construction of the work of art itself.

'Why', asks Jean-Paul Sartre, 'is the first window that opens out on this fictional world the consciousness of an idiot?'[50] By focalising the first narrative through the consciousness of Benjy Compson, Faulkner not only plunges us immediately into a world in which both temporal chronology and relations of cause and effect appear to have evaporated, but he also introduces the crucial theme of absence and loss. As I suggested earlier, absence here also refers to the absence of those elements of literary realism, such as chronology and totality, which modernist fiction tends on the surface to discard. But in this instance it is the absence of Caddy that is most overt. Caddy Compson is almost all that *The Sound and the Fury* contains of love and compassion; and it is the loss of her, as Faulkner writes in his appendix to the novel, that echoes most insistently in Benjy's memory and also, therefore, throughout the novel's opening section:

> BENJAMIN . . . Who loved three things: the pasture which was sold to pay for Candace's wedding and to send Quentin to Harvard, his sister Candace, firelight. Who lost none of them because he could not remember his sister but only the loss of her, and firelight was the same bright shape as going to sleep, and the pasture was even better sold than before because now he and TP could not only follow timeless along the fence the motions which it did not even matter to him were human-beings swinging golfsticks, TP could lead them to clumps of grass or weeds where there would appear suddenly at TP's hand small white spherules which competed with and even conquered what he did not even know was gravity and all the

immutable laws when released from the hand towards plank
floor or smokehouse wall or concrete sidewalk. Gelded 1913.
Committed to State Asylum, Jackson 1933. Lost nothing then
either because, as with his sister, he remembered not the pasture but only its loss, and firelight was still the same bright
shape as sleep.[51]

The loss of Caddy and of the pasture combine in Benjy's reaction
to the cries of the golfers:

> The man said 'Caddie' up the hill. The boy got out of the water
> and went up the hill.
>   'Now, just listen at you.' Luster said. 'Hush up.' (SF, p. 22)

Benjy's wails, as he listens to the call of 'Caddie', are a response
to this reminder of his sister's absence. Benjy grasps at this mistaken echo of his sister's name.

In a sense, though, this is something which we too, as readers,
are led to do throughout the novel. As Frederick R. Karl points
out, each narrative section explicitly 'creates' a Caddy for us;[52] for
all the apparent immediacy of Faulkner's narratives, Caddy's voice
is at best represented to us via her brothers. What I am trying to
suggest is that The Sound and the Fury is itself the evocation of
Caddy Compson, that we should take quite seriously Faulkner's
claim: 'So I, who had never had a sister and was fated to lose my
daughter in infancy, set out to make myself a beautiful and tragic
little girl.' The creation of the novel, it seems to me, is also the
creation of Caddy, the imaginative evocation of a Caddy who is
absent.

Yet if Caddy represents something of love and affection in the
novel, her 'fall' is also a figure for that of the South itself, the loss
of the Civil War and subsequent economic decline. In the reconstruction of Caddy, then, we, as readers, are also engaged in the
reconstruction of a narrative of the South's history, a role which
Susan Willis suggests is common to readers of many of Faulkner's
narratives:

> The fact that so many of Faulkner's works are defined by the
> need to reconstruct history, apparent in so much of Faulkner's
> writings, betrays the inability to any longer experience his-
> tory directly and the haunting remembrance of what this
> relationship to history was in traditional society. Indeed, we
> might compare the Faulknerian narrative to a model kit, where

information about the past is given in bits and pieces and the characters, along with the reader, work to assemble the fragments in a meaningful way.[54]

Just as the Edenic symbolism which runs through *The Sound and the Fury* suggests both Caddy's and the South's loss of innocence, the fragmentary narrative reinforces in the reading experience of the novel a sense of decay, for which the Tower of Babel might offer a more appropriate biblical allusion. The reader's imaginative re-creation of Caddy would thus run parallel to the reconstruction of a historical narrative which charts the decline of the old Southern landowners during the early decades of the twentieth century (for example, the Compsons' pasture is sold to make a golf-course, the proceeds paying for Caddy's wedding). What must be stressed here, though, is the extent to which this whole process is subject to that dialectic of utopian wish-fulfilment and ironic reinscription of totality described in the previous section.

It is worth taking a moment to look again at some of the ways in which *The Sound and the Fury* problematises the assumption of direct mimesis which Lukács associates with stream-of-consciousness narration. In Benjy's section, for example, we find his description of the incident which leads to him being gelded: 'They came on. I opened the gate and they stopped, turning. I was trying to say, and I caught her, trying to say, and she screamed and I was trying to say and trying and the bright shapes began to stop and I tried to get out' (*SF*, pp. 53–4). Faulkner here stresses Benjy's inability to speak; elsewhere, Luster says, 'He deef and dumb' (*SF*, p. 50). The incapacity to use language is precisely one of the things that Faulkner portrays as most characteristic of Benjy, and the root cause of his mutilation. Yet it is of course only through language that his experiences can be conveyed. Likewise, as Sartre notes of the second section: 'Quentin thinks of his last day in the past, like someone who is remembering. But in that case, since the hero's last thoughts coincide approximately with the bursting of his memory and its annihilation, who is remembering?'[55] The implausibility of either of these sections really representing directly the consciousnesses of the characters (an implausibility which the novel itself seems to suggest) pushes to the foreground the role of the artist himself and the aestheticising function of the novel. 'Everyone agrees', writes Richard Brodhead,

that *The Sound and the Fury* is the book in which Faulkner first fully discovers how to write like Faulkner. Part of the reason is that it is the novel in which he latches onto his distinctive rhythm of recreation – calculating, with great deliberateness and ingenuity, a style in which his work can be rendered (what we call the characters or points of view in *The Sound and the Fury* – Benjy, Quentin, Jason – are really so many distinctive ways of composing a world through words), then giving a virtuoso performance in that style, then abruptly abolishing it and going on to construct another (and another, and another) in its place.[56]

The novel's narrative structure thus suggests simultaneously the possibility of the characters' self-expression and the reality of that self-expression's fictionality, its status as the aesthetic product of 'an act of style'.

Tempting though it might be to claim, with an exaggerated sweep of the cape, that Faulkner's novel thus reveals itself as a mere fiction, just words on a page, such an act would not remain true, in any meaningful sense of the word, to the experience of reading *The Sound and the Fury*. 'Art', writes Adorno in *Aesthetic Theory*, 'is the promise of happiness, a promise which is constantly being broken.'[57] In its evocation of an ungraspable Caddy, its intimation of a social history of Southern decline in all its 'epic plenitude', and its suggestion of the impossible expression of the Compsons' suffering, *The Sound and the Fury* enacts precisely the promise and betrayal with which Adorno identifies works of art. Here aesthetic autonomy produces a work which almost seems to lament its own helpless alienation from social life, while nonetheless exposing all that is empty in the state of the latter. Exiled from the real life of social relations, Faulkner's novel releases us from the world of aesthetic constructs back into the unredeemed world of actuality, fated to chase, like Benjy, after misheard echoes of Caddy's name.

Adorno and the Culture Industry

The *promesse du bonheur* with which Adorno so gratefully associates works of art can only be retained so long as the 'necessary illusion' of art's autonomy is held to be credible. Here it is worth calling again to mind Lukács's opening essay in *History and Class Consciousness*, 'What is Orthodox Marxism?' Lukács's insistence that the study of separate aspects of the social totality (such as art or literature) must take into account the relation of that sphere to others (such as the socio-economic) would suggest that any change in that relation should be reflected in a change in our understanding of the significance of, or modes of signification in, each social sphere. What we see in a number of novelists during the 1930s and 1940s is an increasing self-consciousness that their art is subject to precisely such a transformation: the illusion of autonomy loses its last shred of credibility and we witness the ageing of the new.

In *After the Great Divide* Andreas Huyssen suggests that modernist art and literature developed to a large extent as a reaction to the burgeoning culture industry of the nineteenth century.[58] The antipathy of many modernist artists to 'low' culture (or to 'the masses' in general) and the painstakingly achieved *difficulty* of their work would both serve as markers in support of Huyssen's thesis. It was partly to distance their work from the more easily consumable cultural goods on offer, runs this argument, that writers from Flaubert to Eliot adopted styles and techniques which would frustrate the more conventional expectations of a reader: Flaubert's stylistic labours are unlikely to have been intended to appeal to a reader such as Emma Bovary; in fact, the opposite is true. But, in the absence of any radical transformation in the economic mode of production, the attempt to retain for art some autonomous space largely outside the market could be successful for a limited time span only. The modernist claim to autonomy, with its grandiose and touching pretension to the making of supreme fictions, appears in retrospect more of a last gasp than a bold, artistic assertion.

The writings of Adorno on the culture industry provide perhaps the most cogent and consistent critique of the process by which art is fully absorbed into the market. In an essay written in response to Walter Benjamin's identification of the radical potential of mechanically reproduced art – an essay entitled 'On the Fetish Character of Music and the Regression of Listening' – and (with Max Horkheimer) in the 'Culture Industry' chapter of *Dialectic of Enlightenment*, Adorno describes the changes that art must undergo in response to its new position within the social totality. 'The culture industry', he writes,

> can pride itself on having energetically executed the previously clumsy transportation of art into the sphere of consumption, on making this a principle, on divesting amusement of its obtrusive naïvetés and improving the type of commodities.[59]

Art, then, whose autonomy had already been a consequence of its fetishisation, becomes a commodity in a new way. Whilst that previous claim to autonomy had at least expressed some form of negation of actuality, in the distance it established between the aesthetic and the external world of suffering and market exchange, the refusal now to indulge in that illusion seems, for Adorno, to represent a chilling assent to the values and conditions of the present. What adds perhaps even further to the melancholy character of this cultural critique is the suggestion of its virtual inexorability.

According to Jay Bernstein, Adorno's 'aesthetic theory was, almost from the outset, self-consciously delineating the ageing of modernism'.[60] Writing throughout the 1930s and 1940s, Adorno describes how the logic of commodification had required art to appear autonomous in order to fulfil that ideological role which Herbert Marcuse calls art's 'affirmative character'. However, the needs of the market change; and it is at this time, the high-point of the totalitarian era, during which Adorno writes, that the necessity that the world of art and of aesthetics be absorbed by the market and be made purposeful becomes more and more overt. The irony which saw Adorno flee the ubiquitous propaganda of Nazi Germany only to find the same principles of domination at work in US advertising is less the product of Adorno's prejudices than of history itself. The increase in commodity production that is the result of assembly-line methods or, perhaps more properly, of Fordism requires a similar increase in consumption. After all, '[w]hat was special about Ford,' writes David Harvey, '(and what ultimately separates Fordism from Taylorism), was his vision, his explicit recognition that mass production meant mass consumption'.[61] To this end, all elements of society must be mobilised; autonomous art, for all its wonderful ideological potential, is sacrificed to the needs of the market. The world of the culture industry and of advertising awaits.

Bernstein's dark appraisal of Adorno's aesthetic theory would appear to be borne out by an early passage in the 'Fetish Character in Music' essay:

> The categories of autonomously oriented art have no applicability to the contemporary reception of music; not even for that of the serious music, domesticated under the barbarous name of classical so as to enable one to turn away from it again in comfort.[62]

The desperate attempts by those such as Schönberg to evade absorption are very much a last, desperate stand, for '[w]here [listeners] react at all,' writes Adorno, 'it no longer makes any difference whether it is to Beethoven's Seventh Symphony or to a bikini'.[63] It is not, then, simply the continuing growth of mass culture to which Adorno is reacting, but a transformation in the position and status of culture itself. This offers a redefinition of both 'high' and 'low' art; it also transforms the subject's understanding of her or his relationship to her or his social environment.

Explaining that latter point, Adorno and Horkheimer write the following:

> The whole world is made to pass through the filter of the culture industry. . . . The more intensely and flawlessly [the movie producer's] techniques duplicate empirical objects, the easier it is today for the illusion to prevail that the outside world is the straightforward continuation of that presented on the screen.[64]

It is not merely the redefinition of art and culture to which Adorno and Horkheimer's fears are directed, but also to this qualitative shift in the means by which we, as individual cognitive subjects, perceive and reflect on our social relations. The vision which this model suggests of the reconciled worlds of aesthetic images and social praxis is one of barbaric harmony. The previous alienation of art has now been erased in favour of its harmonious reconciliation in the false totality of an unjust society. The same, they suggest, is the fate of the individual subject:

> Life in the late capitalist era is a constant initiation rite. Everyone must show that he wholly identifies himself with the power which is belaboring him. . . . Everyone can be like this omnipotent society; everyone can be happy, if only he will capitulate fully and sacrifice his claim to happiness. In his weakness society recognizes its strength, and gives him some of it. His defenselessness makes him reliable. . . . But the miracle of integration, the permanent act of grace by the authority who receives the defenseless person – once he has swallowed his rebelliousness – signifies Fascism.[65]

The integration of art and the socio-economic – the insistence on art's socio-economic purpose – has a further, internal, consequence for art. Adorno and Horkheimer write of 'a shift in the internal structure of cultural commodities' which follows from this process,[66] principally relating to the dissolution of the division between 'high' and 'low' art. Just as the alienation of art from other social spheres had expressed some form of 'truth content', a melancholy expressiveness which Bernstein evokes in the phrase 'beauty bereaved', the false distinction within art itself between 'high' and 'low' had also reflected a social truth of irreconciled contradiction. Art, doubly alienated, had embodied the social and internal alienation of the beleaguered individual under capitalism. Now, however, the situation is very different.

In one of his most quoted phrases – from a letter to Benjamin – Adorno writes of 'high' and 'low' culture as the 'torn halves of an integral freedom, to which however they do not add up'.[67] The popular caricature of Adorno as a cultural mandarin, blind to the beauties of all but the most difficult and inaccessible of artworks, is as misconceived as that which portrays him denouncing those who write poetry after Auschwitz. The true object of Adorno's scorn is the easy reintegration of 'high' and 'low' that the culture industry achieves. This, he argues, is yet another marker of false utopian resolution – one which, as Bernstein writes, 'forsakes the promise of happiness in the name of the degraded utopia of the present'.[68]

The truly utopian yearning of relatively autonomous art is discarded by the culture industry in its fusion of the aesthetic and the socio-economic. In its disavowal of autonomy, the culture industry indicates its refusal to posit the image or semblance of any alternative to actuality. What is expressed, therefore, is a form of flight: 'not, as is asserted, flight from a wretched reality, but from the last remaining thought of resistance'.[69] (Here, in passing, it is worth noting the similarity of Adorno's critique of the culture industry to Lukács's of modernism. This is a point to which I will later return.) The integration of the socio-economic and the aesthetic abolishes the critical distance which art's autonomy had established. By allowing us to experience a sense of disappointment and frustration as social actuality proved unable to redeem the promise of happiness offered by works of art, that critical distance presented to us starkly those utopian possibilities which were denied to us. In the age of the culture industry, however, disappointment and frustration have been banished. Now that the worlds of aesthetics and of social praxis have been absorbed by one another, the aesthetic act is depicted as fully sufficient in itself; after all, there is no longer any separate, external reality of which it might be said to be critical.

Following Adorno, a discussion of the implications of these changes to the position and status of art for novelists of the 1930s and 1940s would do well also to concentrate on the respective situations in Germany and the United States. What is to come is intended to be less representative than symptomatic. The following discussion of some German and American fiction does not necessarily show that writing to be typical of its time, but it does at least attempt to highlight the ways in which some of the artistic dilemmas described above in theoretical terms begin to find expression in the work of some of the important writers of the 1930s and 1940s. As we shall see, these dilemmas are such that they impose a significant measure of self-consciousness in their delineation. As well as providing, then, examples of the fictional treatment of the aesthetic issues raised by the culture industry, a consideration of these novels should also indicate something of the literary-historical logic of the development of literary postmodernism. The novelists at whose work I shall be – albeit briefly – looking are John Dos Passos and Thomas Mann. For in their work we see a self-conscious reflection of what Fredric Jameson has called 'the nature of tragedy in modern times': 'the possession of man by historical determinism, the intolerable power of history itself over life and over artistic creation, which is not free not to reflect what it reacts against'.[70]

John Dos Passos' USA

[T]here's such a gigantic tradition of hokum behind political phrasemaking that the antihokum phrases are about as poisonous as the hokum phrases.

(John Dos Passos, *The Fourteenth Chronicle*)

The association of the burgeoning American culture industry with fascistic European forces is one which Adorno and Horkheimer make quite pointedly in *Dialectic of Enlightenment*, but it can also be found in the fiction of John Dos Passos. In the short biography of the media magnate William Randolph Hearst in the third instalment of *USA*, *The Big Money*, Dos Passos writes of Hearst's voice 'praising the comforts of Baden-Baden under the blood and bludgeon rule of Handsome Adolph (Hearst's own loved invention, the lowest common denominator come to power out of the rot of democracy)'.[71] Dos Passos' novel, though, cannot fully escape association with that same culture industry. Instead, Dos Passos exploits his work's inability, in Jameson's phrase, 'not to reflect what it reacts against' by foregrounding the mimetic element of the relationship of the novel's form to its social content to such an extent that the reader is forced to recognise a further level to the novel, the ironic stance assumed by Dos Passos in relation to his own literary form. The novel, written in what Alfred Kazin calls 'a machine prose for a machine world',[72] is thus constructed in such a way that the overt (and even excessive) manipulation of both character and reader appears to identify it unmistakably with the deterministic social forces it also appears to criticise.

A consistent feature of *The 42nd Parallel*, part 1 in the *USA* trilogy, is a meditation on the practical, ideological functions that culture (and literary culture in particular) is made serve. Throughout the novel, the reader finds presented a whole series of characters whose particular skills or whose occupations involve them in some way in the production of public forms of discourse: Mac, the linotype operator; Gene Debs; Woodrow Wilson; Doc Bingham, the book salesman; 'The Boy Orator of the Platte'; J. Ward Moorhouse. There are also repeated references to William Randolph Hearst, whose newspaper empire was the most extensive and powerful of its time, and of whom Dos Passos felt able to write in 1934, 'Hearst is handsome Adolph's schoolteacher'.[73] The way in which the individual subject is caught not only within a mechanistic class and economic system, but also within a network of ideological, cultural discourses thus develops as a major theme of the novel.

Implicit, of course, in the elaboration of this theme is the acknowledgement of literary culture as functional. From Doc Bingham's presentation of literature as commodity to J. Ward Moorhouse's avowed wish 'to educate the public by carefully planned publicity over a term of years' (*USA*, p. 211), emphasis is placed on the political and economic motivations that underlie such cultural production. What we are seeing, then, is the novel's focus on the American culture industry and its inevitably violent domination of individual subjects. One example of the novel's overt foregrounding of these concerns is in the opposition portrayed between Gene Debs and Woodrow Wilson. Dos Passos writes that 'Woodrow Wilson had him [Debs] locked up in Atlanta for speaking against war'. Wilson, the politician whose rhetoric helps convince Americans to support entry into the war in Europe, has his aims threatened by another's rhetoric. The biography of Debs goes on to explain his former supporters' avoidance of him:

but on account of the flag
  and prosperity
  and making the world safe for democracy,
  they were afraid to be with him,
  or to think much about him for fear they might believe him;
  for he said:
  While there is a lower class I am of it, while there is a criminal class I am of it, while there is a soul in prison I am not free. (USA, p. 39)

Debs' supporters avoid him because they are convinced by Wilson's slogans – 'making the world safe for democracy' – and also because they fear that they might find his slogans equally convincing. The subject is here portrayed as a pawn of rhetoric. Inherent in the Debs biography is the fear that there is something intrinsic to the production of discourse aimed at a mass audience that is incompatible with the retention of some form of autonomy for the individual subjects who make up that audience.

It is not only, though, those to whom such discourses are directed who find themselves manipulated and stripped of even a residual subjectivity. On various occasions, the reader sees characters attempt to influence the reactions of other characters through the construction of a fiction, yet who then find themselves more prey to that fiction than are their intended victims. This is what happens to Doc Bingham when he is sent to spend the night in a barn, having claimed to be a travelling clergyman. We are told that 'Doc Bingham's face was as black as thunder as he wrapped himself in a horseblanket, muttering about "indignity to a wearer of the cloth"' (USA, p. 53). The 'muttering' signals that it is unlikely that Doc is keeping up the pretence for others. Instead, he has begun to refer to himself *in private* using terms dictated by the very fiction he has created to manipulate others. His indignation is, therefore, caused not by their treatment of him, but by their treatment of his fiction – a distinction which he is, comically, unable to make.

Of greater significance, though, are the ways in which characters are shown to be caught within an inescapable mechanistic structure. Their fictional status is foregrounded by the narrator's tendency to repeat phrases or establish explicit parallels in his descriptions of different characters. Thus, Mac is linked to J. Ward Moorhouse by the echo of the narrator's description of Yuma, a stopping-point on Mac's trip to Mexico, as 'hotter'n the hinges of hell' (*USA*, p. 114) in the phrase 'hot as the hinges of Delaware' (*USA*, p. 153); Delaware being the birthplace of J. Ward Moorhouse. Moreover, the role of the reader in establishing this association is also prominent at such times: it is left to the reader to make a mental note of these descriptive echoes, thereby rendering him or her complicit with the construction of a textual network of association that binds the characters every bit as tightly as does the industrial capitalist system. This aspect of the reader's role is further emphasised by the fact that the phrase 'hot as the hinges of Delaware' appears in a Camera Eye section and not in a chapter on Moorhouse himself. It is left for readers to make the connection when, in the very next chapter, they read that Moorhouse was born there. Later, Charley Anderson is also included when the narrator describes New Albany, on Charley's arrival, as 'hot as the hinges of hell' (*USA*, p. 326).

Characters' fates are made coincide with a regularity that serves to foreground their helplessness. The use of Mexico as a destination is particularly striking: Mac goes there; J. Ward Moorhouse takes Janey there on a business trip; and Charley Anderson at one point plans to go to the Mexican border with the American militia. Examples of this sort abound throughout the *USA* trilogy so much so that it is not long before the reader learns to expect that each new character will in some way be forcefully integrated into the social sphere of the others. It appears to matter little whether or not they belong to the same class or share similar aspirations; characters are made to enter a mechanistic narrative system in which everything and everyone is reduced to the status of a functional cog, where nothing escapes the most utter absorption and rationalisation; a social predicament described in prose which, as Kazin writes, 'bears along and winds around the life stories in the book like a conveyor belt carrying Americans through some vast Ford plant of the human spirit'.[74]

Even economic success is unable to provide characters with an effective escape route. Throughout the novel, a succession of short biographies of some of the capitalist system's 'success stories' – Andrew Carnegie, for example – is paraded before us. The inspirational value of these vignettes is somewhat hampered, however, by their regular (and surely unnecessary) intimations of mortality:

> Andrew Carnegie became the richest man in the world
> and died. (*USA*, p. 225)

This pattern is repeated with reference to Luther Burbank, Bill Haywood, 'The Boy Orator of the Platte', Minor C. Keith, Steinmetz and Bob La Follette. The novel insists on the hopelessness even of its more successful characters: no matter what success or distinction they attain, each of them must be shown to reach their use-by date.

In Dos Passos' novel, then, it is the explicit parallels created between the fictional characters and the historical subjects of these biographies that emphasise the futility of any narrated act or achievement. The description of the young J. Ward Moorhouse (initially 'Johnny') as the 'class orator' at school (USA, p. 155) ironically identifies him with 'The Boy Orator of the Platte', the subject of the previous biography which concludes, 'He was a big eater. It was hot. A stroke killed him' (USA, p. 153). Likewise, the reader is later told that Moorhouse is attending a course 'in the care of fruit trees' (USA, p. 211) soon after the biography of Minor C. Keith, 'the pioneer of the fruit trade', which begins and ends with mention of his death. Characters' fates are thus portrayed as predetermined, a suggestion principally achieved through the structural composition of the novel. In effect, the reader is forced to make the connections that highlight each character's hopelessness and mock their continuous and pitifully strenuous efforts, while those same characters continue, oblivious to their predestined fate, to act out the same search for success that establishes those very connections.

The retention of some form of individual autonomy, of the subject's non-identity, is undermined in Dos Passos' novel not only through this overtly manipulative plot structure and repeated use of similar descriptive phrases, but also through the absence of any distinctive relation between characters and their terms of expression. Thus, when the narrator writes of Alice that '[s]he said it made her feel freer to spend a few hours with broadminded people' (USA, p. 130), the reader would appear to have learned something of that particular character; especially as she or he is aware that Janey's parents are in fact bigots who had prevented their daughter bringing home a black girl. However, the effect of this technique changes when, later in the novel, the narrative is focalised through Eleanor Stoppard and we read, 'Doctor Hutchins was a Unitarian minister and very broadminded and Mrs Hutchins did watercolors of flowers that were declared to show great talent' (USA, p. 187). Free indirect speech works here not to distinguish characters, but to blur the lines between them, to indicate a condition rather than a particular perspective.

The overt transformation of human subjects into replaceable components in an aesthetic structure – Dos Passos' novel – is a reflection of the social effects of 'Hearstian demagoguery'[75] and the Taylorisation of American industry. The effect of assembly-line production on the workers is, for Dos Passos, clearly analogous to that of the emergent mass media upon the consciousnesses of the American public. The novel thus depicts the ideological collusion of that culture industry in which it is itself produced and by which it is to a large extent defined. Modernism's necessary lie of autonomy is no longer sustainable; *The 42nd Parallel* acknowledges this in its formal mimicry of the forces of domination and reification associated with assembly-line production methods.

The mimesis of novel and society in *The 42nd Parallel* is so complete that we have little choice but to recognise it as primarily an ironic work. Dos Passos allows the novel's mimesis of its subject to provide an ironic self-commentary on its own tarnished moral standing, thereby justifying its status as, simultaneously, commodity and instrument of social critique. He suggests that, without this ironic retreat from the ideological collusion of aesthetic form, all art (and particularly that which is politically engaged) must be self-devouring and lead effectively to silence. *The 42nd Parallel* shows similar stories repeated under different names: Mac, Janey, J. Ward Moorhouse, Charley Anderson. The system that is both the novel and society continually repeats the same processes on its way to the temporary conclusion of war. The 1914–18 war is presented as the goal towards which capitalist societies were slowly and inexorably heading; it is present all along as an inevitability – of course, for both author and reader, it is from the very start a historical fact – and for the novel's characters, for Charley Anderson, it is what finally enforces understanding of what is wanted: 'The lookout put his hand over his mouth. At last he made Charley understand that he wasn't supposed to talk to him' (*USA*, p. 341). Here is the logic not only of industrial utilitarianism's easy adaptation to a wartime situation, but also that of culture's own complicity in the market reification and rationalisation of humanity: all that is left, without Dos Passos' self-critical detachment, is resignation to the futility of expression. In the culture industry the voice of protest can be no more effective than Charley's affirming silence.

Thomas Mann's *Doctor Faustus*

> Thoughts on holding art up to mockery, breaking out of it,
> dissolving it – all the while remaining absolutely and ruthlessly
> devoted to it.
>
> (Thomas Mann, *Diaries*)

The novel's formal mimicry of dehumanising social forces is justifiable for Dos Passos as long as it is subject to the ironic stance of the author, since the alternative to this is complete non-expression. There is, however, another, more overtly metafictional alternative that employs the text's self-commentary to extend debate over its ideological function rather than short-circuiting or neutralising it as Dos Passos' option effectively does. In Thomas Mann's *Doctor Faustus* the metafictional element is reinforced by the explicit dramatisation of an artist striving to find a means of regenerating an art that he sees as decadent and debased.

Like Dos Passos, though for different reasons, Adrian Leverkühn, Mann's fictional composer, also relies on a distancing mechanism. Arnold Schönberg's twelve-tone system, whose development is here attributed to Leverkühn, represents an alternative method of insisting on this critical detachment of the artist from his own aesthetic form. The creation of this system allows the artist unlimited freedom as long as he remains within the boundaries determined by the system. Thus, as Adorno writes in *Philosophy of Modern Music*, 'Twelve-tone technique . . . enchains music by liberating it. The subject dominates music through the rationality of the system, only in order to succumb to the rational system itself.'[76] It is precisely this artistic paradox that Mann explores in *Doctor Faustus*, presenting more explicitly its political and historical implications.[77] As Patrick Carnegy puts it:

> Here Mann develops his theme of the artistic and political barbarity that is induced by the irrational adoption of a totalitarian principle, and of the once-and-for-all commitment to this principle which is taken as sufficient reason for the suspension of further moral (or aesthetic) scrutiny.[78]

A similar moral uneasiness over the creation of such a mechanism is also expressed by the novel's narrator, Serenus Zeitblom: 'Quite generally this claim to ironic remoteness, to an objectivity which surely is paying less honour to the thing than to the freedom of the person has always seemed to me a sign of uncommon arrogance.'[79] Here Mann's narrator pinpoints one of the major problems to result from the artists' ironical treatment of their own artistic work: they divorce themselves from the work's listeners/readers and stand alone and aloof in their ability to evade both manipulation by the artform and responsibility for it. The impersonality that follows from this ironical stance thereby reinforces the alienation of artists from both their artistic materials and the work's audience. Furthermore, and most significantly, this is effected through the adoption of another systematic process and leads – as Zeitblom is later aware and as the case of Leverkühn exemplifies – to the artists' rediscovery of themselves as another function of form (or of a metaform), this time unable to escape parody and the stance of ironic detachment.

The problem that Leverkühn attempts to address is nevertheless a valid one. As his own devil states the case: '"Composing itself has got too hard, devilishly hard. Where work does not go any longer with sincerity how is one to work?"' (*DF*, p. 232). This dilemma emerges not only (as we shall see) from Mann's own artistic grapplings, but also from his reading of Adorno's elaboration of the artist's difficulties in *Philosophy of Modern Music*:

> The material transformation of those elements responsible for expression in music, which – according to Schönberg – has taken place uninterruptedly throughout the entire history of music, has today become so radical that *the possibility of expression itself comes into question*. In the process of pursuing its own inner logic, music is transformed more and more from something significant into something obscure – even to itself.[80]

Leverkühn's answer is to be sincere in his insincerity, to construct a formal framework within which he can mock everything while signalling the mockery's dependence upon the form itself and then subjecting to an ironic distance both the form and 'its' mockery. Mann's novel presents as analogous this artistic impersonality that finds some relief in aesthetic alienation and a political bestiality that celebrates the subjugation of the individual (in the name of the 'Volk') while allowing her or his worst excesses to go unchecked. For Mann, therefore, the problematics of modernism are extended to the artist's attempts to resolve those very problems. It is this extension that particularly distinguishes the question of the justification of self-consciously *modernist* art, a self-consciousness which simultaneously identifies the work as modernist and exposes to it the limited historical horizons of the modernist project itself. Or, as Georg Lukács writes:

> Hitherto the tragedy of the artist has, almost without exception, been presented from the standpoint of the relationship and conflict between the artist and life, between art and reality. This is largely true of the early Mann. Here, however, the work of art itself is called into question. Therefore, its genesis and structure must be shown; the tragic predicament of modern art must be demonstrated by the work of art itself.[81]

Unfortunately, Lukács goes on to try to justify the reading of Mann's novel as a realist critique of modernist aesthetics. *Doctor Faustus* is revealed as far more interesting, however, and far more complex than Lukács would have us believe when we recognise the elements that serve to question and to problematise the novel itself; that is, when we perceive the novel not only as the dramatisation but also as the exemplification of the moral and political dilemmas of modernist art.

The key to such a reading lies in the use Mann makes of the parallels between his novel and Leverkühn's compositions, particularly his masterpiece, *The Lamentation of Dr Faustus*. Echoing Leverkühn's lament, '"Why does almost everything sound to me like its own parody?"' (*DF*, p. 131), Mann too in *The Genesis of a Novel* confesses, 'In matters of style I really no longer admit anything but parody.'[82] His novel draws from as many sources as does Leverkühn's music, while the explicit stylisation of Leverkühn's language, whose significance in pointing to Luther and the doctrine of predestination is missed by the narrator, finds an echo in Mann's own use of leitmotif, which also exposes Zeitblom's ignorance of the influence dictating the story he tells. That influence is, of course, diabolic and is signalled in the leitmotif of laughter, Adrian's laughter in particular. An especially striking example of this use of leitmotif to undermine Zeitblom occurs during his account of the visit he and Leverkühn pay to the home of the theology professor, Kumpf, and their reaction to the professor's claim that the devil is also present:

> All this was pretty awful, and I take it Adrian must have thought so too, though his pride prevented him from exposing his teacher. However, when we went home after that fight with the Devil, he had such a fit of laughter in the street that it only gradually subsided with the diversion of his thoughts. (*DF*, p. 97)

Zeitblom is here presented with the image of the devil and with his friend's mocking laughter. At this point, however, he is unable to link them, unable to see the presence already of a demonic spirit that he is later only to recognise through viewing Adrian Leverkühn's mental collapse as analogous to the moral collapse of Germany. In fact, although Zeitblom professes to have learned much since the time of the composer's death, he remains to the very end oblivious to the inevitability, signalled unwittingly in his memoir, of the terrible fate awaiting his friend. It is in this same 'innocent' and oblivious manner that he shrugs off his tendency to narrate prematurely events that do not take place until much later in the plot: 'I have fallen into my old, bad habit and got ahead of my story' (DF, p. 252), he tells us, inadvertently integrating a pattern of predestination into the very narration of that story.

The establishment of an ironic distance between himself and his narrator is an important means through which Mann identifies himself and his creation with Leverkühn and his symphony. As I suggested earlier, the laughter of Leverkühn functions as a leit-motif; one in which, Mann writes, 'the devil, as the secret hero of the book, is invisibly present'.[83] Yet Mann's explanation of the use he makes of his narrator surely raises the question of his own diabolic laughter: 'To make the demonic strain pass through an undemonic medium, to entrust a harmless and simple soul, well-meaning and timid, with the recital of the story, was in itself a comic idea.'[84] Elaborating on the association of himself with Leverkühn, Mann states that the use of Zeitblom as narrator 'removed some of the burden, for it enabled me to escape the turbulence of everything direct, personal and confessional which underlay the baneful conception'.[85] In fact, throughout The Genesis of a Novel the confessional element is emphasised. Mann reports feeling that 'the whole thing has something forbidding about it', that he 'was not at ease about the business'. More to the point, and of far greater centrality in defining the nature of Mann's anxiety, he writes of 'the danger of my novel's doing its part in creating a new German myth, flattering the Germans with their "demon-ism"'.[86] Not only does Mann face the same problem of the regeneration of art as does his fictional composer – he claims to have been particularly struck by Harry Levin's assertion that Joyce '"has enormously increased the difficulties of being a novelist"'[87] – but he is also aware that his attempt to resolve the problem may be morally compromised in a similar way to Leverkühn's.

Having shown how Leverkühn's subjection of musical form to

an ironic distance, culminating in *The Marvels of the Universe* and
the *Apocalypse*, leads to the negation of faith in personal artistic
expression and offers an analogy to the anonymous barbarism of
political totalitarianism, Mann can hardly resolve his anxieties
over *Doctor Faustus* by himself retreating to an ironic distance
in the manner of Dos Passos. Zeitblom explains how *The Marvels of
the Universe* appears to embody 'a luciferian sardonic mood, a
sneering travesty of praise which seems to apply not only to the
frightful clockwork of the world-structure but also to the medium
used to describe it: yes, repeatedly with music itself, the cosmos of
sound' (*DF*, p. 266); similarly, of the *Apocalypse*, he writes that 'in
the searing, sussurant tones of spheres and angels there is not one
note that does not occur, with rigid correspondence, in the hellish
laughter' (*DF*, p. 364). He adds immediately, 'That is Adrian
Leverkühn. Utterly.' Leverkühn is thus defined not by musical
form, for that he parodies, but by his role as the parodist of that
form. In other words, Leverkühn pays the price of accepting
that personal expression is no longer possible so that, through
parody, he might escape absorption into his musical system; but
he does so only to find that he is absorbed into a metasystem,
fated to distance himself eternally from all that his art supposedly expresses. The art for which Leverkühn searches, that is
'per du' with humanity, is consequently further than ever from
reach as a result of his attempt to create it from a position of
aloofness and detachment.

In his final work, however, Leverkühn does, according to
Zeitblom, achieve true expression: 'expression as lament'. He
does so by finally renouncing ironic distance and submitting
to his musical form. This act of submission is nonetheless a
true expression of Leverkühn's despair, of his conclusion that
expression is now truly impossible. For Zeitblom, though not for
Leverkühn himself, *The Lamentation of Dr Faustus* offers 'a hope
beyond hopelessness'.

Mann, too, clings to this same, barely perceptible ray of hope.
He attempts no clear resolution of his moral and artistic dilemma,
the dilemma of a morally tainted art. Instead he accepts responsibility for a work whose possible aesthetic complicity with forces
of social domination charts the end of autonomous art itself. In *The
Genesis of a Novel* Mann ponders the possibility that artists'
submersion of themselves in art rather than in human relations
marks them as inhumane, and asks whether the guilt that this
knowledge provokes in artists is enough to redeem them. He adds,
'Here is a speculation impious enough to be ascribed to Adrian

Leverkühn.'[88] Unable to stand aloof from his literary form, Mann accepts definition by that form, as Leverkühn does, aware however that such acceptance might well provide a further allegorical parallel to political domination, the willing submersion of the subject in the impersonal aesthetic structure. As with his hope that the artist's sense of guilt might 'reconcile others . . . even win their affection', Mann is here left hoping that his awareness of the problems inherent in his acceptance of literary form and renouncement of ironic distance might be enough to express a lamentory ambivalence, an ambivalence that is directly expressive of his thoughts on the future of art and of Germany. That Mann is, then, unable to find a means of resolution to his moral dilemma and consequently submits to his tainted artistic form while still questioning the morality of that submission is surely for him to integrate within his work of art the perpetual moral self-enquiry that is properly his own. The novel itself must, therefore, actually be about the justification of art and can never reach resolution, for at that point the author is guilty of an outright affirmation of, and active collusion in, the violent forces of domination.

Postmodernism and the Avant-Garde

In order to understand the terrible irony of the relationship of the postmodern to modernity and the culture of modernism, it is necessary, as Terry Eagleton suggests, to take into account the whole critique of aesthetic or cultural autonomy as proposed by the work of the historical avant-garde.[89] In his *Theory of the Avant-Garde* Peter Bürger argues that the art of the revolutionary avant-garde in the early twentieth century was based on an explicit denunciation of art's claim to autonomy or social transcendence. Bürger begins by citing Marx's critique of religion as ideology in the *Critique of Hegel's Philosophy of Right* – which asserts dialectically that '[t]he wretchedness of religion is at once an expression of and a protest against real wretchedness' – and offers the following commentary:

> It is in religion that this twofold character of ideology is brought out. 1. Religion is an illusion. Man projects into heaven what he would like to see realized on earth. To the extent that man believes in God who is no more than an objectification of human qualities, he succumbs to an illusion. 2. But religion also contains an element of truth. It is 'an expression of real

wretchedness' (for the realization of humanity in heaven is merely a creation of the mind and denounces the lack of real humanity in human society). And it is 'a protest against real wretchedness' for even in their alienated form, religious ideals are a standard of what ought to be.[90]

Bürger then shows how such ideology critique (*Ideologikritik*) has been applied in the writings of Western Marxism to the sphere of culture. His principal example is Herbert Marcuse's 'The Affirmative Character of Culture'.[91] 'It is not difficult', writes Bürger, 'to recognize that Marcuse is guided by the Marxist model of the critique of religion.'[92] He explains Marcuse's argument that (just as Marx says of religion) bourgeois, autonomous culture is simultaneously affirmative and critical of the society in which it is produced: 'Marcuse demonstrates', writes Bürger, 'that bourgeois culture exiles humane values to the realm of the imagination and thus precludes their potential realization'; while he adds that 'Marcuse views the humane demands of great bourgeois works of art as a protest against a society that has been unable to live up to them'.[93]

It is important to grasp, however, that what both Bürger and Marcuse are referring to is not the significance or status of individual artworks in themselves, but the general categorisation of *culture* itself. '[W]orks of art', writes Bürger, 'are not received as single entities, but within institutional frameworks and conditions that largely determine the function of the works.'[94] Bürger terms these conditions the 'institution of art' and it is to this 'institution', this categorisation of what is deemed 'cultural' in bourgeois society, that he attempts to portray the avant-garde as an explicit and critical response:

> with the historical avant-garde movements, the social sub-system that is art enters the stage of self-criticism. Dadaism, the most radical movement within the European avant-garde, no longer criticizes schools that preceded it, but criticizes art as an institution, and the course its development took in bourgeois society. The concept 'art as an institution' as used here refers to the productive and distributive apparatus and also to the ideas about art that prevail at a given time and that determine the reception of works. The avant-garde turns against both – the distribution apparatus on which the work of art depends, and the status of art in bourgeois society as defined by the concept of autonomy.[95]

An example of such critique is offered by Andreas Huyssen in
After the Great Divide. Huyssen cites Marcel Duchamp's ready-
made *L. H. O. O. Q.*, which consists of a reproduction of Leonardo's
Mona Lisa complete with additional moustache and goatee beard.
The title, as Huyssen points out, when spoken in French makes
even more apparent the satiric intent: elle a chaud au cul/she has a
hot ass.[96] 'It is not', writes Huyssen, 'the artistic achievement of
Leonardo that is ridiculed by moustache, goatee and obscene
allusion, but rather the cult object that the *Mona Lisa* had
become in that temple of bourgeois art religion, the Louvre.'[97]
Bürger argues that this process is historically driven. Although the
autonomy of art as an institution was established in the eighteenth
century, Bürger writes that it was really only with late nineteenth-
century Aestheticism that the full logic of aesthetic autonomy was
properly expressed. The response of the avant-garde to this
attempts, though, to preserve something of the critical potential
of such autonomy:

> The avant-gardistes proposed the sublation of art − sublation in
> the Hegelian sense of the term: art was not simply to be
> destroyed, but transferred to the praxis of life where it would
> be preserved, albeit in a changed form. The avant-gardistes
> thus adopted an essential element of Aestheticism. Aestheticism
> had made the distance from the praxis of life the content of
> works. The praxis of life to which Aestheticism refers and
> which it negates is the means−ends rationality of the bourgeois
> everyday. Now, it is not the aim of the avant-gardistes to
> integrate art into *this* praxis. On the contrary, they assent to
> the aestheticists' rejection of the world and its means−ends
> rationality. What distinguishes them from the latter is the
> attempt to organize a new life praxis from a basis in art.[98]

What is perhaps most striking in this formulation of the avant-
garde project is its similarity to Adorno's horrified description of
the achievements of the culture industry. This is acknowledged by
Bürger, who notes that '[d]uring the time of the historical avant-
garde movements, the attempt to do away with the distance
between art and life still had all the pathos of historical progres-
siveness on its side'.[99] The situation of the culture industry, as
Bürger realises, is quite different. It has effected not merely the
sublation of art, but also of the avant-garde's radicalism: today, as
Huyssen points out, 'an assiduous audience admires *L. H. O. O. Q.*
as a masterpiece of modernism in the museum'.[100] Or, as Bürger

would have it, 'now the protest of the historical avant-garde against art as institution is accepted as *art*'.[101] That this 'art' is no longer autonomous – as the avant-gardistes wished – yet remains fetishised as 'culture' in an economically productive culture industry, whose 'means–ends' rationality remains undisturbed, is perhaps the final cruel irony of the avant-garde's failure-in-success.

Terry Eagleton, in one of the most overtly polemical analyses of the postmodern, describes postmodernism as 'among other things a sick joke at the expense of such revolutionary avant-gardism'.[102] For Eagleton, postmodernism is the culture industry triumphant. 'In its early stages', he writes,

> capitalism had sharply severed the symbolic from the economic; now the two spheres are incongruously reunited, as the economic penetrates deeply into the symbolic realm itself, and the libidinal body is harnessed to the imperatives of profit. We are now, so we are told, in the era of postmodernism.[103]

Eagleton's writings on postmodernism are an explicit response to those of Jameson. As we shall see in a moment, Jameson attempts to recuperate some sense of political radicalism for the postmodern, some space for the aesthetic expression of social conflict. For Eagleton, though, the postmodern is quite utterly bereft of conflict (just as the culture industry is for Adorno). This postmodernism is less a condition than an attitude, less the cultural logic of a stage in historical development (as Jameson would have it) than the product of conscious political will. Thus Eagleton hypothesises a political form of contemporary art which combines both modernist and avant-gardist impulses in a quite different way to the postmodern, creating an alternative response to the culture of modernity and taking a different turn from that of postmodernism.[104] This, as we shall see, is very different from Jameson's insistence on the need for a political art today to be produced through an engagement with postmodernism itself. For Eagleton, postmodernism is – both politically and culturally – the false resolution of the dilemmas of modernism. The whole problematic of autonomy is here resolved by the postmodern with a chilling indifference:

> If the work of art really is a commodity then it might as well admit it, with all the *sang froid* it can muster. Rather than languish in some intolerable conflict between its material reality

and its aesthetic structure, it can always collapse that conflict on one side, becoming aesthetically what it is economically.[105]

A resolution of this sort can be seen by briefly comparing Hermann Broch's *The Death of Virgil* with a contemporary, post-modernist text, Christoph Ransmayr's *The Last World*. Broch's work, written almost contemporaneously with Mann's *Doctor Faustus*, is a tortured (and, at times, tortuously difficult) response to the fate of an art which can no longer pretend to the autonomy of a discrete aesthetic sphere. Broch's Virgil wants to destroy the *Aeneid* because he believes his art to be inimical to the historical age: 'the time', he tells Caesar,

> determines the direction in which the task [of the artist] lies, and he who goes contrary to it must collapse . . . an art that is consummated outside these limits, evading the real task, is neither perception nor help — in short it is not art and cannot endure.[106]

There is, though, a younger generation of poets in whom Virgil seems to see art's future: the love poets Tibullus, Propertius and 'young Ovid who is so full of poor taste' have, he says, 'struggled through to an originality which I am unable to approach' (*DoV*, p. 254). The case against is made by Lucius, who views Ovid and the others as weak, ephemeral and, perhaps above all, irredeemably imitative: 'They are imitators of Theocritus, pupils of Catallus, and whatever they can take from our Virgil, that they take' (*DoV*, p. 256).

If *The Death of Virgil* really is a novel which charts, in a displaced form, the death of modernism, it is not surprising that the young Ovid (before whom lies the writing of the *Metamorphoses*) should be in some way associated with the future of poetry. Virgil's attempt to make of the *Aeneid* a supreme fiction does not any longer seem credible when the actuality of the Roman state imposes so much more powerfully an image of reality's possibilities on the minds of the citizens. Ovid's *Metamorphoses*, however, will reassert art's ability to offer new images of the real by insisting on the fluidity and unceasing mutability of reality itself.

The Last World by Christoph Ransmayr is a novel in which the newness of Ovid's work is depicted as itself a transformation of the world. A young Roman dissident named Cotta comes to the island of Tomi in search of the banished Ovid. Ransmayr's Ovid (here called Naso) has been punished for his accidental act of democratic rebellion; he has forgotten to address the Emperor first in the introduction of his speech and has begun instead with the words 'Citizens of Rome'. Cotta comes to Tomi in search not only of Ovid, but also of his final poem – the *Metamorphoses* – which he understands as a work of political subversion – and which the poet has burned.

As Cotta's search progresses, it becomes clear to the reader that the inhabitants of Ransmayr's Tomi are reworked, debased versions of characters from the *Metamorphoses*. Here, as Salman Rushdie writes in his review of the novel, we see 'Ransmayr's vision of art conquering defeat by remaking the world in its own image'.[1] In fact, the world of Tomi *is* Ovid's work of art. The anxieties which haunted Broch's Virgil have gone. The contemplation of art's destruction in the face of an overwhelming reality can now be borne with all the *sang froid* that Terry Eagleton fears; for the world of images and the world of political punishment are one, and the dream of the avant-garde – 'the attempt to organize a new life praxis from a basis in art' – has finally been realised. And unto Caesar is rendered what is still Caesar's.

Jameson's Postmodernism

As I suggested earlier, Fredric Jameson is probably the best known of Marxist theorists to have written at length on postmodernism. Following Adorno's writings on the culture industry, Jameson portrays the postmodern as a new and more complete stage of capitalist commodification; while, citing Guy Debord's *The Society of the Spectacle*, he writes that

> the ultimate form of commodity reification in contemporary consumer society is precisely the image itself. With this universal commodification of our object world, the familiar accounts of the other-directedness of contemporary conspicuous consumption and of the sexualization of our objects and activities are also given: the new model car is essentially an image for other people to have of us, and we consume less the thing itself, than its abstract idea, open to all the libidinal investments ingenuously arrayed for us by advertising.[108]

The postmodern is that stage when what had once been thought – however problematically – as real, genuine or authentic has been lost completely, not even remaining (as it does with modernism) in the form of a longing or lament for what is now absent. 'Postmodernism', writes Jameson, 'is what you have when the modernisation process is complete and nature is gone for good.'[109] The end of art's autonomy has, then, led not only to the commodification of culture, but also to the aestheticisation of the external object world, producing what we saw Jameson call earlier 'a society of the image or simulacrum', an aspect of the postmodern which, as Jameson acknowledges, has been dealt with most comprehensively by Jean Baudrillard.[110]

Thus far Jameson is little different from either Adorno or Eagleton. Where he takes a step that is quite original is in his insistence on a *dialectical* approach to the study of postmodernism. Taking his cue from *The Communist Manifesto* – 'Marx powerfully urges us to do the impossible, namely, to think this development [of capitalism] positively *and* negatively all at once' – Jameson argues that it is the duty of any Marxist analysis of the postmodern to attempt to 'identify some "moment of truth" within the more evident "moments of falsehood" of postmodern culture'.[111] This produces in Jameson's critique not a paralysing ambivalence, but the desire to trace the expression of some element of conflict, of irreconciled ideological significance in the cultural products of the postmodern. If Jameson can trace those, he believes that Marx's insistence on the capitalist mode's necessary contradictions will be shown to remain true, thereby reasserting the validity of Marxist critique itself and identifying postmodernism quite firmly as 'the cultural logic of late capitalism'.

This is not the place to discuss Jameson's identification of postmodernism's principal stylistic characteristics in any detail; instead, these features (such as pastiche, depthlessness, playfulness, etc.) will be looked at in relation to specific texts in following chapters. For the moment, however, it is worth stressing the quite striking ahistoricism that Jameson associates with postmodernism. 'It is safest', he writes in the opening sentence of the *Postmodernism* book, 'to grasp the concept of the postmodern as an attempt to think the present historically in an age that has forgotten how to think historically in the first place.'[112] What he is to offer us – 'the concept of the postmodern' – is the historicisation of a resolutely ahistorical cultural configuration. To readers of Adorno, the latter should come as little surprise: '[h]istory is extruded from tales which have become cultural commodities, even and especially there where historical themes are exploited.'[113] Just as we saw in the opening pages how Marx depicts the commodity as a

fetishised object wiped clean of the historical markers of its production, Adorno here suggests that such a process might also be
identified in cultural commodities. The various ways in which this
problem might be seen to relate to *specific* postmodernist texts will
be explored in following chapters.

It is worth noting, though, that the critique Jameson offers of
Adorno's analyses of the culture industry is also based on a
perceived inadequacy of historicisation: 'what has been omitted
from the later judgements', he writes, 'is precisely Adorno's
fundamental discovery of the historicity, and in particular, the
irreversible aging process, of the greatest modernist forms.'[114]
Just as Adorno criticised Lukács's ahistorical prejudice for the
realist aesthetic of Balzac and (far more problematically) Mann,
Jameson questions Adorno's own reliance on a modernist mode
whose time would seem to have passed. Where Adorno saw in
the work of modernist writers the expression of a particular
historical experience ('[t]he voice of the age echoes through their
monologues'), Jameson tries to identify in postmodernism a
similar expressiveness:

> [I]nsofar as postmodernism really expresses multinational capit-
> alism, there is some cognitive content to it. It is articulating
> something that is going on. If the subject is lost in it, and if in
> social life the psychic subject has been decentered by late
> capitalism, then this art faithfully and authentically registers
> that. That's its moment of truth.[115]

Jameson's rebuke of Adorno is thus based on what he has called
'the one absolute and we may even say "transhistorical" imperative of all dialectical thought': 'Always historicise!'[116] 'Who, after
all,' as Andreas Huyssen asks, 'would want to be the Lukács of the
postmodern. . . .'[117]

It is with this attempt to historicise both the ahistoricism and
cognitive decentring that he associates with postmodernism that
Jameson also seeks to find something redemptive, some cultural
expression of contemporary social experience. We have already
seen Jameson's identification of that spatial confusion to which
postmodern culture contributes with the individual subject's
decentring in late capitalism. Jameson's well-known and extensive description of John Portman's Westin Bonaventure Hotel in
Postmodernism is a good example of the cultural space–social
space analogy on which this analysis rests.[118] Probably of
greater relevance to the present argument, though, is the way

in which Jameson discusses the ahistoricism of postmodern fiction.

Taking E. L. Doctorow as his principal example, Jameson attempts to interpret such ahistoricism as a feature of cultural and historical necessity. Doctorow's novels do not express for Jameson (as they do for Linda Hutcheon) 'an extended critique of American democratic ideals through the presentation of class conflict',[119] but instead the very inability to sustain such a critique. 'Doctorow', he writes, 'is the epic poet of the disappearance of the American radical past.' For Jameson, then, the 'moment of truth' of a novel such as *Ragtime* is not in its delineation of class conflict, but in its transformation of 'the past into something which is obviously a black simulacrum',[120] and its evocation of the left's 'poignant distress' as it witnesses the disappearance of the historical referent, the disappearance of those historical parameters in which class conflict is situated. Jameson's key claim for Doctorow's writing is as follows:

> What is culturally interesting, however, is that he has had to convey this great theme formally (since the waning of the content is very precisely his subject) and, more than that, has had to elaborate his work by way of that very cultural logic of the postmodern which is itself the mark and symptom of his dilemma.[121]

Above all, Jameson is here stressing the inescapability of the cultural logic that is postmodernism. '[O]ne can't', he writes elsewhere, 'wish this postmodern blockage of historicity out of existence by mere self-critical self-consciousness.'[122] Rather, he insists on the need to work, as he claims Doctorow does, from within postmodernism, using postmodernist techniques and modes of representation to depict the condition of postmodernity itself, and thereby to suggest its own necessary historicisation. What Jameson seems to be claiming for Doctorow's writing is nothing less than a form of aesthetic negative dialectics of the postmodern:

> [Doctorow] suddenly makes us realize that this is the only image of the past we have, in truth a projection on the walls of Plato's cave. This, if you like, is negative dialectics, or negative theology, an insistence of the very flatness and depthlessness of the thing which makes what isn't there very vivid. That is not negligible. It is not the reinvention of some sense of the

past where one would fantasize about a healthier age of deeper historical sense: it is the use of those very limited instruments to show their limits. And it is not ironic.[123]

This is as far as Jameson has yet reached in his attempt to recuperate for Marxist theory some element of postmodernist culture. It is, as we have seen, quite a different form of response to that of both Adorno and Eagleton; the latter, in fact, views Jameson's project as distinctly naïve politically. As Jameson depicts it, at its best postmodernist art and literature can seek to offer a form of 'cognitive mapping' for the decentred subjects of the late capitalist age. This is quite different from those networks of totality that Lukács saw in the novels of Balzac, different even from the solitary (but typical) suffering selves of Adorno's Beckett. Instead, the representation both of totality and of the alienated individual subject is sacrificed for the sake of immanent critique. Although, as we have seen, Jameson identifies it in some examples of postmodern culture, he portrays this form of critique as the goal of a new and truly political postmodernism:

> [T]he new political art (if it is possible at all) will have to hold to the truth of postmodernism, that is to say, to its funda-mental object − the world space of multinational capital − at the same time at which it achieves a breakthrough to some as yet unimaginable new mode of representing this last, in which we may again begin to grasp our positioning as individual and collective subjects and regain a capacity to act and struggle which is at present neutralized by our spatial as well as our social confusion.[124]

In my short concluding chapter I return to the theoretical concept of the postmodern as discussed by Jameson, suggesting some revision of his model. For the moment, though, it suffices to note that the argument pursued in the course of this book is predicated on the assumption that there is adequate complexity in postmodern fiction of the 1980s and 1990s to trace those internal dialectics of complicity and immanent critique without anticipating some 'unimaginable new mode' of representation which will somehow make it all easier for us. Better to start, claimed Brecht, with the 'bad new things' than the 'good old ones', a sentiment cited with ironic approval by Terry Eagleton.[125] Above all, however − since the unimaginable is rarely as anticipated − it is advisable, as the following chapters are intended to demonstrate, to begin with what is to hand.

Notes

1. Theodor W. Adorno, *Aesthetic Theory*, p. 1.
2. Georg Lukács, 'Reification and the Consciousness of the Proletariat', in his *History and Class Consciousness*, p. 83.
3. Karl Marx, *Capital*, Vol. 1, p. 165.
4. See Karl Marx and Friedrich Engels, *The Communist Manifesto*, p. 79: 'The history of all hitherto existing society is the history of class struggles.'
5. Marx, *Capital*, Vol. 1, pp. 164–5.
6. Lukács, 'Reification and the Consciousness of the Proletariat', p. 93.
7. Ibid., pp. 110–11.
8. J. M. Bernstein, *The Philosophy of the Novel*, pp. xiii–xiv.
9. Lukács, 'Reification and the Consciousness of the Proletariat', p. 124.
10. Ibid.
11. Bernstein, *The Philosophy of the Novel*, p. xvii.
12. Lukács, 'Reification and the Consciousness of the Proletariat', p. 134.
13. Ibid.
14. Jürgen Habermas associates this aspect of Lukács's thought with the influence on a strand of Western Marxism of Max Weber's writings on rationalisation (Habermas, *The Philosophical Discourse of Modernity*, p. 75). Weber, writes Habermas,

> described as 'rational' the process of disenchantment which led in Europe to a disintegration of religious world views that issued in a secular culture. With the modern empirical sciences, autonomous arts, and theories of morality and law grounded on principles, cultural spheres of value took shape which made possible learning processes in accord with the respective inner logics of theoretical, aesthetic, and moral-practical problems. (*The Philosophical Discourse of Modernity*, p. 1)

The influence of Weber's writings on rationalisation runs through the early Lukács of *History and Class Consciousness* and the Critical Theory of the Frankfurt School, most notably Adorno and Horkheimer's *Dialectic of Enlightenment*.

The extent to which this narrative has now, in Western Marxist circles, become something of a truism is attested by Terry Eagleton's half-parodic summary in *The Ideology of the Aesthetic*:

> Let us tell, in crude and fabular form, a Weberian kind of story. Imagine a society sometime in the indeterminate past, before the rise of capitalism, perhaps even before the Fall, certainly before the dissociation of sensibility, when the three great questions of philosophy – what can we know? what ought we to do? what do we find attractive? – were not as yet fully distinguishable from

one another. A society, that is to say, where the three mighty
regions of the cognitive, the ethico-political and the libidinal-
aesthetic were still to a large extent intermeshed. (p. 366)

See also, for an extended treatment of these themes: J. M. Bernstein,
*The Fate of Art: Aesthetic Alienation from Kant to Derrida and
Adorno*.
15. Lukács, 'What is Orthodox Marxism?', in his *History and Class
    Consciousness*, p. 6.
16. Ibid., pp. 12–13.
17. Ibid., p. 13.
18. Bernstein, *The Philosophy of the Novel*, p. 91.
19. Lukács, *The Theory of the Novel*, pp. 38–9.
20. Ibid., p. 88.
21. Ibid., p. 60.
22. Ibid., p. 56.
23. Bernstein, *The Philosophy of the Novel*, p. 46 (emphasis added).
24. Ibid., p. 229.
25. Ibid., p. 242.
26. Andreas Huyssen, *After the Great Divide: Modernism, Mass Culture,
    Postmodernism*.
27. John Carey, *The Intellectuals and the Masses: Pride and Prejudice
    among the Literary Intelligentsia, 1880–1939*.
28. Bernstein, *The Philosophy of the Novel*, p. 241.
29. Theodor W. Adorno, 'Reconciliation under Duress', in Ernst Bloch et
    al., *Aesthetics and Politics*, p. 160.
30. Georg Lukács, 'Critical Realism and Socialist Realism', in his *The
    Meaning of Contemporary Realism*, p. 96.
31. Erich Auerbach, *Mimesis: The Representation of Reality in Western
    Literature*, p. 473.
32. Fredric Jameson, 'Beyond the Cave: Demystifying the Ideology of
    Modernism', in *Contemporary Marxist Literary Criticism*, ed. Francis
    Mulhern, p. 174.
33. Auerbach, *Mimesis*, p. 548.
34. Ibid., p. 545.
35. Georg Lukács, 'The Ideology of Modernism', in his *The Meaning of
    Contemporary Realism*, p. 25.
36. Ibid., p. 26.
37. Ibid., p. 36.
38. Ibid., p. 31.
39. Ibid., p. 30.
40. Adorno, 'Reconciliation under Duress', pp. 162–3.
41. Ibid., p. 166.
42. Jameson, 'Beyond the Cave', pp. 174–5.
43. Ibid., p. 175.
44. Ibid., p. 183.

45. Ibid., pp. 183–4.
46. William Faulkner, 'Introduction to *The Sound and the Fury*', cited in Frederick R. Karl, *William Faulkner: American Writer*, p. 318.
47. Jameson, 'Beyond the Cave', p. 184.
48. Adorno, 'Reconciliation under Duress', pp. 160–1.
49. Richard H. Brodhead, 'Introduction: Faulkner and the Logic of Remaking', in his *Faulkner: New Perspectives*, p. 5.
50. Jean-Paul Sartre, 'On *The Sound and the Fury*: Time in the Work of Faulkner', in his *Literary and Philosophical Essays*, p. 84.
51. William Faulkner, 'Appendix', in his *The Sound and the Fury*, pp. 299–300. Further references to the text are from the same edition and will be cited in the main text, prefixed by the abbreviation *SF*.
52. Karl, *William Faulkner*, p. 328.
53. William Faulkner, 'Introduction to *The Sound and the Fury*', cited ibid., p. 318.
54. Susan Willis, 'Aesthetic of the Rural Slum', in Broadhead, *Faulkner: New Perspectives*, p. 182.
55. Sartre, 'On *The Sound and the Fury*', p. 91.
56. Brodhead, *Faulkner*, pp. 5–6.
57. Adorno, *Aesthetic Theory*, p. 196.
58. See Huyssen, *After the Great Divide*, pp. vii–viii. For a discussion of the irony which attends the novel's increasing respectability as a literary genre in the nineteenth century and its simultaneous increasing commodification in a culture industry, see Terry Lovell, *Consuming Fiction*, pp. 78–81. Huyssen's analysis of the continuity of thematic preoccupations from late nineteenth-century to early twentieth-century literature is also suggested by Peter Keating (in *The Haunted Study*, p. 4) when he writes of 'the overwhelming force of democratic consumerism' which exerts a continuous influence on literature of the Victorian and modernist periods.
59. Adorno and Horkheimer, *Dialectic of Enlightenment*, p. 135.
60. J. M. Bernstein, 'Introduction', in Theodor W. Adorno, *The Culture Industry: Selected Essays*, p. 19.
61. Harvey, *The Condition of Postmodernity*, pp. 125–6.
    See also Henry Ford, *My Life and Work*; especially Chapters VIII, IX and XI. The following, for example, is from Chapter XI ('Money and Goods'):

    > The factory must build, the sales department must sell, and the dealer must buy cars all the year through, if each would enjoy the maximum profit to be derived from the business. If the retail buyer will not consider purchasing except in 'seasons', *a campaign of education* needs to be waged, proving the all-the-year-around value of a car rather than the limited-season value. And while the educating is being done, the manufacturer must build, and the dealer must buy, in anticipation of business. (p.165; emphasis added)

62. Theodor W. Adorno, 'On the Fetish Character in Music and the Regression in Listening', in his *The Culture Industry*, pp. 26–7.
63. Ibid., p. 33.
64. Adorno and Horkheimer, *Dialectic of Enlightenment*, p. 126.
65. Ibid., p. 154.
66. Ibid., p. 158.
67. Theodor W. Adorno, 'Letters to Walter Benjamin', in Ernst Bloch et al., *Aesthetics and Politics*, p. 123.
68. Bernstein, 'Introduction', p. 8.
69. Adorno and Horkheimer, *Dialectic of Enlightenment*, p. 144.
70. Fredric Jameson, *Marxism and Form: Twentieth-Century Dialectical Theories of Literature*, p. 37.
71. John Dos Passos, *USA*, p. 1116. Further references to the text will be to the same edition and will be marked in the main text, prefixed by the abbreviation *USA*.
72. Alfred Kazin, 'Dos Passos and the Lost Generation', in Barry Maine (ed.), *Dos Passos: The Critical Heritage*, p. 226.
73. T. Ludington (ed.), *The Fourteenth Chronicle: Letters and Diaries of John Dos Passos*, p. 441.
74. Kazin, 'Dos Passos', p. 229.
75. Ludington, *The Fourteenth Chronicle*, p. 441.
76. Theodor W. Adorno, *Philosophy of Modern Music*, pp. 67–8.
77. For a discussion of Adorno's influence on the musical sections in *Doctor Faustus*, see Thomas Mann, *The Genesis of a Novel*, and T. W. Adorno, 'Toward a Portrait of Thomas Mann', in his *Notes to Literature*, Vol. 2, pp. 12–19.
78. Patrick Carnegy, *Faust as Musician: A Study of Thomas Mann's Novel 'Doctor Faustus'*, p. 108.
79. Thomas Mann, *Doctor Faustus*, p. 69. Further references to the text are to the same edition and are marked in the main text, prefixed by the abbreviation *DF*.
80. Adorno, *Philosophy of Modern Music*, p. 19 (emphasis added).
81. Georg Lukács, *Essays on Thomas Mann*, p. 67.
82. Thomas Mann, *The Genesis of a Novel*, p. 47.
83. Ibid., p. 60.
84. Ibid., p. 29.
85. Ibid.
86. Ibid., p. 48.
87. Ibid., p. 76.
88. Ibid., p. 144.
89. Terry Eagleton, 'Capitalism, Modernism and Postmodernism', in his *Against the Grain*, pp. 131–47.
90. Peter Bürger, *Theory of the Avant-Garde*, p. 7.
91. Herbert Marcuse, 'The Affirmative Character of Culture', in his *Negations: Essays in Critical Theory*, pp. 88–133.
92. Bürger, *Theory of the Avant-Garde*, p. 11.

93. Ibid., pp. 11–12.
94. Ibid., p. 12.
95. Ibid., p. 22.
96. Huyssen, *After the Great Divide*, p. 147.
97. Ibid.
98. Bürger, *Theory of the Avant-Garde*, p. 49.
99. Ibid., p. 50.
100. Huyssen, *After the Great Divide*, p. 147. See also Huyssen's description of Andy Warhol's use of Duchamp in the serial portrait *Thirty Are Better than One*, pp. 146–8.
101. Bürger, *Theory of the Avant-Garde*, p. 53.
102. Eagleton, 'Capitalism, Modernism and Postmodernism', p. 131.
103. Terry Eagleton, *The Ideology of the Aesthetic*, p. 373.
104. Eagleton, 'Capitalism, Modernism and Postmodernism', p. 147.
105. Ibid., pp. 140–1.
106. Hermann Broch, *The Death of Virgil*, p. 335. Further references to the text are to the same edition and are marked in the main text, prefixed by the abbreviation *DoV*.
107. Salman Rushdie, 'Christoph Ransmayr', in his *Imaginary Homelands: essays 1981–1991*, p. 293.
108. Fredric Jameson, 'Reification and Utopia in Mass Culture', in *Signatures of the Visible*, pp. 11–12.
109. Fredric Jameson, *Postmodernism, or, the Cultural Logic of Late Capitalism*, p. ix.
110. See ibid., p. 234; see also Jean Baudrillard, 'Simulations and Simulacra', in his *Selected Writings*, pp. 166–84.
111. Jameson, *Postmodernism*, p. 47.
112. Ibid, p. ix.
113. Theodor W. Adorno, 'The Schema of Mass Culture', in his *The Culture Industry*, pp. 66–7.
114. Jameson, 'Reification and Utopia in Mass Culture', p. 14.
115. Anders Stephanson and Fredric Jameson, 'Regarding Postmodernism: A Conversation with Fredric Jameson', in D. Kellner, *Postmodernism/Jameson/Critique*, p. 55.
116. Fredric Jameson, *The Political Unconscious: Narrative as a Socially Symbolic Act*, p. 9.
117. Huyssen, *After the Great Divide*, p. 43.
118. Jameson, *Postmodernism*, pp. 38–45.
119. Linda Hutcheon, *A Poetics of Postmodernism*, pp. 61–2.
120. Stephanson and Jameson, 'Regarding Postmodernism', p. 61.
121. Jameson, *Postmodernism*, p. 25.
122. Stephanson and Jameson, 'Regarding Postmodernism', p. 61.
123. Ibid, p. 62.
124. Jameson, *Postmodernism*, p. 54.
125. Eagleton, 'Capitalism, Modernism and Postmodernism', p. 141.

II   Postmodern Reflections: Thinking after Marxism

Lukács's Kant is primarily a bourgeois thinker. The antinomies of Kant's thought, as we have already seen, represent for Lukács the internal contradictions of bourgeois society, the construction of a private, rational moral order which remains cut off from an external world of social and economic relations. Such a description, however, is perhaps more dependent on the Marxist *concept* of history to which Lukács subjects his reading of Kant than it is on the Kantian texts themselves. It is on the ground of this conceptual domination of particulars that the postmodern, postmarxist critique of traditional Marxist ideology critique proceeds.

At the centre of this critique is the suggestion that the Marxist concept of history is itself ahistorical. Jameson, of course, acknowledges this at least to some degree in the opening sentence of *The Political Unconscious*: 'Always historicize! This slogan the one absolute and we may even say "transhistorical" imperative of all dialectical thought will unsurprisingly turn out to be the moral of *The Political Unconscious* as well.'[1] However, it is not the simple act of historicisation that postmarxists attack, but the domination of historical acts and conditions by the Marxist schema of relations of production. As will be clear throughout the course of this and following chapters, postmodern and postmarxist thought interprets Marxist historicisation as an escape from history rather than an engagement with it. Thus it is possible to interpret Jameson's comments on the relationship between Marxism and feminism as the ahistorical imposition on the latter of the former's conceptual framework:

> The affirmation of radical feminism . . . that to annul the patriarchal is the most *radical* political act insofar as it includes and subsumes more partial demands, such as the liberation from the commodity form is thus perfectly consistent with an expanded Marxian framework, for which the transformation

of our own dominant mode of production must be accompanied and completed by an equally radical restructuration of all the more archaic modes of production with which it structurally coexists.[2]

Jameson here grasps little of the distinctive history of feminist struggle, acknowledging its radical credentials only to the extent to which its agenda is compatible with the Marxist categories of modes and relations of production. Such thinking, for the post-marxist, is really an evasion of thought and an imposition of transhistorical, reified concepts onto particular and distinct historical experiences. In this sense, as we shall see later, the conceptual domination of Marxist categories over specific and heterogeneous experiences or conditions can be interpreted by the postmarxist as analogous to the domination under exchange value of objects' heterogeneous use-values in the process of capitalist commodification. It is not surprising, therefore, to find that postmarxist theory frequently insists on Marxism's complicity, in the final instance, with the capitalist system it professes to critique.

It is in this sense that postmarxism identifies the Marxist tradition with the legacy of European Enlightenment, extending Adorno and Horkheimer's critique of the rationalisation of thought in *Dialectic of Enlightenment* to Marxism itself. This aspect of postmarxist thought is neatly summarised by Thomas Docherty:

Since the Enlightenment, thought has been rigorously policed or disciplined, 'conventionalised'. The discipline of thinking the province of intellectual practice has been established within rigorously conventionalised boundaries whose function is the legitimisation and, indeed, recuperation of all thought such that it is made to conform to the norms of 'Enlightenment'. The incipient radicalism of thinking as such, of a mode of thinking which escapes or questions dogma or ideology, becomes an impossibility: its status is that of 'illegitimate' thought, schizophrenia or madness. All so-called 'thought' now takes place under the sign of a dominant schema or ideology a 'logic'. As in mathematical logic, no real critical thinking is required; for, given the counters at work in any mathematical situation, it is the *system* of mathematical logic which does the thinking and which provides the answers. The subject has no thoughts or stakes in this matter. Postmarxism, like postmodernism, strives to make the possibility of thinking of an unpoliced, undisciplined thought, or of thinking differently available once more.[3]

Postmarxist thought attempts to evade the rationalised conditions of Marxist critique through a return to Kant. Where Lukács concentrates on Kant's *Critique of Pure Reason* and *Critique of Practical Reason*, postmarxism stresses the significance of the third *Critique*, *The Critique of Judgement*. Jean-François Lyotard proposes Kant's model of aesthetic judgement as a critical response to the systematic application of a critical method (such as Lukács's Marxist critique of Kant). '[A]esthetic judgement conceals', suggests Lyotard, 'a secret more important than that of doctrine, the secret of the "manner" (rather than the method) in which critical thought proceeds in general.'[4]

Critical thought, for Lyotard, is predicated on what Kant calls 'reflective' judgement. Kant distinguishes between '*determinant*' and '*reflective*' judgement. The former, he argues, '*subsumes merely under given laws, or concepts, as principles*'.[5] In this case, the method, system, or set of *a priori* concepts (for example, the Marxist schema of relations of production) determines the judgement; the role of the subject is confined to the rationalised application of these 'given laws'. Truly critical thought, however, is predicated on 'reflective' judgement which 'has to subsume under a law that is not yet given'.[6] For the postmarxist Lyotard: 'The mode of critical thought should by definition be purely reflective (it does not *already* have the concepts it seeks to use).'[7] Postmarxist thought thus proceeds in a manner that is open to the heterogeneity of its object(s) and has no necessary stake in the legitimisation of its own method. In this way, postmarxism can be characterised as a mode of thinking which discovers its legitimisation in the act or event of its own inquiry rather than in the pre-determined confirmation it finds in its results or conclusions. From this standpoint, it is hardly surprising that Kant appears to Lukács as such an exemplar of bourgeois thought; such a result legitimises the Marxist premises of Lukács's critical method.

This chapter will describe in greater detail some of the ways in which postmodern theory – in particular, that of Jean-François Lyotard and Jean Baudrillard – attempts to develop a form of postmarxist critical thinking which engages with the limitations of Marxist ideology critique. Works of fiction by Toni Morrison (*Beloved*) and Don DeLillo (*White Noise* and *Libra*) will be read in the light of these ideas, exploring their implications for our interpretation of such fictional texts. The chapter begins, though, with the work of Lyotard and the issues it raises both for questions of legitimation and, in his description of the postmodern sublime, for aesthetic representation.

Jean-François Lyotard and the
Problem with Grand Narratives

Simplifying to the extreme, Jean-François Lyotard defines 'postmodern' as 'incredulity toward metanarratives'.[8] 'By metanarratives or grand narratives,' he explains, 'I mean precisely narrations with a legitimating function.'[9] Lyotard thus identifies the postmodern with a sceptical stance towards the legitimating function of narrative. More specifically, he posits the postmodern as a critique of narrative legitimation that extends beyond the specific instance or condition of that particular narrative to encompass a general or totalising truth. Lyotard offers an exemplary list of those metanarratives with which he is concerned:

> the progressive emancipation of reason and freedom, the progressive or catastrophic emancipation of labour (source of alienated value in capitalism), the enrichment of all humanity through the progress of capitalist technoscience, and even if we include Christianity itself in modernity (in opposition to the classicism of antiquity) – the salvation of creatures through the conversion of souls to the Christian narrative of martyred love.[10]

These narratives (for example, liberalism, Marxism, Christianity) are portrayed as markers of modernity; and thus modernity is characterised, for Lyotard, by the desire to construct a total and totalising narrative which will legitimise a political, philosophical or ethical project. In fact, it is this faith in the *project* that is modernity's most striking characteristic. In this sense, Lyotard can be seen to continue the critique of Enlightenment thought that Adorno and Horkheimer develop in *Dialectic of Enlightenment*. It is hardly coincidental that both Lyotard and the Frankfurt School thinkers concentrate on the privileged status in modernity of scientific discourse and rationality. For both, that status is predicated on the illegitimate and ideological identification of scientific truth with some generalised and overarching notion of Truth itself.

Lyotard expands this critique into areas Adorno and Horkheimer addressed less directly through his description of the complicity of Marxist critique with the capitalist system it professes to oppose. Assessing the critical impact of Marxist struggle, Lyotard writes:

> in countries with liberal or advanced liberal management, the struggles and their instruments have been transformed into regulators of the system; in communist countries, the totalizing model and its totalitarian effect have made a comeback in the name of Marxism itself, and the struggles in question have simply been deprived of the right to exist. Everywhere, the Critique of political economy (the subtitle of Marx's *Capital*) and its correlate, the critique of alienated society, are used in one way or another as aids in programming the system.[11]

The project of modernity, characterised by 'the realisation of universality', encompasses both the increasing globalisation of the capitalist system and its critique in the form of the Marxist narrative of class conflict and the central role of the mode of production.

For Lyotard, truly critical thinking must accept that '[t]he grand narrative has lost its credibility, regardless of what mode of unification it uses, regardless of whether it is a speculative narrative or a narrative of emancipation'.[12] It is only through the acceptance of heterogeneity, the abandonment of any universal criteria for judgement, that critical thinking again becomes possible. We can see, then, that Lyotard's discussion of metanarratives or grand narratives, and his definition of the postmodern condition as the loss of such narratives' credibility, is analogous to his insistence on the necessity of 'reflective' judgement, a form of critique which is not determined by pre-established laws or underpinned by a legitimising metanarrative. The grand narratives of modernity can thus be read as the 'given laws' or set of *a priori* concepts that inform 'determinant' judgement, legitimising its conclusions in advance and (re)constructing the thinking subject as simply the vehicle for the laws' or narratives' enactment and fulfilment.

Significantly, too, Lyotard refuses to define the postmodern strictly in terms of historical chronology. 'Ultimately,' explains Thomas Docherty, 'it is mistaken to conceive of postmodernism as a periodising concept. . . . The postmodern is not synonymous with the contemporary.'[13] That Western Marxist narrative summarised in the previous chapter, describing a historico-cultural transition from modernism to postmodernism, is posited by postmarxism as a crude and erroneous historicisation. Instead, in a passage endlessly recycled by subsequent commentators, Lyotard defines the postmodern as 'not modernism at its end, but in a nascent state, and this state is recurrent.'[14] The postmodern, thus understood, is a particular mode of representation rather than, as Jameson would have it, the 'cultural logic' of a specific stage in capitalist economic development. In fact, Docherty describes as naïve the Marxist position which assumes that, because the 'current wave' of postmodernism is taking place simultaneously with the development of 'late capitalism', the former should be seen as the latter's cultural or aesthetic expression. Lyotard, associating the decline of grand narratives with 'the blossoming of techniques and technologies since the Second World War', concludes that '[a]nytime we go searching for causes in this way we are bound to be disappointed'.[15] Postmodernism, in this case, is a mode of thought and of aesthetic representation, a mode that demands what Lyotard calls the 'pleasure in reason exceeding all presentation'.[16] This postmodernism cannot be explained away as the effect of a stage in economic development, but challenges the reader/listener/viewer to discover ways of interpreting a particular text in the event of its confrontation, rather than by the application of pre-established categories (such as Marxist historicisation). This, ironically, opens the text up to a more dramatic historical dimension: namely, that of the subject's engagement with the work or text, now no longer determined by adherence to a transhistorical, reified set of interpretative criteria.

That engagement, as we have just seen Lyotard describe, is also a recognition of the inadequacy of aesthetic representation to present certain objects or forms of experience. This is at least part of what Lyotard means when he describes the postmodern in terms drawn fom Kant's definition of 'the sublime'. The following section will describe Lyotard's discussion of the relation of postmodernism to the sublime and explain how this might help in understanding his work in relation to that of both Fredric Jameson and Theodor Adorno. The chapter will then go on to explore some of these ideas in a reading of Toni Morrison's *Beloved*, suggesting that in Morrison's narrative of slavery we can see the abandonment of any legitimising grand narrative (whether based, like Richard Wright's *Native Son*, on Marxist premises, or founded on the historical assumption of white guilt and black innocence). The relevance of some notion of the sublime to an appreciation of the text will also be discussed.

Lyotard, Postmodernism and the Sublime

Lyotard explains the aesthetics of the sublime in the following terms:

> a pleasure mixed with pain, a pleasure that comes from pain. In the event of an absolutely large object the desert, a mountain, a pyramid or one that is absolutely powerful a storm at sea, an erupting volcano which, like all absolutes, can only be thought, without any sensible/sensory intuition, as an Idea of reason, the faculty of presentation, the imagination, fails to provide a representation corresponding to this Idea. The failure of expression gives rise to a pain, a kind of cleavage within the subject between what can be conceived and what can be imagined or presented. But this pain in turn engenders a pleasure, in fact a double pleasure: the impotence of the imagination attests *a contrario* to an imagination striving to figure even that which cannot be figured, and that imagination thus aims to harmonize its object with that of reason and that further- more, the inadequacy of the images is a negative sign of the immense power of ideas.[17]

This conception of the sublime is crucial to the postmarxist under- standing of postmodernism. It is precisely this concentration on the inadequacy of aesthetic representation, putting forward 'the unpresentable in presentation itself', that for the postmarxist is the defining feature of the postmodern aesthetic.

The association of postmodernism with an aesthetic of the sublime reinforces that sense of the postmodern as a mode rather than as a period style or periodising concept. 'The postmodern artist or writer', writes Lyotard,

> is in the position of a philosopher: the text he writes or the work he creates is not in principle governed by pre-established rules and cannot be judged according to a determinant judge- ment, by the application of given categories to this text or work. Such rules and categories are what the work or text is investigating.[18]

The ceaseless aesthetic experimentation on which such a model of the postmodern is based might not, however, prove too different from the Marxist argument, found in the work of both Jameson and Eagleton, that postmodernism expresses the ever-new modes of production and consumption that are necessary in the age of consumer capitalism. In fact, Lyotard acknowledges something of this sort himself:

> there is a kind of collusion between capital and the avant-garde. The force of scepticism and even of destruction that capitalism has brought into play, and that Marx never ceased analysing and identifying, in some way encourages among artists a mistrust of established rules and a willingness to experiment with means of expression, with styles, with ever-new materials. There is something of the sublime in capitalist economy.[19]

He adds:

> This is how innovation in art operates: one re-uses formulae confirmed by previous success, one throws them off balance by combining them with other, in principle incompatible, formulae, by amalgamations, quotations, ornamentations, pastiche. . . . In this way one thinks that one is expressing the spirit of the times, whereas one is merely reflecting the spirit of the market.[20]

Lyotard seems to accept that the avant-garde experimentation with form no longer necessarily creates a critical aesthetic of the sublime. In fact, the playful eclecticism that for the Marxist critical tradition is such a marker of postmodernism is interpreted by Lyotard as a realism, a realism 'of money'. 'This realism', he explains, 'accommodates every tendency, just as capital accommodates every "need".'[21] Much of this sounds similar to Adorno's warnings against the seductive power of the culture industry. In fact, Lyotard's critical postmodernism – difficult, ascetic, 'that which denies itself the solace of good forms' – bears a greater resemblance to Adorno's late modernism (for example, Beckett) than to the playful, populist postmodernism analysed by Jameson (for example, Jonathan Demme's *Something Wild* and Steven Spielberg's *Jaws*).

Unimaginable Guilt: Toni Morrison's *Beloved*

Beloved is a novel about guilt and judgement. It is a novel which insists on the necessity of ethical judgement, forcing us to confront both violence and racism, while denying us any consistent, overarching criteria on which to base these necessary judgements. Again and again, Morrison's text depicts comparable scenes, similar events; yet this repetition always involves some variation. It is impossible, reading *Beloved*, to construct a grand narrative that will account for the complexities of guilt and victimisation in the novel, or legitimise any general criteria of ethical or political judgement. Such judgements, the novel seems to suggest, must be specific to each event and cannot be based on criteria equally applicable to other events or situations.

As we shall see, this distinguishes *Beloved* from earlier Afro-American 'protest fiction', such as that of Richard Wright in the 1940s. Unlike such earlier fiction, *Beloved* articulates no single, pre-determined ideological perspective; instead, it allows us to engage in a reading process of constructing various, inescapably ideological explanations of characters' acts, while continuously revising these explanations and experiencing the inadequacy of any single set of criteria for interpreting the events represented. Moreover, *Beloved* is concerned at least as much with issues of representation as it is with the evaluation and interpretation of those events it represents. The following pages will show not only how the complexities of questions relating to guilt and suffering in *Beloved* evade the comforting analyses of fixed criteria tied to class or race, but also how the novel explores the very limitations of what might be adequately represented, articulating a sense of the inadequacy of aesthetic representation itself. *Beloved* thus reflects both on the absence of a grand narrative with which to legitimise the necessary ethical judgements involved in the represented world of the novel, and on the limitations of artistic expression and the imagination. The events of the novel exist in the reader's confrontation with impossible but necessary ethical judgements; yet that confrontation is one made even more opaque by the inexpressible and unimaginable feelings and experiences of the novel's principal protagonists.

These features are highlighted when placed in the broader context of Afro-American fiction since the 1940s. It is perhaps no accident that Morrison refuses the sort of sociological justification for Sethe's crime that Richard Wright provides for Bigger Thomas's murder of two young women in *Native Son*. The Marxian social analysis which dominates the end of Wright's novel is too crude a polemical tool to allow any real imaginative interaction on the part of the reader; it is as though we have arrived to find that everything has already been understood and explained. The girls' violent deaths are thus reduced to necessary, if lamentable, stages in the demystification and denunciation of a racially and economically oppressive social system. Here the production of social critique is all. As we shall now see, *Beloved*, in its refusal to sacrifice aesthetic and ethical complexity to the sureties of polemical critique, follows a particular strain of Afro-American reaction to Wright's fiction. That is not to say that Morrison's novel is in any way written as a deliberate response to *Native Son* – such a suggestion would be far too limiting and almost certainly wrong. Instead it is to indicate the extent to which this contrast illuminates certain peculiarities of *Beloved*, highlighting some of its most striking and distinctive features. Some of those features, though, can already be seen in the responses to Wright's fiction by both James Baldwin and Ralph Ellison.

In 1940 *Native Son* was published to the resounding acclaim of white, liberal America. Irving Howe's judgement in 'Black Boys and Native Sons' remains an accurate appreciation of the novel's polemical impact on a generation of white, liberal literary critics and cultural commentators:

> The day *Native Son* appeared, American culture was changed forever. No matter how much qualifying the book might later need, it made impossible a repetition of the old lies. In all its crudeness, melodrama, and claustrophobia of vision, Richard Wright's novel brought out into the open, as no one ever had before, the hatred, fear, and violence that have crippled and may yet destroy our culture.[22]

Wright's novel set out, in an almost naturalistic form, the squalor, degradations and daily humiliations of life for Afro-Americans in Chicago's slums. The story of Bigger Thomas serves as a an overt warning to white, middle America that the racialist policies of social, cultural and economic segregation will produce a violent backlash to fulfil their most extreme visions of racial paranoia.

The reproduction of those racial fantasies in Wright's narrative led, though, to stringent criticisms of his polemical and aesthetic strategies by a younger generation of Afro-American writers. For James Baldwin, Wright offered Bigger Thomas quite simplistically and naïvely as 'the monster created by the American republic, the present awful sum of generations of oppression'. Baldwin argues, though, that Wright thus 'fall[s] into the trap of making him [Bigger] subhuman'. He concludes:

It seems to me that this idea carries, implicitly, a most remark-
able confession: that is, that Negro life is in fact as debased and
impoverished as our theology claims; and further, that the use
to which Wright puts this idea can only proceed from the
assumption – not entirely unsound – that Americans, who
evade, so far as possible, all genuine experience, have therefore
no way of assessing the experience of others and no way of
establishing themselves in relation to any way of life which is
not their own.[23]

There is, for Baldwin, a sense of naïve complicity in Wright's use
of such a crudely polemicised narrative and, in particular, in his
use of the all too violent and stereotypical Bigger Thomas.

This, too, was precisely the complaint of Ralph Ellison. Ellison,
though, goes perhaps a little further, suggesting that Wright's
adoption of what is basically a naturalist literary mode is to
some extent responsible for the novel's limitations. 'In *Native
Son*,' writes Ellison,

Wright began with the ideological proposition that what whites
think of the Negro's reality is more important than what
Negroes themselves know it to be. Hence Bigger Thomas was
presented as a near subhuman indictment of white oppression.
He was designed to shock whites out of their apathy and end
the circumstances out of which Wright insisted Bigger
emerged. Here environment is all – and, interestingly enough,
environment conceived solely in terms of the physical, the
non-conscious. . . . Wright could imagine Bigger, but Bigger
could not possibly imagine Richard Wright. Wright saw to
that.[24]

The very nature of the experiences that *Native Son* describes is
seen by Ellison as too limiting. Wright's novel, published eighteen
years after *Ulysses* and eleven after *The Sound and the Fury*, seems
to suggest a static, fixed and immovable identity for its protago-
nist, Bigger Thomas. The character is defined and lives out the
logic of his social situation. This, for Ellison, conforms far too
closely to convenient white stereotypes. Ellison, conversely, is
interested in transformation. Bigger Thomas lives out the essential
truth of his predicament and finds some form of existential fulfilment in accepting his role as violent social outcast. If *Native Son*
offers solace, it is in the discovery of a character's true being: at
the novel's conclusion, Bigger tells his lawyer, '"When a man

kills, it's for something . . . I didn't know I was really alive in this world until I felt things hard enough to kill for 'em.'''[25]

As the extract from Ellison quoted above shows, at least part of what both Ellison and Baldwin react against in *Native Son* is the exclusion of the transformative powers of the imagination. The stylistic virtuosity of Ellison's narrator in *Invisible Man* is an indication of his discovery that he can reconstruct himself for us, the readers, through his artistic medium itself. In this sense, the stylistic fluctuations and improvisations of his narrative serve as literary analogues for the self-assertion and self-discovery that Ellison associates with great jazz in the essays collected in *Shadow and Act*. The most cursory reading of James Baldwin's fiction – for example, *Go Tell It on the Mountain*, 'Sonny's Blues', *Another Country* – shows a very similar desire to identify and explore strategies of social and aesthetic transcendence. Toni Morrison's *Beloved* addresses comparable issues. As we shall see, the question of the scope and the limitations of the imagination's powers is of quite central importance to Morrison's novel.

It is quite easy to see *Beloved* as an example of what Linda Hutcheon calls 'historiographic metafiction'. This is clearly a form of historical novel which also reflects on the construction of various kinds of narratives. But perhaps the most startling aspect of Morrison's novel is the way in which it seems to ask us to join in making sense of what is utterly irrational and perhaps (to most readers at least) utterly incomprehensible.

For Morrison, the novel is necessarily a kind of dialogue. She writes in *Playing in the Dark*:

> The imagination that produces work which bears and invites rereadings, which motions to future readings as well as contemporary ones, implies a shareable world and an endlessly flexible language. Readers and writers both struggle to interpret and perform within a common language shareable imaginative worlds.[26]

Morrison stresses here the process of this imaginative dialogue, the construction of a relationship between author and reader which is constantly shaping and reshaping the boundaries of what each can imagine and, perhaps, feel. As we'll see a little later, this is a relationship dramatised in the novel itself, when Denver tells Beloved the story of her own birth. It is this emphasis on the relationship between reader and author that I am taking as the starting point of my reading of *Beloved*. Key to this reading will be

the notion of 'shareable imaginative worlds' that Morrison discusses above. And it is precisely this notion which it is necessary
to extend to the relationship of the reader to the characters
themselves. The extent to which there is an imaginative world
that we can share with the characters, with Sethe or Beloved,
becomes, it seems to me, one of the central dilemmas of the
novel. Again in *Playing in the Dark* Morrison points to this very
question:

> As a reader (before becoming a writer) I read as I had been
> taught to do. But books revealed themselves rather differently
> to me as a writer. In that capacity I have to place enormous
> trust in my ability to imagine others and my willingness to
> project consciously into the danger zones such others may
> represent for me. I am drawn to the ways all writers do this:
> the way Homer renders a heart-eating cyclops so that our hearts
> are wrenched with pity; the way Dostoevsky compels intimacy
> with Svidrigailov and Prince Myshkin. I am in awe of the
> authority of Faulkner's Benjy, James's Maisie, Flaubert's
> Emma, Melville's Pip, Mary Shelley's Frankenstein − each of
> us can extend the list.
>
> I am interested in what prompts and makes possible this
> process of entering what one is estranged from − and in what
> disables the foray, for purposes of fiction, into corners of the
> consciousness held off and away from the reach of the writer's
> imagination.[27]

The following analysis of *Beloved* focuses on precisely this tension
in the novel between what it is possible − and maybe even
necessary − to imagine and what lies out of reach, beyond the
boundaries of 'shareable worlds' and imaginative empathy.

Beloved is a kind of Afro-American *Crime and Punishment*. We
are told that 'To Sethe, the future was a matter of keeping the past
at bay.'[28] Beloved herself, then, is a revisiting of that past, as
though Raskolnikov's guilt had taken human form and could
also somehow come to represent a whole cultural and historical
past. Beloved, as we'll see, is the guilty past not only of Sethe, but
also of the white American community; and it is precisely this
issue of the ambiguity and complexity of guilt and victimisation
that the novel, in a sense, 'works on'.

Early in the novel some kind of representative status for the
sufferings of Sethe's family is indicated:

'We could move,' she [Sethe] suggested once to her mother-in-law.

'What'd be the point?' asked Baby Suggs. 'Not a house in the country ain't packed to its rafters with some dead Negro's grief. We lucky this ghost is a baby. My husband's spirit was to come back in here? Or yours? Don't talk to me. You lucky. You got three left. Three pulling at your skirts and just one raising hell from the other side. Be thankful, why don't you? I had eight. Every one of them gone away from me. Four taken, four chased, and all, I expect, worrying somebody's house into evil.' Baby Suggs rubbed her eyebrows. 'My first-born. All I remember of her is how she loved the burned bottom of bread. Can you beat that? Eight children and that's all I remember.' (*B*, p. 5)

What initially seems to be a situation characterised by its extra-ordinariness is now portrayed as commonplace. What is being suggested here is the grotesque leap in logic that is necessary to grasp the nature of an everyday reality for those subjected to slavery.

On the very first page, we are told of the break-up of Sethe's family. In a sense, this is hardly significant, since we later find out that the family had never been together out of slavery: even before the death of Beloved, Sethe had had to live without Halle. So the novel begins with us being told of the break-up of a family which had already been broken up. Sethe's sons, Howard and Buglar, leave the house when they can no longer put up with the presence of the ghost. In a way, then, the ghost of Beloved forces the family to re-enact the disruption that we can associate with her own murder. Repetition and re-enactment thus become crucial to the novel thematically and to the structure of the narrative. In the end, of course, Sethe deliriously re-enacts the coming of the Schoolteacher which led to the murder of Beloved, attacking Edward Bodwin this time with an ice-pick.

The complexities of our responses to the characters' situations and experiences are highlighted in the novel's articulation of one of its most important themes, that of dehumanisation. We are given some sort of insight into precisely what horror is here involved when Sethe talks about Schoolteacher's instructions to one of his pupils:

I couldn't help listening to what I heard that day. He was talking to his pupils and I heard him say, 'Which one are you doing?' And one of the boys said, 'Sethe.' That's when I stopped because I heard my name, and then I took a few steps to where I could see what they was doing. Schoolteacher was standing over one of them with one hand behind his back. He licked a forefinger a couple of times and turned a few pages. Slow. I was about to turn around and keep on my way to where the muslin was, when I heard him say, 'No, no. That's not the way. I told you to put her human characteristics on the left; her animal ones on the right. And don't forget to line them up.' (*B*, p. 193)

It is worth noting Schoolteacher's final instruction '"And don't forget to line them up"' a detail that reinforces the association of a rhetoric of scientific rationality with the justification of a racist institution. The novel itself renders these kinds of representations of dehumanisation more complicated, though, by offering a similarly dehumanised portrait of the whites; for example, Stamp Paid reflects on the white murderers of a young, black girl: '"What *are* these people? You tell me, Jesus. What *are* they?"' (*B*, p. 180). Perhaps more significantly, Paul D's reaction to Sethe's confession that she killed her own daughter offers a clear echo of Schoolteacher's unforgotten humiliation of Sethe:

'What you did was wrong, Sethe.'
  'I should have gone on back there? Taken my babies back there?'
  'There could have been a way. Some other way.'
  'What way?'
  'You got two feet, Sethe, not four,' he said, and right then a forest sprang up between them; trackless and quiet. (*B*, p. 165)

Paul D's insult echoes, but is not precisely the same as, School-teacher's identification of Sethe as inhuman or bestial; similarly, Sethe's murder of Beloved is not exactly comparable to the whites' murder of the child whose curl and ribbon Stamp Paid finds. The novel, though, constructs these complicated echoes, thereby undermining any pattern or schema of guilt that we might feel tempted to impose on the narrative. The guilt of *Beloved* cannot be understood merely as that of a slaveholding society's institutional racism. The representation of guilt in Morrison's novel is nuanced and shaded; we cannot fully absolve Sethe of Beloved's murder just because of the circumstances in which she found herself; those circumstances, perhaps unimaginable in their extremity, nonetheless do not provide *a priori* legitimation for the murder of a child.

In this way, *Beloved* can be seen as a truly postmodern alternative to a novel such as Wright's *Native Son*. *Beloved* produces no
single critical perspective from and by which characters and
events might be judged. In fact the novel's own representational
strategies enact something of the same ethical and ideological
complexity that is associated with the characters. Beloved herself,
perhaps the principal victim in the novel, victimises Sethe by
choking her – and, most significantly, she appears as a demonic
succubus, feeding at others' expense and sexually draining Paul D.
Yet this depiction of Beloved clearly affects our interpretation of
her representative function. What can it mean to have a figure
who also represents a violently victimised community portrayed
as a succubus, feeding on the life blood of others?

The dilemmas and inadequacies of the novel's capacity for
representing the events and experiences it depicts are raised too
in those sections where Sethe and Denver try to explain Beloved's
significance and meaning for them, and in which Beloved
describes her experiences (*B*, pp. 200–17). The following is from
Beloved's narration:

> All of it is now   it is always now   there will never be a time
> when I am not crouching and watching others who are crouch-
> ing too   I am always crouching   the man on my face is dead
> his face is not mine   his mouth smells sweet but his eyes are
> locked   some who eat nasty themselves   I do not eat   the
> men without skin bring us their morning water to drink   we
> have none (*B*, p. 210)

Beloved is describing a state of death, her own state; but it is also a
description of the experience of being on a slave ship, of being
transported into slavery (the 'men without skin' are the white
crew). The defining, inescapable moment is stressed ('All of it is
now   it is always now'). Slavery, it is implied here, is itself a
kind of death. The fragmentation of the narrative, the absence of
regular grammar and punctuation, suggest something of the difficulty of expressing this state, this experience. For readers too
there is a difficulty in working out what is going on, in trying
to make sense of what we're being told. And this, it seems to me, is
crucial. The novel is describing, repeatedly, experiences which
are, to a readership separated from the slaves by history, incomprehensible and perhaps even unimaginable. This is part of what
the novel is about: the limitations of expression and of the imagination, the impossibility of our sharing, even vicariously, the same

imaginative space as the characters. We can never quite grasp, and
the novel can never quite express, the full horror of these characters' experiences. In this sense, Beloved herself is a manifestation of the postmodern sublime. Her ghostly presence personifies
the sublime mode of *Beloved*, a text in which we find that, as we
have already seen Lyotard write of the sublime, '[t]he failure of
expression gives rise to a pain, a kind of cleavage within the
subject between what can be conceived and what can be imagined
or presented'. We can conceive of the pain and suffering that
Sethe and Beloved have experienced; but we cannot truly imagine
them, neither can the text properly present them.

Commenting on her reworking of the slave narrative in *Beloved*,
Morrison says:

> [Slave narratives] had to be very understated. So while I looked
> at the documents and felt *familiar* with slavery and over-
> whelmed by it, I wanted it to be truly *felt*. I wanted to translate
> the historical into the personal. I spent a long time trying to
> figure out what it was about slavery that made it so repugnant,
> so personal, so indifferent, so intimate and yet so public.
>
> In reading some of the documents I noticed frequent refer-
> ences to something that was never properly described – *the bit*.
> This thing was put into the mouths of slaves to punish them
> and shut them up without preventing them from working. I
> spent a long time trying to find out what it looked like . . .
>
>   . . . Then I realized that describing it would never be help-
> ful: that the reader didn't need to *see* it so much as *feel* what it
> was like. I realized that it was important to imagine the bit as an
> active instrument, rather than simply as a curio or a historical
> fact. And in the same way I wanted to show the reader what
> slavery *felt* like, rather than how it looked.[29]

The reading experience of *Beloved* becomes an experience of re-
creating the ethical dilemmas the novel depicts, forcing the reader
to adopt different ethical standpoints and sometimes incompatible
criteria of judgement. Perhaps above all, though, it is a confrontation with the limitations of the imaginable; our struggles with the
halting inarticulacy of Beloved create some sense of the ungraspable and incommunicable nature of her experiences – experiences
which are, of course, not hers alone. Our relationship with the
novel comes, in fact, to resemble that between Denver and Beloved
as the young girl tells her sister the story of her (Denver's) birth.
Neither of the girls really know what happened, but their inter-

action as storyteller and listener creates for both of them an experience of the event:

> Denver was seeing it now and feeling it – through Beloved. Feeling how it must have felt to her mother. Seeing how it must have looked. And the more fine points she made, the more detail she provided, the more Beloved liked it. So she anticipated the questions by giving blood to the scraps her mother and grandmother had told her – and a heartbeat. The monologue became, in fact, a duet as they lay down together. . . . Denver spoke, Beloved listened, and the two did the best they could to create what really happened, how it really was, something only Sethe knew . . . (B, p. 78)

We too engage in the creation of what we can never really know, a creation haunted by a sense of its inadequacy, its incapacity to represent the full complexity and horror of history. As a later chapter will make clear, though, this is how the postmodern novel engages with issues of history, eschewing what we think we already know and discovering a historical experience in the act of reading itself.

Jean Baudrillard: Ideology and Simulacra

The Marxist tradition of ideology critique is based on the demystification of ideological discourses, practices and apparatuses. Such demystification is, though, dependent on a viable and ultimately identifiable distinction between illusion and reality. The later work of Jean Baudrillard, focusing on questions of simulacra and the hyperreal, attempts to undermine the credibility of this distinction and therefore the very foundations of traditional, Marxist ideology critique. Baudrillard describes a social sphere so saturated by images and signs that a resultant crisis in representation has overtaken its capacity to insist on the real, on truth, and on meaning:

> All of Western faith and good faith was engaged in this wager on representation: that a sign could refer to the depth of meaning, that a sign could *exchange* for meaning and that something could guarantee this exchange – God, of course. But what if God himself can be simulated, that is to say, reduced to the signs which attest his existence? Then the whole system becomes

weightless; it is no longer anything but a gigantic simulacrum: not unreal, but a simulacrum, never again exchanging for what is real, but exchanging in itself, in an uninterrupted circuit without reference or circumference.[30]

Simulation, crucially, is not illusory or false; it does not produce images which distort some underlying reality. Instead, simulation works in opposition to representation; in simulation, the image 'bears no relation to any reality whatever'. It is the reality principle itself which is negated in simulation. Baudrillard uses the model of Disneyland to show the redundancy of ideology critique and the reality/illusion distinction on which it is based. He cites the ideology critique of Disneyland as 'digest of the American way of life, panegyric to American values, idealized transposition of a contradictory reality'.[31] But in fact, argues Baudrillard, 'Disneyland is there to conceal the fact that it is the "real country", all of "real" America, which *is* Disneyland.'[32] He is interested in the scandal that the denial of the real entails. 'Disneyland', he writes,

> is presented as imaginary in order to make us believe that the rest is real, when in fact all of Los Angeles and the America surrounding it are no longer real, but of the order of the hyperreal and of simulation. It is no longer a false representation of reality (ideology), but of concealing that fact that the real is no longer real, and thus of saving the reality principle.[33]

The denial of a primary reality, its substitution by simulacra that do not rely on some reference to the 'real', can thus be used as a critique of both the 'reality' of social conventions and institutions and of the demystificatory power of ideological analysis. In this way, Baudrillard suggests the shared vested interest that the power of capital and the ideological analysis of Marxism hold in the preservation of the reality principle and faith in the possibility of truth.

A further example of simulation offered by Baudrillard is the scenario of someone who feigns an illness. This, he argues, is not simply a feigning, as the subject may subsequently develop the precise symptoms of the 'feigned' illness. 'Since the simulator produces "true" symptoms,' asks Baudrillard, 'is he or she ill or not?'[34] We shall see later how in Don DeLillo's *White Noise* a comparable scene is depicted, but for the moment we need only note the way in which the production of a 'truth' or 'reality' is compromised by simulation. In fact, rather than this model of production (whether of truth, reality or meaning), Baudrillard proposes an alternative model of seduction. 'Seduction', he writes, 'is that which extracts meaning from discourse and detracts it from its truth.'[35] Baudrillard's depiction of the postmodern is in this respect similar to that of Fredric Jameson; both point to postmodernity's expulsion of models of 'depth' and 'truth' in favour of surface and contingency. Crucially, though, Baudrillard's analysis suggests the illegitimacy or redundancy of Jameson's Marxist critique. The Marxism that underpins Jameson's definition of the postmodern is interpreted by Baudrillard as just as reliant on an outdated model of truth and reality as is the rationalism of bourgeois thought. Baudrillard thus points to aspects of the complicity of Marxist critique with the bourgeois, capitalist ideology it claims to oppose; both are seen as allies in conflict with the more radical, discomforting logic of simulation:

> It is always the aim of ideological analysis to restore the objective process; it is always a false problem to want to restore the truth beneath the simulacrum.
> This is ultimately why power is so in accord with ideological discourses and discourses on ideology, for these are all discourses of *truth* — always good, even and especially if they are revolutionary, to counter the mortal blows of simulation.[36]

The remainder of this chapter will explore the relationship between postmodern fiction and theoretical models of the postmodern. More particularly, it will offer an extended discussion of novels by Don DeLillo, highlighting some of the problems that such fiction raises for Marxist ideology critique.

'Now More than Ever': Death and Cultural Consumption in Don DeLillo

The late President Richard Nixon campaigned in 1968 with the slogan 'Now More than Ever'. As a number of writers have since pointed out, Nixon's campaign team had taken the slogan (perhaps unwittingly) from Keats' 'Ode to a Nightingale': 'Now more than ever seems it rich to die.' To read, in Don DeLillo's most recent novel *Underworld*, J. Edgar Hoover's fevered response to a magazine reproduction of Bruegel's painting *The Triumph of Death* is to find something of that very same irony laid bare before us:

Edgar reads the copy block on the matching page. This is a sixteenth-century work done by a Flemish master, Pieter Bruegel, and it is called *The Triumph of Death*.

A nervy title methinks. But he is intrigued, he admits it – the left-hand page may be even better than the right.

[. . .]

Dear germ-free Edgar, the man who has an air filtration system in his house to vaporize specks of dust – he finds a fascination in cankers, lesions and rotting bodies so long as his connection to the source is strictly pictorial.

[. . .]

Edgar loves this stuff. Edgar, Jedgar. Admit it – you love it. It causes a bristling of his body hair. Skeletons with wispy dicks. The dead beating kettledrums. The sackcloth dead slitting a pilgrim's throat.[37]

Godfearing J. Edgar tries so very hard to be appalled by the gratuitously violent magazine picture, but he must confess that 'the left-hand page may be even better than the right'. We see here the possibility of political truths being exposed by the power of art. Hoover's sexualised apocalyptic fantasies, representative of a political attitude that saw the unsentimental Henry Kissinger claim that power was the greatest aphrodisiac, become representable through the effect on J. Edgar of the reproduction of Bruegel's painting.

But if there is the suggestion here that art can still retain some element of critical power, DeLillo's fiction has also explored – and, I'll be arguing, has to some extent exemplified – a contrary position, a sense that contemporary, postmodern culture has been emptied of critical content, has become a culture of social assent or affirmation. Time and again in these novels, aesthetic creativity, the construction of narratives or images, is shown to be absorbed into a culture of consumerism. This theme of the artist's difficulty in standing apart from dominant social forces, in being distanced enough from them to offer social critique, is one that Don DeLillo shares with some of the great, European writers of late modernist fiction, fiction which charts the disintegration of a modernist, aesthetic critical distance. Two novels in particular – Thomas Mann's *Doctor Faustus* and Hermann Broch's *The Death of Virgil* (both published in 1947) – would seem to offer reflections on the relationship of artistic impulses to historical forces which are, to me at least, strikingly similar to those found in DeLillo's work. In fact, that work often seems to share in the expression of what

Fredric Jameson, writing of Thomas Mann, called 'the nature of tragedy in modern times: . . . the intolerable power of history itself over life and over artistic creation, which is not free not to reflect what it reacts against'.[38]

This reading of DeLillo's work will attempt to trace those moments of ideological complicity and cultural commodification. I'll be focusing principally on *White Noise*, though there will be references to other works, such as *Running Dog, Libra* and *Mao II*. In conclusion, I want to suggest some way of viewing the problems that fiction such as DeLillo's poses for Marxist criticism.

A Portrait of the Postmodern: Goods and Simulacra

The title of Don DeLillo's *White Noise* perhaps resembles more a deflationary label than any aesthetic or artistic adornment. It is as though DeLillo does not want us, as readers, to expect too much. More accurately, perhaps, it is the acknowledgement that his text competes for our time in the same realm as TV ads and computer games; the status of the literary text itself has been transformed and it is to this state of affairs that the title of *White Noise* stands testament.

Of course, it is precisely that society in which such a situation has come to pass which also provides the subject-matter of the novel. In its opening paragraph, Jack Gladney, the narrator, describes the return of the students to the College-on-the-Hill:

> The roofs of the station wagons were loaded down with care-fully secured suitcases full of light and heavy clothing; with boxes of blankets, boots and shoes, stationery and books, sheets, pillows, quilts; with rolled-up rugs and sleeping bags; with bicycles, skis, rucksacks, English and Western saddles, inflated rafts.[39]

The list of goods, products and belongings continues for some time: 'personal computers . . . controlled substances . . . Dum Dum pops, the Mystic mints'. Books are included in this list, sandwiched between footwear and bedding, but they are hardly conspicuous. As Frank Lentricchia rightly observes, 'these books are things like other things, commodities, too, or – in the most question-begging of all economic terms – *goods*'.[40] *White Noise* is therefore a book written about, and written from within, a society in which books have no more worth than, and cannot be differentiated from, any other consumer commodity item: from neither 'small refrigerators and table ranges' nor from 'Waffelos and Kabooms'.

DeLillo's novel can lay no claim to the status of the autonomous work of art. Instead, it is a product of the contemporary, American culture industry. Early in the novel, Jack and Babette go shopping in the supermarket, where they meet Murray Jay Siskind, an ex-sportswriter and recent appointee to the college's popular culture department. While Murray talks to them about the packaging of the peanuts and the peaches in his basket, a woman falls into 'a rack of paperback books' (*WN*, p. 19). No explanation is given for her fall. As Jack leaves with Babette and Murray, he comments, 'The three of us left together, trying to maneuver our shopping carts between the paperback books scattered across the entrance.' The only thing in the passage that distinguishes the books from the peaches in Murray's basket is the fact that they are now lying on the floor, dislodged from their proper place on the supermarket racks. Here, art has finally become functional, a commonplace, everyday, untroubling feature of late capitalist existence, like tinned peaches or the background white noise emitted by the TV.

Two novels later, in *Mao II*, DeLillo proves to be no less preoccupied by this ever-closer relation of the work of art to ordinary commodities. Bill Gray, the character on whom the novel is principally focused, is an author. In the manner of a J. D. Salinger or a Thomas Pynchon (the two role models most frequently cited by the novel's reviewers), Gray has become an obsessive recluse. His status as such renders him more sought-after than ever: for others, it becomes his gimmick, maybe serving as an inadvertent example of niche marketing. Gray is tracked down by Scott, an event which precedes the novel's point of narration, and is persuaded to employ him as an assistant. It is with the novel's introduction of Scott, who is killing time in a bookstore while on the way to a meeting with the photographer chosen for Bill's first photographs in over thirty years, that DeLillo signals in *Mao II* his acknowledgement of the loss of art's autonomy in the society in which Bill (and, by implication, DeLillo too) finds himself writing:

He examined books stacked on tables and set in clusters near the cash terminals. He saw stacks on the floor five feet high, arranged in artful fanning patterns. There were books standing on pedestals and bunched in little gothic snuggeries. Bookstores made him slightly sick at times. He looked at the gleaming bestsellers. People drifted through the store, appearing caught

in some unhappy dazzlement. There were books on step-ter-
races and Lucite wall-shelves, books in pyramids and theme
displays. He went downstairs to the paperbacks, where he
stared at the covers of the mass-market books, running his
fingertips erotically over the raised lettering. Covers were
laquered and gilded. Books lay cradled in nine-unit counter-
packs like experimental babies. He could hear them shrieking
Buy me.[41]

Here, downstairs, in the 'section on modern classics', Scott finds
copies of Bill's two novels 'in their latest trade editions'. They are
not, it seems safe to presume, quite as shameless in matters of self-
promotion as their laquered and gilded cousins, but the bookstore
generously finds room to accommodate even such a pair 'banded
in austere umbers and rusts'. Like the market itself, the bookstore
into which Scott has wandered offers a place for all, but at a price:
namely, the substitution of specific, artistic value by the abstract
exchange or commodity value; in other words, submersion in the
commodity structure. The loss of cultural autonomy can, then,
here be perceived in those few easy strides from 'best seller' to
'modern classic'.
   It would, though, be wrong to view this loss of cultural or
artistic autonomy merely as the integration of what would formerly have been self-avowedly autonomous works of art into the
commodity structure. Rather, as Fredric Jameson argues, it should
be understood dialectically, as a fundamental transformation in
the *relation* of two aspects of the social totality. Thus, on one level,
the novel (for example, *White Noise*) becomes indistinguishable
from economic products or commodities; while, at the same time,
those same commodities, as Jameson writes elsewhere, take on 'an
aesthetic dimension'. Here we leave the reality/illusion distinction
upon which so much Marxist ideology critique is based, and enter
a world described by the postmarxist Jean Baudrillard in which
'[i]llusion is no longer possible, because the real is no longer
possible'.[42] How this loss of cultural autonomy should properly
be imagined, then, is not as a simplistic, one-sided integration of
the cultural realm into the commodity structure or merely as the
absorption of that commodity structure by cultural or aesthetic
forms; instead, it must be grasped as the operation of both these
processes at once.
   If it is true, as I have been suggesting, that these are novels
which reflect the loss of cultural autonomy, we would perhaps
expect to see, in the light of Jameson's model, the depiction of a

society permeated by Baudrillardian simulacra and culturally mediated forms of experience occurring simultaneously with the transformation that we have already witnessed of art into mere commodity. In fact, that is exactly what we find. As I plan to show, DeLillo consistently portrays a society in which simulations and images of 'the real' increasingly take precedence over 'the real' itself. A good place to start is at 'the most photographed barn in America'.

Jack Gladney, the first-person narrator of *White Noise*, undergoes in the course of the novel, at the hands of Murray Jay Siskind, a rite of passage into the study of contemporary cultural phenomena (TV, advertising, commodity packaging). His education begins in earnest when he and Murray take a trip to a local tourist attraction: 'THE MOST PHOTOGRAPHED BARN IN AMERICA'. While driving there, they pass signs advertising the forthcoming attraction. Arriving, Jack and Murray find themselves among a crowd of tourists, each photographing 'the most photographed barn in America'. There is a man in a booth who sells postcards and photographic slides of the barn to the tourists; there is an elevated spot – a grassy knoll – from which the barn might be viewed or, indeed, photographed. Murray feels compelled to explain the significance of what they are witnessing:

'No one sees the barn,' he said finally.
   A long silence followed.
   'Once you've seen the signs about the barn, it becomes impossible to see the barn.'

Murray's monologue is punctuated by lengthy silences; we cannot be sure whether he is considering his next point or stringing out a performance:

'They are taking pictures of taking pictures,' he said. He did not speak for a while. We listened to the incessant clicking of shutter release buttons, the rustling clank of levers that advanced the film. 'What was the barn like before it was photographed?' he said. 'What did it look like, how was it different from other barns, how was it similar to other barns? We can't answer these questions because we've read the signs, seen the people snapping the pictures. We can't get outside the aura. We're part of the aura. We're here, we're now.' (*WN*, pp. 12–13)

As such passages suggest, Murray serves as a would-be post-modern guru. His is the celebratory voice of mass, consumer culture; for not only is Murray attuned to the dissolution of the object world into so many images and simulacra of itself, as we have seen above, but he is willing to act as an enthusiastic advocate of this new 'reality'. '"You have to learn how to look"', he tells Jack. '"You have to open yourself to the data"' (*WN*, p. 51). This advocacy of the primacy of image extends, though perhaps unconsciously, even to Murray's dress sense. Jack tells us that Murray dresses 'almost totally in corduroy'. He adds: 'I had the feeling that since the age of eleven in his crowded plot of concrete he'd associated this sturdy fabric with higher learning in some impossibly distant and tree-shaded place' (*WN*, p. 11). Like Jack himself, who has changed his name to J.A.K. Gladney in order to approximate more closely the image of a head of 'Hitler Studies', Murray is the simulacrum of an academic. The difference between them is that Murry, were he aware of the false shadow he casts (and we cannot be sure that he is not), would no doubt react positively and find the whole thing amusing; Jack, on the other hand, is disquieted when he finds his identity thus uncertain: 'I am the false character that follows the name around', he says (*WN*, p. 17).

As the novel progresses, Jack discovers that his environment is coming to resemble more and more that alien and disconcerting world described to him by Murray. When the 'Airborne Toxis Event' forces the Gladneys and others to abandon their homes, Jack finds that the evacuation procedure is being overseen by SIMUVAC, an organisation which is using the evacuation to practise the simulated evacuations which are their 'real' job. The same group later employ Steffie, one of the Gladney children, to act as a victim in one of their simulations. But this might be the second time that she has played such a role, as neither Jack nor Babette can be sure whether the medical symptoms shown by the girls at the time of the toxic cloud were genuine or merely provoked by radio broadcasts which listed possible symptoms. Even Jack's exposure to the toxic waste has uncertain consequences which destabilise his own claim to victimhood: in response to the question '"Am I going to die?"' he receives the answer '"Not as such"' (*WN*, p. 140). In a rather perverse way, then, the role of victim that Steffie plays for SIMUVAC may be the more authentic as it can at least be attributed to a 'real' simulation and has an identifiable outcome (Steffie is carried to an ambulance and then goes home). It has a shape and substance lacking in both the girls' nausea and Jack's toxic infection.

For Leonard Wilcox, the depiction of society in *White Noise* is
recognisable from, and comparable to, the analysis of contemporary society offered by the French philosopher Jean Baudrillard. In
a study entitled 'Baudrillard, DeLillo's *White Noise* and the End of
Heroic Narrative' he writes thus:

> The informational world Baudrillard delineates bears a striking
> resemblance to the world of *White Noise*: one characterized by
> the collapse of the real and the flow of signifiers emanating from
> an information society, by a 'loss of the real' in a black hole of
> simulation and the play and exchange of signs. In this world
> common to both Baudrillard and DeLillo, images, signs and
> codes engulf objective reality; signs become more real than
> reality and stand in for the world they erase. . . . Moreover,
> for both Baudrillard and DeLillo a media-saturated conscious-
> ness threatens the concept of meaning itself.[43]

It is significant that Wilcox should speak of a 'media-saturated
consciousness', suggesting that those cultural or mass-cultural
forms now act as determining agents of the human psyche itself,
an argument that we saw earlier proposed by Fredric Jameson.

In *White Noise*, the embodiment of this media-constructed self
is the character of Willie Mink (a.k.a. Mr Gray), sexual black-
mailer of Babette and victim of Jack's gunslinging frenzy. As
Wilcox notes, Mink is 'a repository for the rambling, metonymic
discourses of a consumer culture'. At times, for no reason, Mink
will suddenly start spouting random snatches of TV-speak.
'"Some of these playful dolphins have been equipped with radio
transmitters"', he says. '"Their far flung wanderings may tell us
things"' (*WN*, p. 310). He claims to have learned English by
watching TV, but it would appear that he has been less educated
than fully reconstructed by the Tube.

It is with Mink, too, that Jack witnesses one of the more bizarre
side-effects of Dylar, the drug which is meant to suppress fear of
death. Mink responds to words as though they need no longer
correspond to an external reality but, instead, have themselves
replaced that reality. Thus, Jack can cry out, '"A hail of bullets"',
and Mink dives to the floor; he assumes 'the recommended crash
position' on hearing the words '"Plunging aircraft"'. It is perhaps
this latter feature above all, this side-effect, that justifies Wilcox's
analysis that in the world of *White Noise* meaning itself has been
dissipated and that, in truth, once they've seen the signs, no one
need see the barn.

It is not, however, until DeLillo's next novel – *Libra* – that the theme of the constructed self becomes the central preoccupation around which the novel is developed. In *White Noise* it is necessary for DeLillo first to delineate a social milieu and to depict, as convincingly as possible, the modes of behaviour that such a society encourages or even necessitates; only then can the means by which the inner-consciousnesses of men and women are socially conditioned properly become the book's subject. In *Libra*, by contrast, the thematic structure unfolds in precisely the opposite direction. Lee Harvey Oswald's place in American history is secure; his name is known. Simply by writing a novelistic account of the life of America's most notorious assassin, DeLillo indicates that there is something else to know, something beyond the moment of the assassination itself. From the opening description of the young Lee Oswald riding the subway, it is clear that the Oswald to be portrayed in the pages of *Libra* is to be conspicuously passive, a cipher for external sensations and influences. In other words, the very subject-matter of *Libra* implies an interest in the artificiality or constructedness of the self, an interest elevated to the thematic level by the subsequent treatment of that subject-matter – that is, the portrayal of a passive Oswald, daily prey to the whirling babble of voices that leads him to the Texas School Book Depository and which constitutes the authentic expression of corporate, anti-communist America. The narrative journey that takes us in *White Noise* from the heart of American institutional life to the random mess of media-speak that is Willie Mink thus finds its reverse mirror image in a plot which follows the life of the impressionable young Oswald through the travails and neon-lit dreams of Middle America to the death of an American president and the power games which dictate the courses of lives.

We shall come in a moment to the haphazard cultural formation of Lee Harvey Oswald, but it is worth while noting that Oswald is far from alone in *Libra* in his characterisation as a 'false' or 'unnatural' self. The unwitting partner in Oswald's bloody rite of passage, Kennedy himself, is exposed as another constructed persona, primarily a photo-fit president. Guy Bannister, reflecting disgustedly on his president's civil-rights programme, grasps at a stroke the image-consciousness that is his great political skill: 'You could photograph a Kennedy all right. That's what a Kennedy was for.'[44] Later, on that fateful day in November, he is again described in terms of his media 'self'; in fact, like the photographic barn in *White Noise*, the real Kennedy has long been supplanted by images of himself: 'He moved along the fence, handsome and tanned, smiling famously into the wall of opened mouths. He looked like himself, like photographs, a helmsman squinting in the sea-glare, white teeth shining' (*L*, p. 392).

In his essay '*Libra* as Postmodern Critique', Frank Lentricchia argues convincingly that DeLillo's portrayal of America is that of a society in which one is taught to yearn for a second, transformed self. 'Left with a book more about Oswald than conspiracy,' he writes, 'we learn that the question is not what happened in Dallas on 22 November 1963 – DeLillo gives us a theory about that. The question is not even, who is this Oswald? It is, who is *Lee Harvey Oswald*?'[45] Oswald, himself, is peculiarly susceptible to the belief that he can constantly be remade. When Dr Braufels teaches him Russian, he begins to feel that the very enunciation of these new sounds might have a transformative effect: 'he could almost believe he was being remade on the spot, given an opening to some larger and deeper version of himself' (*L*, p. 113). And later, when the dream of entering history via the Soviet Union has faded, Oswald sits alone in a room in New Orleans and routinely narrates fictitious versions of himself on the pages of job application forms (*L*, pp. 305–6).

When the transformation or reconstruction of Oswald is completed, it follows not from his part in the class struggle but from his absorption and subsequent image-projection by the mass-media. Long before Oswald is to be classified as a lone, crazed gunman, we, as readers, witness the shock – to which our own daily experience has numbed us – felt by Oswald's Russian wife, Marina, as she passes by a department store window and sees herself and her husband on the TV screen inside. An everyday event, she suddenly finds, has been made part of the TV world, the world of *Racket Squad* and *Dragnet*, shows that the young Lee Oswald would watch with his mother. This is an incident which foreshadows what is perhaps the most disturbing passage of the novel: Oswald's death. As he lies with a bullet in his stomach, the ambulance speeding towards a hospital, Oswald watches his shooting replayed on TV: 'He could see himself shot as the camera caught it. Through the pain he watched TV. . . . Through the pain, through the losing of sensation except where it hurt, Lee watched himself react to the auguring heat of the bullet' (*L*, p. 439). Here, the moment of his murder itself becomes a cultural product, a TV-event, later to be rescreened countless times.

But if the media-coverage is to destabilise the authenticity of the moment of his actual murder, it is also responsible for the birth of that new self of which Lee Oswald had always dreamt and which 'Lee Harvey Oswald' represents. The time between his arrest for the assassination of President Kennedy and his own death at the hands of Jack Ruby is a time like no other for Oswald, a time of new beginnings and uncluttered opportunity. Once arrested, he is soon given a hint of the full transformation that awaits: 'Whenever they took him down, he heard his name on the radios and TVs. Lee Harvey Oswald. It sounded extremely strange. . . . No one called him by that name. Now it was everywhere' (L, p. 416). Earlier in the novel, while in the Soviet Union, Oswald is given a foretaste of what it might mean to enter into the official history of notoriety recognised by the media:

> It occurred to Oswald that everyone called the prisoner by his full name. The Soviet Press, local TV, the BBC, the Voice of America, the interrogators, etc. Once you did something notorious, they tagged you with an extra name that was ordinarily never used. You were officially marked, a chapter in the imagination of the state. Francis Gary Powers. In just these few days the name had taken on a resonance, a sense of fateful event. It already sounded historic. (L, p. 198)

Now transformed, in Lentricchia's phrase, into 'a triple-named echo of another media child, "John Fitzgerald Kennedy"', Oswald discovers his true vocation: he will study the assassination in minute detail, 'vary the act a hundred ways, speed it up and slow it down, shift emphasis, find shadings, see his whole life change' (L, p. 434). 'His life', we are told, 'had a single clear subject now, called Lee Harvey Oswald' (L, p. 435).

By the end of the novel, the very means by which Oswald grasps his own identity are so thoroughly mediated by consumer-cultural forms that it seems only fitting that his body should be laid to rest under a false name, 'William Bobo', and that the coffin should be carried to the graveside by a team of journalists. Lee Oswald, now renamed (for the very last time) 'William Bobo', may be dead, but Lee Harvey Oswald lives on.

Postmodern Forms: Pastiche and Electronic Reproduction

Thus far I've been describing DeLillo's portrayal of, and meditation upon, late capitalist society and what Jameson describes as its attendant 'cultural logic', postmodernism. I now want to go further and suggest that White Noise is a text whose very form implicates it in that same social and cultural configuration that it is intent on depicting. In more precise terms, it has become time to note the relevance to the postmodern novel of the critique of the culture industry contained within Adorno and Horkheimer's *Dialectic of Enlightenment*. The force of that critique, as Fredric Jameson writes, 'lies in its demonstration of the unexpected and imperceptible introduction of commodity structure into the very form and content of the work of art itself'.[46] I now want to trace those formal aspects of *White Noise* which betray its postmodern status and, through that, the reflection of late capitalist reification in its very own inner-structure.

It seems useful to start by identifying at least one of those formal features associated with the postmodern: namely, a new depthlessness that repulses or repudiates the sort of hermeneutic enquiry, based on multitudinous layers of signification, for which the modernist work of art seemed to cry out. Jameson writes of 'the emergence of a new kind of flatness or depthlessness, a new kind of superficiality in the most literal sense, perhaps the supreme formal feature of all the postmodernisms'.[47] One example of that depthlessness, for Jameson, is what he identifies as a form of postmodern pastiche that has replaced the modernist predilection to parody:

> Pastiche is, like parody, the imitation of a peculiar or unique, idiosyncratic style, the wearing of a linguistic mask, speech in a dead language. But it is a neutral practice of such mimicry; without any of parody's ulterior motives, amputated of the satiric impulse, devoid of laughter and of any conviction that alongside the abnormal tongue you have momentarily borrowed, some healthy linguistic normality still exists.[48]

Jameson's pastiche refuses to construct or to impose an order to which its content might be subjected: it becomes impossible to identify a determinate object of irony; we do not know who or what is being ironised, who or what is the object of the joke, or even if there is one.

To see how this might operate in postmodern textual practice, we need look no further than *White Noise* and some interpretative difficulties raised by Jack Gladney's narration. Frank Lentricchia, in 'Tales of the Electronic Tribe', studies the uses served by DeLillo's choise of first-person narrative in some depth. Gladney is, in Lentricchia's words, 'the less than self-possessed voice of a culture that he would subject to criticism and satire'.[49] The implications of Gladney's original satiric intentions needn't detain us for now, but it is important to note, with Lentricchia, that Gladney's narration must itself be held suspect, saturated as it is by the values and aesthetic conventions of the society on which it is to reflect. Lentricchia points to a sentence of Gladney's early in the novel: 'It was a cold bright day with intermittent winds out of the east' (*WN*, p. 4). 'Straight or deadpan?' he asks:

> A joke about the way we talk these days about the weather, with our voices indentured to the jargon of what is called meteorology? A joke that stings us for our inability to muster 'real' voice, 'real' speech, even about – or is it especially about? – matters so ordinary? Or is the sentence delivered unawares, just the way Jack talks sometimes, like a weatherman. Self-parody or a weird, because unconscious, form of 'pastiche', a term whose very meaning assumes an act of deliberation?[50]

As Lentricchia suggests, we are left here unable to situate either the origin or object of the irony.

To support this point a bit more fully, I want to look at one more extract from Jack Gladney's narrative – this time unprompted by Lentricchia. At the end of *White Noise* Jack describes the sensation of waiting in line at a supermarket checkout:

> And this is where we wait together, regardless of age, our carts stocked with brightly colored goods. A slowly moving line, satisfying, giving us time to glance at the tabloids in the racks. Everything that we need that is not food or love is here in the tabloid racks. The tales of the supernatural and the extra-terrestrial. The miracle vitamins, the cures for cancer, the remedies for obesity. The cults of the famous and the dead. (*WN*, p. 326)

We have already been made aware of Jack's weakness for parody and for ironic put-down; yet, similarly, we have witnessed the falsity underlying that ironic distance that DeLillo's narrator sometimes attempts to construct (and which the reader is at times all too willing to presuppose). The passage quoted above might well parody the 'Aristotelianism of bubble gum wrappers and detergent jingles' which, for Jack, constitutes the work of the college's popular culture department, but by this stage in the novel such confidence and self-assertion in the use of irony on Jack's part would be unlikely. In fact, the tone is neither caustic nor satiric, but rather elegiac. The blank content of these sentences

is akin to the message of mass-culture triumphalism that Murray
Jay Siskind preaches throughout – the tone of reverence and
quasi-religious awe is the same – but the celebratory fervour
that characterises Murray's sermons is entirely lacking. Instead,
there is a placid acceptance, a weary assent to the world as it is.
The years consumed by fear of death; the mad, frantic search for
Dylar; the long, slow immersion in the life and writings of Hitler
have all taken their toll. Jack perhaps sees finally that to ape, in a
sincere way, the truths of his friend Murray and of Alfonse (Fast
Food) Stompanato need take no considerable effort and might at
least retain an authenticity to which the cultural satirist, the
sardonic parodist, can no longer pretend.

It is not only, however, in the prevalence of pastiche or suspensive irony that *White Noise* betrays itself as formally postmodernist. Earlier, we noted that Fredric Jameson extends the notion of
postmodern depthlessness beyond the specific example of pastiche
or 'blank parody' to include a general repudiation of meaning and
signification. The result is what Jameson calls 'schizophrenic art',
an art in which meaning itself ('the interlocking syntagmatic series
of signifiers which constitutes an utterance or a meaning'[51]) has
broken down and what we are left with is 'schizophrenia in the
form of a rubble of distinct and unrelated signifiers'. The examples
which Jameson offers range from the music of John Cage to Samuel
Beckett's novel *Watt* and Bob Perelman's poem 'China'. Although
DeLillo's *White Noise* is nowhere near as extreme as these texts in
its disruption of the hermeneutic process – a disruption that is
here periodic rather than constant – we can nonetheless identify a
similar formal feature at work.

Interspersed at various intervals throughout DeLillo's text, we
find mysterious codas or brand names such as the following:
'Dacron, Orlon, Lycra Spandex' (*WN*, p. 52); 'Mastercard, Visa,
American Express' (*WN*, p. 100); 'Leaded, unleaded, super
unleaded' (*WN*, p. 199); 'Random Access Memory, Acquired
Immune Deficiency Syndrome, Mutual Assured Destruction'
(*WN*, p. 303). They appear, as John Frow observes ('The Last
Things Before the Last: Notes on *White Noise*'), 'in the midst of
the mundane world of novelistic narrative, detached, functionless,
unmotivated . . . without any marker of a speaking source'.[52] The
origin of these corporate inscriptions has been the cause of some
dispute: for Michael Valdez Moses ('Lust Removed from Nature'),
'[i]t is clear that these incursions cannot be directly credited to
Jack Gladney's narrative voice';[53] while Frank Lentricchia insists
that '[i]t is, of course, Jack who speaks the line[s] because *White*

Noise is a first-person novel, and it could therefore be no-one else'. 'Jack in these moments is possessed,' adds Lentricchia, 'a mere medium who speaks.'[54] It seems to me that it is Lentricchia who is right. Valdez Moses associates these 'consumerist mantras' with 'the "white noise" of postmodern America that envelops the Gladneys and the inhabitants of Blacksmith', but Lentricchia, I suspect, grasps the insidious potential of that 'white noise' more fully when he associates these mantras with Jack's own unconscious self.

This is a notion which also suggests itself to Leonard Wilcox, who writes:

> These 'eruptions' in the narrative imply the emergence of a new form of subjectivity colonized by the media and decentered by its polyglot discourses and electronic networks. They imply the evacuation of the private spheres of self, in Baudrillardian terms 'the end of interiority'.[55]

Moreover, this interpretation is supported by an incident which occurs while the Gladneys are spending the night with the town's other evacuees. Sitting beside his sleeping daughter Steffie, Jack hears her murmuring two initially incomprehensible words: '*Toyota Celica*' (*WN*, p. 155). He realises that she is chanting the name of a car in her sleep. 'She was only repeating', he thinks, 'some TV voice. Toyota Corolla, Toyota Celica, Toyota Cressida.' A distinction must be drawn, however, between these two examples. Steffie's nocturnal chants, like the later TV-chatterings of Willie Mink, are an example of the novel's *representation* of the colonisation of the unconscious by the commodity structure. Jack's own 'consumerist mantras', on the other hand, actually determine the very *form* of the narrative surface itself. The novel thus betrays itself both as a representation and as exemplar of the American culture industry.

A similarly 'schizophrenic' effect is produced by the scattered, apparently random and meaningless transcriptions of utterances emitted by the TV or radio: 'The TV said: "And other trends that could dramatically impact your portfolio"' (*WN*, p. 61); 'The radio said: "It's the rainbow hologram that gives this credit card a marketing intrigue"' (p. 122).[56] As the narrator of DeLillo's later *Mao II* comments on the rush of sensations he experiences while walking through the (post)modern city, 'Nothing tells you what you are supposed to think of this' (*MII*, p. 94). That, of course, is the point. DeLillo's portrait of contemporary America is, as we have seen, one of a society in which meaning and signification have been dissipated. The replication of that same sense of disjointedness in the reading experience of *White Noise* – an inability on the part of the reader to see how such snatches of electronic media-speak might illuminate (perhaps ironically), or at least stand in some meaningful relationship to, their immediate textual surroundings (see, for a contrasting example, uses of montage in Malcolm Lowry's late modernist novel *Under the Volcano*) – is thus a means of foregrounding this aspect of the novel's social critique in the mind of the reader, while also allowing the form of that critique to be determined by a cultural logic which repudiates and discourages any attempt cognitively to establish interrelations and to reach, on that basis, determinate conclusions regarding the nature of the social and/or textual environment in which we find ourselves.

In his *Constructing Postmodernism* Brian McHale cites, in the midst of an essay on Umberto Eco's *Foucault's Pendulum*, Fredric Jameson's identification of a trend in postmodern textual production towards 'narratives which are *about* the processes of reproduction and include movie cameras, video, tape recorders, the whole technology of the production and reproduction of the simulacrum'.[57] We have already noted the media saturation of DeLillo's texts, but it is necessary to go beyond this and to insist that the texts are themselves at times actually generated by those same 'processes of reproduction'. Again referring ostensibly to *Foucault's Pendulum*, McHale writes of texts in which 'certain narratological functions that would normally be carried out by the verbal text have been entrusted to some secondary medium (movie, television, computer) represented *in* the verbal text'.[58] We shall now see briefly the relevance of such remarks to DeLillo's *Libra* and *Mao II*.

Although Michael Valdez Moses is surely wrong to associate certain sections of the narrative in *White Noise* with the 'white noise' of postmodern America rather than with Jack Gladney's commodity-saturated consciousness, his judgement highlights a determination of narrative by media of reproduction which it is necessary to acknowledge in some of DeLillo's other novels. In *Libra*, for instance, a surrogate author figure called Nicholas Branch is introduced. He has been 'hired on contract' by the CIA to write a secret history of the Kennedy assassination, a project near enough to that of the novel's author to invest Branch's efforts with a certain measure of analogical significance. Branch researches files, films, tapes and books *en masse*; any document that he requires is brought to him by the Curator. His technique for trying to understand, and to reach conclusions about, the assassination is described thus: 'We shall build theories that gleam like jade idols, intriguing systems of assumption, four-faced, graceful. We will follow the bullet trajectories backwards to the lives that occupy the shadows, actual men who moan in their dreams' (L, p. 15). The possible elision of the narratorial voice at such moments with that of Branch and (presumably) those in the CIA who originally issued his instruction is a topic to which we shall return in a few moments, but for now we need only note of this passage the way in which it anticipates the methodology not only of Branch's study, but also of *Libra* itself. The formal structure of the novel, then, would appear to be modelled on that of the secret history of the Kennedy assassination to be found on Nicholas Branch's computer files.

Moreover, passages in *Libra* may themselves be direct representations of Branch's computer text. For example, the chapter in which Branch is introduced is called '17 April', a date which situates temporally not the narrative of Branch's study and its progress, but that of a completely new character, Win Everett, and the genesis of the plot to kill Kennedy. This other narrative would seem to be generated by Branch's own computer:

> He [Branch] enters a date on the home computer the Agency has provided for the sake of convenient tracking. April 17, 1963. The names appear at once, with backgrounds, connections, locations. The bright hot skies. The shady street of handsome old homes framed in native oak.
>
> American kitchens. This one has a breakfast nook, where a man named Walter Everett Jr. was sitting, thinking – Win, as he was called – lost to the morning noises collecting around him, a stir of the all familiar, the heart-beat mosaic of every happy home, toast springing up, radio voices with their intimate and busy timbre, an optimistic buzz living in the ear. (L, p. 16)

The narrative of the conspiracy that Everett instigates certainly follows chronologically from that of Branch and his studies, and seems in some way to be prompted by it, but we cannot say with absolute confidence that we are reading a direct representation of the computer text that Branch has just called up on his screen, although it is clearly a suspicion that the novel provokes. Rather, the start of the Everett narrative can be viewed as a concrete example, no longer dependent on the reader's recognition of methodological analogues, of the unsettling complicity of the narrative structure that is *Libra* with the secret CIA project on which Branch has embarked and which is itself a narrated subject. The question of the text's broader complicity with that which it narrates might also be provoked when the reader goes on to discover that the Everett narrative is that of the secret project of ex-CIA operatives, themselves intent, in Everett's words, on '"script[ing] a person or persons out of ordinary pocket litter"' (*L*, p. 28).

In *Mao II*, though, matters are somewhat more direct. There, on three separate occasions, the narrative describes TV news reports as seen by some of the characters. First it is the disaster at Hillsborough, the football fans crushed to death (*MII*, pp. 32–4):

> They show the fence from a distance, bodies piling up behind it, smothered, sometimes only fingers moving, and it is like a fresco in an old dark church, a crowded twisted vision of a rush to death as only a master of age could paint it. (*MII*, pp. 34)

Later we read the description of the TV coverage of the Tiananmen Square massacre (*MII*, pp. 176–8): 'They show the bicycle dead, a soldier's body hanging from a girder, the row of old officials in Mao suits' (p.178). Finally, there is the report of the Ayatollah Khomeini's funeral (*MII*, pp. 188–93):

> The helicopter landed with the body in a metal casket, which revolutionary guards carried on their shoulders a short distance to the grave. But then the crowds surged again, weeping men in bloody headbands, and they scaled the barriers and overran the gravesite.
>
> The voice said, Wailing chanting mourners. It said, Throwing themselves into the hole. (*MII*, p. 191)

These passages must be distinguished from their counterparts in those novels by Umberto Eco (*Foucault's Pendulum*) and Thomas Pynchon (*Vineland*) cited by McHale. Such examples in DeLillo's fiction distinguish themselves by their relative brevity (the longest is five pages) and also by their frequent reminders that what we are reading is a literary representation of a TV report. In fact the narrative shuttles between offering representations of what is on the screen and descriptions of the character's act of watching that TV-screen. Yet although these distinctions are necessary, *Mao*

II ought nonetheless to be counted, along with *Libra*, among those postmodernist novels in which the narrative is, at least momentarily, 'entrusted to some secondary medium (movie, television, computer) represented *in* the verbal text'.

Don DeLillo and Self-Conscious Postmodernism

What we saw in the previous section is the expression *formally* in DeLillo's fiction of the conventions, values and assumptions of a postmodernist, consumerist culture and a late capitalist, commodity-saturated social configuration. This expression comes as a result, as we noted earlier, of the integration of the commodity structure itself into the very form of the work of art, now redesigned as a *text*. In other words, we have been busy indicating some of the *ideological* features of the text.

We shall see later, with the help of Paul Cantor, how a self-conscious recognition of the ideological complicity is expressed in *White Noise*; for now, though, we remain with *Libra* and *Mao II* in order to indicate the means by which a similar self-consciousness finds expression there too. A recurrent figure in DeLillo's novels is that of the author or artist, the 'men in small rooms' who are also Nicholas Branch's subject. Film-makers figure prominently in both *Americana* and *The Names*; *Great Jones Street* is the story of a rock star, *Ratner's Star* that of a child maths prodigy; in *Libra* we find Branch, Everett and Oswald, each in his own way attempting to write (or to rewrite) certain narratives; *Mao II*, attaining a new level of explicitness, is about a novelist. To define Win Everett as some sort of 'author', the creator of a conspiratorial 'fiction', is also to highlight the double significance that DeLillo allocates to the word 'plot'. Everett muses on his own plot, secretly suspecting that what has begun as the simulacrum of an assassination conspiracy will nonetheless result in a death. 'There is a tendency of plots to move towards death', he thinks. 'He believed that the idea of death is woven into the nature of every plot. A narrative plot no less than a conspiracy of armed men' (*L*, p. 221). These thoughts match those of Jack Gladney in *White Noise* (*WN*, p. 26), and offer a further indication of the analogy DeLillo implicitly draws between the construction of his own fiction and that of Everett (not to mention Branch).

'Win Everett', we read,

was at work devising a general shape, a life. He would script a gunman out of ordinary dog-eared paper, the contents of a wallet. Parmenter would contrive to get document blanks from the Record Branch. Mackey would find a model for the character Everett was in the process of creating. They wanted a name, a face, a bodily frame they might use to extend their fiction into the world. (*L*, p. 50)

In a sense, *Libra* is full of authors. As well as attending to the as-yet-fictional 'other' that he wants to become, Oswald himself plans to write a book and is somewhat put out when his mother announces her own authorial ambitions (*L*, pp. 277–8). Yet, really, they are all authors-*manqués*, their own stories taken over by others and ultimately submerged in the impersonal totalising dynamic of late capitalist history and society.

Perhaps an even more extreme case of the author's inability to evade submersion in the consumerist society of the image or simulacrum is that of Bill Gray, the novelist, in *Mao II*. Gray's reclusiveness, the distance he imposes between himself and the outside world, ironically becomes the reason for his unintended prominence in the world. He agrees to be photographed in order to dispel, if only a little, the burdensome mystique that has developed. His re-entrance into the public world, though, when it extends to a planned public appearance in support of a kidnapped French poet, leads eventually to his death. It is curious to reflect on the novel in the light of Ernst Bloch's remarks on the novel of the artist, a genre to which *Mao II* might reasonably be expected to belong: 'That which moves one in the novel of the artist itself . . . is the desire to break new ground, with knights, death, and the devil, to head for the envisioned utopian castle or to that which corresponds to its formation in shape, sound, or word.'[59] But *Mao II* is not really a novel of the artist in Bloch's sense; rather, it is a novel of both the end of the artist and the mass production of artists, a novel in which the loss of cultural autonomy has led inevitably to the artist's direct complicity with, and destruction by, the social forces to which she or he responds.

To point out these aspects of DeLillo's novels, though, is only to indicate the presence on the level of thematics or content of that self-conscious acknowledgement of ideological complicity of which I have been writing. Perhaps even more significant are the means by which such self-consciousness is expressed formally, through the narrative, structural and stylistic techniques the novels employ. In this respect, it is the systematic nature of DeLillo's novels that is most significant. Often, the texts seem to foreground the extent to which they, themselves, constitute a totalising dynamic, a textual mechanism in which characters – and even the narrator – become mere functions of an apparently abstract and impersonal narrative structure.

In DeLillo's novels characters sometimes seem to merge into one another; they can become almost indistinguishable in the course of a short dialogue. We see this, for example, when the two Jacks (Karlinsky and Ruby) discuss Oswald and the death of Kennedy (*L*, pp. 431–2). Lentricchia is surely right when he writes that '[t]he two Jacks are hard to tell apart, which is the point'.[60] In fact, we find that the whole narrative operates in this manner. Lentricchia makes much of DeLillo's overall narrative strategy in the novel: a third-person narration with frequent recourse to free indirect discourse. He points out that the narrative voice in *Libra* does not retain the distinct critical distance from its subject(s) that we might normally expect. 'For the narrator in *Libra* is not DeLillo,' he writes, 'but DeLillo in quotation marks: "DeLillo" as a voice crafted to perform virtuoso changes of point of view that function as disconcerting repetitions of his characters' obses-sive shifts from first-person to third.'[61] The effect is to reduce the supposedly authoritative voice to the status of another character.

We can see quite clearly what Lentricchia means if we look at the framing of one of Marguerite Oswald's monologues:

Marguerite sat on the sofa watching TV.

It griped him to move to New York, which we travelled all the way in that 1948 Dodge, but that's where John Edward was stationed with his wife and baby and we are a family that has never been able to stay together . . . I have made my best effort to raise my boy in this manner, regardless. Whatever is said by them, and they are at it all the time, he knows who has been his main support from the moment I took him home from the Old French Hospital on Orleans Avenue. I am not the looming mother of a boy's bad dreams.

George Gobel appeared on the screen, stubby, crew-cut, with a wholesome smirk, right hand raised to the middle of his forehead in some kind of fraternal small town salute.

Lee was in his room reading about the conversion of surplus value into capital, following the text with his index finger, word by word by word. (*L*, pp. 48–9)

The narrative shifts from a third-person description of what Marguerite is doing to her own first-person interior monologue and then back again to the third-person narration without such shifts being marked in any way. This is quite typical of the text; as Lentricchia notes, '"DeLillo's" voice fades into his major characters, he becomes Ruby or Oswald, or the crowd gaping at Kennedy, or Mrs. John Connolly in the limousine speeding to Parkland Hospital ("those men dying in our arms").'[62]

In *Mao II* we see a similar technique at work. Scott's girlfriend, Karen, is watching a TV programme on physical fitness; the narrator starts to comment on her reactions: 'She took it all in, she believed it all, pain, ecstasy, dog food, all the seraphic matter, the baby bliss that falls from the air. Scott stared at her and waited. She carried the virus of the future. Quoting Bill' (*MII*, p. 119). The penultimate sentence of this passage would appear to be an example of free indirect discourse – the narrative is focalised through Scott – but what about the last sentence? 'Quoting Bill' may be Scott's own comment on his mental description of Karen, but it might equally be the narrator's. In a sense, of course, this is just another instance of suspensive irony; but here it serves to indicate, albeit subtly – through the reduction of characters and narrator to mere transient functions of an impersonal, totalising narrative – those social conditions of systematic absorption and domination upon which the cultural dominant of postmodernism (and its characteristic textual strategies, such as pastiche) is predicated.

Yet while DeLillo's texts may indicate these social forces, it must be borne in mind that they do so through their own overt and utterly self-conscious reflection and expression of them. In other words, the social critique implicit in the text's mimicry of forms of systematic absorption is here expressed in terms of a further acknowledgement of the literary text's own ideological complicity with such forms and processes. Tom LeClair, in *In the Loop: Don DeLillo and the Systems Novel*, writes in a very different vein of the systematic construction of DeLillo's texts, preferring to explore the affinities of those texts with 'systems theories'. Nonetheless, the extent to which he highlights as a characteristic feature of DeLillo's texts the absorption of characters into a larger impersonal structure is, I think, incisive and potentially productive for more materialist analyses.

Rather than proposing, then, a general preoccupation in DeLillo's novels with systems and systems theory, I would prefer to interpret that undoubted interest in terms of a more specific response to the systematic structures of late or consumer capitalism. Discussing his novel *Ratner's Star*, DeLillo, in a rare interview, offers the following comments:

I was trying to produce a book that would be naked structure. The structure would be the book and vice versa. I wanted the book to become what it was about. Abstract structures and connective patterns. A piece of mathematics in short. To do this, I felt I had to reduce the importance of people. The people had to play a role subservient to pattern, form, and so on.[63]

This is also as far as LeClair takes us, noting of the novel that '[n]arration slips rapidly and cleanly without transition among the characters, effectively implying the continuous.'[64] Modes of thought and aesthetic forms are, however, intimately related to social and economic formations. We have already seen how, in *White Noise* and *Libra*, characters are portrayed as the haphazard constructions of dominant and ubiquitous social forces. It is precisely these social conditions of which the subservience of character to abstract pattern and form in DeLillo's texts – extending beyond *Ratner's Star* to *Libra* and to *Mao II* – is expressive. That *Ratner's Star* itself follows through the logic of its own formally expressed domination of characters should be evident from the attempt by the scientist Cheops Feeley to convince the 14-year-old maths prodigy Billy Twillig to have implanted in his brain a device that will help the business cartel which Feeley represents to manipulate the international money curve, but which has the added side-effect of allowing Billy only to experience and to perceive things in abstract terms.[65] Mathematical or scientific abstraction (which the text itself attempts to mimic) thus serves to reinforce man's subservience to a global capitalist network; or, as Theodor Adorno and Max Horkheimer write in *Dialectic of Enlightenment*, 'The more the machinery of thought subjects existence to itself, the more blind its resignation in reproducing existence.'[66]

Adorno and Horkheimer insist repeatedly on the relation – which is an expressive one – of abstract, scientific or enlightened categories of thought to 'the corresponding conditions of social reality – that is, of the division of labour'.[67] The common feature they share, as DeLillo's texts also attest, is the domination of the specific or individual by general or abstract categories or forms. 'What is done to all by the few', write Adorno and Horkheimer, 'always occurs as the subjection of individuals by the many: social repression always exhibits the masks of repression by a collective. It is this unity of the collectivity and domination . . . which is expressed in thought forms'.[68] While recognising that this is the form in which social domination commonly manifests itself, it

must equally be borne in mind that 'even the threatening collective belongs only to the deceptive surface, beneath which are
concealed the powers which manipulate it as an instrument of
power'.[69] What ultimately concerns here both the authors of
Dialectic of Enlightenment and DeLillo are methods of reification,
that process by which, in the words of Georg Lukács, 'a relation
between people takes on the character of a thing'.[70]

In order to grasp substantially the means by which such a
concept might illuminate DeLillo's work, it is necessary to understand the complex and mystificatory forms that social domination
(and, subsequently, reification) takes. The logic, therefore, of the
last two quotations from *Dialectic of Enlightenment* might be adequately synthesised in the following passage: 'It is not merely that
domination is paid for by the alienation of men from the objects
dominated: with the objectification of spirit, the very relations of
men – even those of the individual to himself – were bewitched.'[71]
Although the human subject might appear to be the dominating
agent – whether through the application of rational abstraction or
technology, or in the guise of the baiting crowd – she or he is in
fact dominated by those very same structures of domination. It is
in the figure of the crowd that DeLillo demonstrates this in his
novels.

The opening pages of *White Noise* depict one of DeLillo's many
crowd scenes. The families file to the College-on-the-Hill in their
station wagon, each bearing the products and belongings that
identify their owners as sharers in the good life. As Jack Gladney
reflects, 'This assembly of station wagons, as much as anything
they might do in the course of the year, more than formal liturgies
or laws, tells the parents they are a collection of the likeminded
and the spiritually akin, a people, a nation' (*WN*, pp. 3–4). Like
those who assemble in their local supermarkets, the students'
parents became a crowd (or late capitalist community) as a result
of commodity consumption. The same is also true of the Gladney
family, which is united through a shared experience of commodity
and image consumption. The family nights in front of the TV and
the communal shopping expedition are, in *White Noise*, enough to
forge and to maintain a familial bond.

The first chapter in *Mao II*, depicting a mass wedding of
Moonies, ends portentiously: 'The future belongs to crowds.'
But in the course of the novel there are no more crowd scenes.
Instead, there are descriptions of characters watching crowds on
TV. For the most part these characters witness violence and
destructiveness, which the crowds are sometimes responsible for

and at other times are subjected to. But just as important as the crowds on the screen is the other crowd – that of voyeurs – that the text implies. In *Libra*, Beryl Parmenter, watching the replay of Lee Oswald's murder on TV, is convinced that Oswald looks straight into the camera just before his death and that he seems now to be staring at her out of the screen. She thinks that this in some way unites Oswald with the viewers, that they all somehow form a crowd. If they do, it is surely the modern (or postmodern) form of the 'baiting crowd' of which Elias Canetti writes in *Crowds and Power*. Canetti's crowd is one of newspaper readers, but its features remain broadly applicable to the Tube-watching populus of DeLillo's texts:

> Disgust at collective killing is of very recent date and should not be over-estimated. Today everyone takes part in public executions through the newspapers. Like everything else, however, it is more comfortable than it was. We sit peacefully at home and, out of a hundred details, can choose those to linger over which offer a special thrill. We only applaud when everything is over and there is no feeling of guilty connivance to spoil our pleasure. We are not responsible for the sentence, nor for the journalists who report its execution, nor for the papers which print them. None the less, we know more about the business than our predecessors, who may have walked miles to see it, hung around for hours, and, in the end, seen very little. The baiting crowd is preserved in the newspaper reading public, in a milder form it is true, but, because of its distance from events, a more responsible one. One is tempted to say that it is the most despicable and, at the same time, the most stable form of such a crowd. Since it does not even have to assemble, it escapes disintegration; variety is catered for by the daily reappearance of the papers.[72]

Through the mass consumption of images, then, as much as through that of Waffelos and the Mystic mints (a distinction which, in the age of simulacra, is no longer particularly necessary), the characters of DeLillo's texts are drawn into the structures and thought patterns of the crowd. These characters are, in a sense, reified and dominated by their individual submersion in the crowd of commodity/image consumers.

Yet, as members of a crowd – and particularly of the (post)-modern form of the baiting crowd – the characters of DeLillo's novels must at least appear as agents as well as victims of domination.

Canetti notes, in connection with such crowds, the following reflection: 'The threat of death hangs over all men and, however disguised it may be, and even if it is sometimes forgotten, it affects them all at the time and creates in them a need to deflect death onto others. The formation of baiting crowds answers this need.'[73] Jack Gladney, in the course of a seminar he shares with Murray, comes to a near identical conclusion (*WN*, p. 73). To be part of a crowd is to be dominated, reified, but it is also to attempt to dominate death and may therefore take the form of a need to displace death through the murderous domination of others. The taking of Dylar, then, the consumption of a medication that dispels one's fear of death, works in the novel as a metaphor for any form of consumption (the means by which one becomes part of a crowd).

When Jack finds that Babette's supply of Dylar has been extinguished, he is led to carry out the extreme logic of the equation between the suppression of fear of death that the consumption of Dylar offers and the displacement of death resulting from the violent domination of others: he decides to kill Willie Mink and to steal his stash of Dylar. In doing so, Jack is living out the theoretical speculations of his friend Murray:

> I believe, Jack, there are two kinds of people in the world. Killers and diers. Most of us are diers. We don't have the disposition, the rage, or whatever it takes to be a killer. We let death happen. We lie down and die. But think what it's like to be a killer. Think how exciting it is, in theory, to kill another person in direct confrontation. If he dies, you cannot. To kill him is to gain life-credit. The more people you kill, the more credit you store up. It explains any number of massacres, wars, executions. (*WN*, p. 290)

Murray's ideas are borrowed directly from Canetti's *Crowds and Power*, where they are discussed in the chapter on 'The Survivor'. In Canetti's portrayal the survivor usually manifests himself as a murderous psychopath for whom killing becomes a passion; the unspoken exemplar of such a figure, haunting Canetti's book as he does more overtly *White Noise*, is of course the subject of Jack Gladney's study: Adolf Hitler.

Where these lead Jack – the conspiring forces of consumption and domination – is to the motel room of Willie Mink and there to the very brink of murder. It is at this point in the novel, though, that DeLillo depicts the inter-relation of those forces and the loss

of cultural autonomy that we noted earlier providing both the
cultural context and subject-matter of *White Noise*. It is worth
looking closely at the scene of the shooting:

> I fired the gun, the weapon, the pistol, the firearm, the auto-
> matic. The sound snowballed in the white room, adding on
> reflected waves. I watched blood spurt from the victim's mid-
> section. A delicate arc. I marveled at the rich color, sensed the
> color-causing action of non-nucleated cells. The flow dimin-
> ished to a trickle, spread across the tile floor. I saw beyond
> words. I knew what red was, saw it in terms of dominant
> wavelength, luminance, purity. Mink's pain was beautiful,
> intense. (*WN*, p. 312)

The violence is experienced by Jack in terms of its aesthetic
features: he notes the blood's colour, its viscosity, the 'delicate
arc' in which it spurts; to Jack, his victim's pain is beautiful. In
a sense, then, the side-effect of Dylar that forces Mink to react
to words as though they were their own referents is merely a
more acute reflection of the state of mind that Jack has adopted
as a side-effect of commodity reification and the dialectical
interpenetration of the object and cultural realms – an association which offers yet further evidence of the function Dylar
plays in the novel as a metaphor for commodity/image consumption, and therefore for participation in late capitalist society in
general.

In the 'Culture Industry' chapter of *Dialectic of Enlightenment*,
Adorno and Horkheimer insist on the violence that is a consequence of the culture industry. This association of the culture
industry, or a cultural realm that no longer claims for itself the
autonomy it once did, with forces of domination and terror is one
that is distinctly recognisable from the pages of DeLillo's fiction. In
Mao II this takes the form of a kidnap which is staged from the
very outset as a media event. Rather more indirectly, it is an
association that might be inferred from the discussions between
Bill Gray, the novelist, and George Haddad, the academic spokes-
person for the group responsible for the kidnap. George asks Bill
whether he uses a word processor; Bill does not. George recom-
mends one: '[T]he machine helps me organise my thoughts,' he
says, 'gives me a text susceptible to revision' (*MII*, pp. 137–8).
Later he brings the subject up again: 'I'm still convinced you
ought to get one. Instant corrections . . . the text, is lightweight,
malleable. It doesn't restrict or inhibit' (*MII*, p. 161). The text, he

says, 'is lightweight, malleable'; 'the machine helps me organise
my thoughts.' What thoughts are these? George goes on to speak
of Mao: Mao the poet, Mao the cult. The novelist replies:

> The question you have to ask is, How many dead? How many
> dead during the Cultural Revolution? How many dead after the
> Great Leap Forward? And how well did he hide his dead? This
> is the other question. What do these men do with the millions
> they kill? (*MII*, p. 163)

On the one hand, there are lightweight, malleable texts; on the
other: violence, mass murder. In *White Noise* this same juxtaposition is achieved through the figures of Elvis and Hitler.

What Jameson has called 'the relief of the postmodern' – lightweight texts, art as commodity – is placed side by side with the
icons of terror. The particular question of the juxtaposition in
White Noise of Elvis and Hitler has provoked somewhat troubled
musings among DeLillo's critics. It is therefore worth looking
briefly at two diametrically opposed critical responses while
noting that both are quite breathtakingly wide of the mark.
Both, in fact, proceed from the same, fatally flawed premis:
namely, that Elvis and Hitler represent two alternatives in direct
opposition to one another. For Bruce Bawer ('Don DeLillo's
America'), DeLillo posits contemporary, late capitalist America as
the destroyer of man's natural, savage state. 'In DeLillo's overly
diagrammatic world,' he writes, 'savagery is the only alternative to
depersonalization by means of sensory overload; only through a
pure, brutal physicality can one reclaim one's selfhood.' Speculat-
ing on the ubiquity of Hitler throughout DeLillo's œuvre, Bawer
writes, 'The reason is obvious: Hitler is the ultimate example of
twentieth-century man reverting to primitivism.' DeLillo's point,
therefore, is equally obvious (or 'unmistakable' in Bawer's words):
'Hitler was just like us. We are all Hitler.' For Bawer, then,
DeLillo's fiction can be summed up in the following terms: 'A
craving for primitive destructiveness dwells deep in all our hearts
. . . it is what makes us human.' Given the choice of Elvis or
Hitler, Bawer seems in little doubt that DeLillo would plump for
the greater authenticity of the latter.[74]

Frank Lentricchia, in 'Tales of the Electronic Tribe', comes to
precisely the opposite conclusion. Referring to the periodic note of
awe and sense of mystery in Jack's voice as he speaks of those
commodity cultural forces that bind his family and community
together – principally the supermarket and the TV – Lentricchia

contends that DeLillo offers us the choice of consumer culture or authoritarian terror:

> Would we prefer that Jack give up the supermarket, the mall, his family, the nights gathered around the TV, for another, chilling guarantor of community, who lurks in the background of *White Noise*, as in the background of a number of modernist literary monuments – the specter of the totalitarian, the gigantic charismatic figure who triggers our desire to give in, to merge our frightened selves in his frightening authority? Hitler, another kind of epic hero, voice of national solidarity, is the other object of Jack's awe.[75]

Lentricchia's DeLillo, like that of Bawer, juxtaposes the figures of Elvis and Hitler primarily in order to contrast them, to posit one as the other's contrary alternative. In truth, of course, DeLillo does nothing of the sort. That these two critics should reach opposite conclusions is therefore relatively unimportant; somewhat more significant instead is their unwillingness to grapple with the far more troubling and more complex relationship constructed in DeLillo's fiction – and particularly in *White Noise* – between the contemporary American culture industry and German Nazism.

This is a relationship treated with rather more attentiveness in an article called 'Adolf, We Hardly Knew You' by Paul Cantor. Cantor points to certain problems with Bawer's thesis, particularly to the difficulty of claiming that DeLillo implicitly associates Hitler with a vision of human authenticity in relation to which Elvis and the inauthentic American consumer culture stand in unflattering contrast. Nazi Germany, he writes, is shown to have been just as much a facade as contemporary America. He cites Jack's comments on Albert Speer's architectural plans for the German Reich (*WN*, pp. 257–8). 'We see here', writes Cantor, 'that the Nazis were themselves imitating a model of earlier greatness, namely, ancient Rome (a pattern even clearer in the Italian brand of fascism)'.[76] The aesthetic side of Nazism was, he says, 'a *derivative* aesthetic'. Thus it is the *in*authenticity of the Hitler figure upon which DeLillo dwells, contrary to Bawer's interpretation.

Nevertheless, if DeLillo's text is to offer a proper critique of fascism and the fascist impulse, it must surely note the inauthenticity of the movement while simultaneously insisting on its savagery and barbarism. This *White Noise* is conspicuously unable to do. For all Jack's bluster about the terrifying phenomenon that Hitler represents, the Hitler of *White Noise* remains a curiously domesticated figure, easily assimilated into a university curriculum:

> Advanced Nazism, three hours a week, restricted to qualified seniors, a course of study designed to cultivate historical perspective, theoretical rigor and mature insight into the continuing mass appeal of Fascist tyranny, with special emphasis on parades, rallies and uniforms, three credits, written reports. (*WN*, p. 25)

No one seems to think this strange. Jack and Murray interweave biographical details of Hitler and Elvis as though there are no necessary distinctions to be made between the two; for Jack, the differences are of scale rather than of pathology; he knows that the association of Hitler with Elvis can do nothing but good to the prospects of 'Elvis Studies'.

In one of DeLillo's earlier novels, *Running Dog*, we find another transformation of the Hitler figure. In this novel, a number of different groups are searching for a film reportedly made in Hitler's bunker in Berlin just before the end. There are rumours that the film is pornographic. Eventually it is found:

> The camera is trained on the man's face. Again it moves, coming in for a medium close-up.
> Eyes blank.
> Little or no hair alongside his ears.
> Face pale and lined.
> Flaccid mouth.
> Smoothly curved jaw.
> The famous mustache.
> Head shaking, he acknowledges the presence of the camera. It pulls back. The man moves forward, walking in a screwy mechanical way. Here the camera pans the audience. As the man enters the room, the adults show outsized delight, clearly meant to prompt the children, who may or may not be familiar with Charlie Chaplin.[77]

Hitler is doing a Chaplin impersonation. Citing this passage, Jack's cinema-influenced musings on Attila the Hun in *White Noise*, and his meeting with the postmodern nuns who hold to a mere simulacrum of faith, Cantor points to DeLillo's inability 'to keep postmodernism delimited'. 'As its name indicates,' he writes, postmodernism must be defined in contrast to something else, what came before it. But like many others today, DeLillo keeps wanting to extend the range of postmodernism, above all to keep pushing it farther and farther back into the past, until it threatens to lose all meaning as a distinctive term. This process seems to be the logical outcome of the very concept of postmodernism.[78]

Consequently, for Cantor (in one of the most perceptive comments yet written on DeLillo):

DeLillo himself seems unable to break out of the postmodern circle and offer a convincing alternative to its diminished reality. In short, he can give us a vision of the inauthentic but not, it seems, of the authentic. DeLillo is sufficiently distanced from postmodern existence to want to be able to criticize it, but sufficiently implicated in it to have a hard time finding an Archimedean point from which to do the criticizing.[79]

In a sense, then, DeLillo's position might be compared to that of Jack Gladney once he has finished his monologue on the phenomenon and function of the crowd: 'People gathered round, students and staff, and in the mild din of half heard remarks and orbiting voices I realized we were now a crowd' (*WN*, p. 74).

Central, though, to Cantor's argument is an understanding of the postmodern as a historical stage which repudiates the very concept of history and historical specificity itself. The inability of DeLillo 'to keep postmodernism delimited' ought then to be seen as an example of this dismissal of history in much the same way as we might understand the nonchalance with which Jack and Babette discuss their choice of pornographic reading material: 'Pick your century' (*WN*, p. 29). This ahistoricism, which DeLillo's texts both represent and embody, can be traced to the dissipation of that conflict with economic life which art had previously retained in its radical autonomy and its disavowal of social utility. Thus Adorno writes of 'the emergence of that false reconciliation, the absorption of every negative counter-instance by an omnipotent reality, the elimination of dissonance in the bad totality'.[80] Yet while it is only with this surrender to an utter conflictlessness that art 'turn[s] completely into the lie to which it has always contributed its part in the past', to Adorno the preservation of conflict in the work of art would represent an indefensible lie, 'transfigur[ing] the world into one in which conflict is still possible rather than revealing it as one in which the omnipotent power of production is beginning ever more obviously to repress such a possibility'.[81] This argument leads to an impasse; or, at least, so it would appear. It is time to see, in the concluding section of this chapter, which routes or strategies, if any, might provide an escape to something other than passive acceptance or blind delusion.

DeLillo: From Modernism to Postmodernism

The evolution of cultural forms and its relation to the historical situation is speculatively sketched out by Fredric Jameson in *The Political Unconscious*:

> [T]he relationship of the . . . historical situation to the text is not construed as causal (however that might be imagined) but rather as one of a limiting situation; the historical moment is here understood to block off or shut down a certain number of formal possibilities available before, and to open up determinate new ones, which may or may not ever be realized in artistic practice.[82]

Jameson's formulation can be to some degree rebuked, however, by Raymond Williams' notion of 'residual' and 'emergent' forms which are always to be seen in a dynamic relationship with the 'dominant'.[83] As it appears in *The Political Unconscious*, Jameson's conception of the permissibility or otherwise of artistic forms and techniques does not allow adequate scope for such conflicts, apparently denying at least the validity of 'residual' forms unless they are to be seen as nostalgic deception. In *Postmodernism*, however, he insists on the need to picture the postmodern as 'the force field in which very different kinds of cultural impulses – what Raymond Williams has usefully termed "residual" and "emergent" forms of cultural production – must make their way'.[84]

The slight, but nonetheless significant, confusion of these two passages appears, in the light of Jameson's book on Adorno (*Late Marxism: Adorno, or, the Persistence of the Dialectic*), to be mainly the product of Jameson's reading of the latter's *Aesthetic Theory*. Jameson writes that Adorno's conception of the New is that it originates in the exclusion of older forms or ideas:

> what is new about the *Novum* is less the work itself . . . than these new prohibitions, about which it would therefore be

better to say, not that they tell you what not to do, but rather that they spell out what is *no longer* to be done; what you cannot do any more.[85]

Clearly it is from this model that Jameson takes his own in *The Political Unconscious*. However, Adorno's construction is not, in truth, quite as steel-clad as Jameson's gloss on it (through an interesting omission) would suggest. Having stated precisely what Jameson represents him as doing, Adorno goes on to qualify this:

> It would be a mistake . . . to hypostatise historically grown prohibitions as though they were irrevocable. To do so is to provoke a reaction that is prevalent in Cocteau's brand of modernism and which consists of a favourite slight of hand whereby the prohibited quality is all of a sudden magically pulled out of a hat and presented as though it were brand new – a modernism that gets its kicks from breaking the taboos of modernism. What is valid in this otherwise reactionary modernism is the implicit assumption that taboos are not forever. However, this return of the tabooed should not take the form of a harking back to unproblematic categories and solutions; rather, what may legitimately return are past problems.[86]

The example to which Adorno points is Schönberg's remark that harmony is 'out of the question for the time being'. Denying that this indicates the possibility of a return to triple-chords, Adorno suggests, instead, that it is 'the general question of simultaneity in music' that remains open, making possible a future working-out of this question which might involve the development of a new form of harmony, itself intimately related to a transformed historical situation. As we shall see, this return of 'past problems' is precisely what functions, in a revealing and determinedly historically specific way, as the utopian feature of the internal dialectic of Don DeLillo's postmodernist fiction, thereby producing the potential of that 'alternative or even oppositional relation to the dominant culture' which Raymond Williams associates with certain 'residual' cultural forms.[87]

Before going on to examine how this operates in textual practice, it is worth acknowledging the importance to a proper reading of DeLillo of the subtle distinction between Art in general (particularly as it is grasped abstractly through the construction of a cultural dominant) and the individual text which situates itself in relation to Art and its cultural dominant. Of course, this is my intention throughout this work; in the specific instance of DeLillo, however, it is necessary to go further and to identify that relation, along with Fredric Jameson and Theodor Adorno,[88] as one of dialectical conflict in which the individual work of art 'works on' the guilt (that is, the ideological complicity) of Art while remaining unable ever to disassociate itself from that same guilt of social and class domination.

To demonstrate how this form of critique, whose subject is both the cultural dominant of postmodernism and the individual texts themselves, manifests itself in DeLillo's fiction shall, then, be our chief preoccupation in the brief reminder of this chapter. For Frank Lentricchia the issue is clear-cut; he concludes his 'Introduction' to *New Essays on 'White Noise'* with the following judgement:

> Impulses aesthetic and critical have − classically − stood in starkest opposition, but they go together in the modernist idea of literature, perhaps no more seamlessly than in Don DeLillo, last of the modernists, who takes for his critical object of aesthetic concern the postmodern situation.[89]

Lentricchia's DeLillo, 'last of the modernists', achieves his critical distance unproblematically, through the subjection of a post-modern historical (and historico-cultural) situation to the rigorous scrutiny of modernist critical aesthetics. The whole tenor of Lentricchia's essay on *Libra* ('*Libra* as Postmodern Critique') also conforms to this assumption. Yet, as we have seen, there are both formal and thematic features of the texts that would contradict this all too comfortable conclusion, situating DeLillo's texts firmly within what for Jameson is the 'force-field' of postmodernism rather than seeking some elevated or external aesthetic space that unsullied modernists might occupy and from which their unflinching stare might be trained on contemporary cultural degradation.

The somewhat mistaken conclusion to which Frank Lentricchia holds does, however, highlight one of the most important aspects of DeLillo's texts: namely, the relationship which they establish between modernist and postmodernist aesthetics. Focusing on this same issue, Noel King, in 'Reading *White Noise*: Floating Remarks', asks the sort of question that seems to underlie Lentricchia's comment:

What exactly is the relation of White Noise to the category of the postmodern? Is it to be called a postmodern novel because it talks about postmodern sunsets, semiotics and simulacra? Is it postmodern in the sense that the novels of Pynchon, Gaddis and Coover are termed postmodern?

Or is it, rather, a slyly modernist meditation on postmodern themes?[90]

Although he draws on certain of Fredric Jameson's analyses of the postmodern and alludes once or twice to Walter Benjamin, King's essay is only superficially materialist in approach, evading questions of ideology and seeking to establish a privileged position for what he calls the 'ficto-critical', under whose banner he wishes to situate White Noise. As King depicts it, White Noise offers provisional, hesitant critique, discovering some form of positive worth in a hazy ambivalence of which King himself offers no analysis. While identifying the same dilemma that provokes Lentricchia's remarks, King does not in actual fact ever get around to addressing it in any serious fashion, allowing it instead to float away harmlessly out of sight.

If we are to see a proper engagement of the issue, whose conclusion might be juxtaposed with that of Lentricchia, it is necessary to turn once again to Leonard Wilcox. In 'Baudrillard, DeLillo's White Noise and the End of Heroic Narrative', Wilcox identifies Jack Gladney, the narrator of White Noise, as 'a modernist displaced in a postmodern world'. Even the flight from a threatening external world to a secure, if besieged, inner-consciousness is no longer an option for Gladney, whose own subjectivity, as we have seen, has itself been thoroughly saturated by the white noise of advertising slogans and commodity brand names. Of crucial significance, however, is the step by which Wilcox extends his argument:

Moreover, for Baudrillard and DeLillo the dissolution of a modernist subjectivity in the mire of contemporary media and technology is integrally connected to another issue: the passing of the great modernist notions of artistic impulse and representation, the demise of notions of a 'heroic' search for alternative, creative forms of consciousness, and the idea of art as specially endowed revelation.[91]

It is, then, as we have already noted, precisely that desire, in Ernst Bloch's words, 'to head for the envisioned utopian castle or to that which corresponds to its formation in shape, sound, or word' of which DeLillo, as a postmodernist novelist, no longer has any proper means of expression.

However, moving closer to Lentricchia's position, Wilcox points to a certain ambiguity in DeLillo's work. 'DeLillo's novels', he writes:

> engage historical and political issues; they do not exhibit the ahistoricism and pastiched depthlessness often associated with postmodernism. If his works exhibit the postmodern concern with the unstable nature of subjectivity and textuality, with representation and narrative process, his postmodernism retains the legacy of the modernist impulse to explore consciousness and selfhood and to create an imaginative vision that probes and criticises its subject matter.[92]

Attempting to justify such a claim – a claim which insists on DeLillo's ability to evade those very features of the postmodern (principally ahistoricism and depthlessness) by which we have seen him so firmly constrained – Wilcox invokes DeLillo's 'belief that fictional narrative can provide critical distance from and a critical perspective on the processes it depicts'.[93] A detailed reading, however, as Paul Cantor has shown us, reveals that it is precisely the absence of such a critical distance and the inability to escape from a postmodernist ahistoricism that *White Noise* itself represents. As we are about to see, though, there is a hitherto unsuspected sense in which Lentricchia, Wilcox and Cantor are all in fact correct.

During the course of an interview with Tom LeClair, DeLillo was asked about his literary influences:

> The books I remember and come back to seem to be the ones that demonstrate the possibilities of fiction. *Pale Fire, Ulysses, The Death of Virgil, Under the Volcano, The Sound and the Fury* – these come to mind. There's a drive and a daring that go beyond technical invention. I think it's right to call it a life-drive even though these books deal at times very directly with death. No optimism, no pessimism. No homesickness for lost values or for the way fiction used to be written. These books open out into some larger mystery. I don't know what to call it. Maybe Hermann Broch would call it 'the word beyond speech.'[94]

There is, here, that same attachment to art as mystery that Wilcox emphasises, but there is also – and, for our present purposes, more importantly – a recognition of the power of that which cannot be expressed, that to which at present there is no aesthetic access. In the case of Don DeLillo's fiction, that which can never quite struggle to expression – and whose non-expression renders the texts complicit with those social forms of which they seek to offer a critique – is a meaningful sense of history and historical conflict.

To that extent, Paul Cantor is entirely correct: DeLillo's representations of the postmodern remain determined by the ideology of the postmodern itself. However, it is revealing to view this inability of the texts to oppose such determination in the light of their continual – perhaps, at times, even excessive – meditations upon the transformed relation, and its implications, of the contemporary cultural realm to the political and economic: namely, upon that corner-stone of postmodern ideology, the loss of cultural (semi)autonomy. In the Adornean formulation, as we have seen, it is that loss of autonomy which perverts any aesthetic representation of history. What actually occurs, then, in DeLillo's excessive preoccupation with the interpenetration of the cultural and the economic is a self-conscious meditation upon the ideological forces of the postmodern – from which his texts cannot escape – and the necessary complicity of cultural documents with such forces. This is a form of self-critique. Or, rather, it is not quite so yet. Such a claim remains unjustified until it can be shown that DeLillo's texts, through the self-consciousness of their ideological function and its determining conditions, are able to achieve an internal reflection of the conflicts and contradictions of historical processes; in other words, to achieve a properly historical internal dialectic.

As we saw in Chapter 1, following the arguments of Adorno and Peter Bürger, the coming to self-consciousness of ideological complicity – often expressed as artistic guilt – is essentially a feature of modernist art and aesthetics. The resurrection of such concerns in DeLillo's fiction is, then, somewhat anachronistic. In fact, though, it is precisely through this anachronism that DeLillo justifies, in a curious sense, Frank Lentricchia's definition of him as a modernist. Unable to employ in a plausible way modernist aesthetic strategies of historical representation, DeLillo instead reinvokes modernism in the return of a 'past problem', that of the problematic and ideological relation of the work of art to dominant social forces. His very inability, then, to find an adequate force of opposition to the ideology of the postmodern, the incapacity to retain an inner-conflict which would not be mere nostalgic delusion, results – through a process of 'working on' that same guilty incapacity of the aesthetic sphere in general – in the reinscription in DeLillo's texts of precisely such a force, this time envisaged as the internal conflicts of modernism to which the postmodern itself, as the ahistoric pastiche of the avant-garde that we witnessed in Chapter 1, comes as a false resolution.

Just as in *White Noise* the American culture industry (in the figure of Elvis) is juxtaposed, though necessarily unsuccessfully, with the terrifying manipulation of totalitarian forces (Hitler), the cultural moment of the postmodern is silently brought face to face with its no longer representable origins in the internal contradictions of modernism. Whereas the attempt to establish a critical relationship between Hitler and Elvis must end in failure, through the text's incapacity to represent the former as anything other than a postmodernist cultural construct, the establishment of a paradoxical relationship between modernism and postmodernism is both successful and to some extent liberating – expressing, as it does, the dialectical process of historical *transition* in a way that is critical of, because rendered impermissible by, the cultural dominant of postmodernism and its necessary economic correlative, late capitalism.[95]

There is also, as Frank Lentricchia writes, a similar relationship being evoked in *Libra*:

> One of *Libra*'s more uncanny effects is anachronistic: DeLillo's wager is that we will read the book out of the political history that Watergate and Iran-Contra has made, as if Watergate and Iran-Contra preceded 22 November 1963, as if the novel's narration of the events of twenty-five years past made that day in November contemporaneous with its retelling.[96]

Thus, Lentricchia continues:

> The book's cultural logic encourages us to read JFK as a postmodern figure and Ronald Reagan, the actor who was known to gloss affairs of state with lines from his old movies, as the president we had to have, the chief executive of postmodernism.[97]

The point is made through something of an exaggeration, but is no less valid for that. What DeLillo continually attempts to portray are the dialectical processes of historical development, whereby relations between historical and/or historico-cultural eras might be shown in terms both of their causal progression and of their

radical difference, retaining throughout a sense of the inner contradictions of each era which might lead to either or both of these
possible forms of relation. In *White Noise* that attempt necessarily
fails; there is no narrative recourse to the pre-postmodern. In
Libra the failure is less palpable, more muted; its representation
of history depends, as Lentricchia concedes, on an acknowledgement that cannot be voiced of the text's status as one rooted in the
Reagan 1980s. Never fully present, the relationship that the text
implicitly establishes between the 1960s (Kennedy) and the 1980s
(Reagan) can never achieve the proper gradations of a historical
understanding, implying instead a steel-clad causal relationship
that is more justificatory than analytic. In this respect, Lentricchia
unwittingly highlights the very problem: 'The book's cultural
logic encourages us to reread . . . Ronald Reagan . . . as the president we had to have.'

Yet DeLillo's novels do eventually yield that conflict with the
postmodern that is necessary to affirm their inner dialectic. The
dilemmas of modernism return in these postmodernist texts both
to be absorbed by postmodernist conflictlessness and simultaneously to subject that postmodernist conflictlessness to the
historicising critique of the modernist aesthetic. Historically
speaking, the modernist dilemmas through which that critique
is expressed became in part, as I suggested in Chapter 1, the
precondition of the postmodernist aesthetic, which itself in turn
ruled such critique impermissible. In a recognisable move, then, it
is the impossibility of that critique which becomes in DeLillo's
texts its necessary precondition. Thus DeLillo comprehends
history in terms of a Benjaminian *Jetztzeit*, 'a past charged with
the time of the now which [is] blasted out of the continuum of
history',[98] while recognising that the now can only be understood
in terms of its inheritance from the thought and conditions of the
past. DeLillo's texts occupy an uneasy and critical position some-
where between the now that rewrites its past and the past that
will become the now, while simultaneously – and critically –
dramatising the inter-dependence of these two apparently contradictory stances.

Notes

1. Fredric Jameson, *The Political Unconscious*, p. 9.
2. Ibid., p. 100.
3. Thomas Docherty, *After Theory*, p. 245.

4. Jean-François Lyotard, *Lessons on the Analytic of the Sublime*, p. 6.
5. Immanuel Kant, 'Critique of Teleological Judgement', *The Critique of Judgement*, p. 35.
6. Ibid.
7. Lyotard, *Lessons on the Analytic of the Sublime*, p. 6.
8. Jean-François Lyotard, *The Postmodern Condition*, p. xxiv.
9. Jean- François Lyotard, 'Apostil on narratives', *The Postmodern Explained to Children: Correspondence 1982–1985*, p. 31.
10. Ibid., p. 29.
11. Lyotard, *The Postmodern Condition*, p. 13.
12. Ibid., p. 37.
13. Docherty, *After Theory*, p. 19.
14. Jean-François Lyotard, 'Answer to the Question: What is the Post-modern?', *The Postmodern Explained to Children*, p. 22.
15. Lyotard, *The Postmodern Condition*, pp. 37–8.
16. Lyotard, 'Answer to the Question: What is the Postmodern?', p. 23.
17. Jean-François Lyotard, 'The Sublime and the Avant-Garde', in his *The Lyotard Reader*, pp. 203–4.
18. Lyotard, 'Answer to the Question: What is the Postmodern?', p. 24.
19. Lyotard, 'The Sublime and the Avant-Garde', p. 209.
20. Ibid., p. 210.
21. Lyotard, 'Answer to the Question: What is the Postmodern?', p. 17.
22. Irving Howe, 'Black Boys and Native Sons', accessible online at www.english.upenn.edu/~afilreis/50s/howe-blackboys.html
23. James Baldwin, 'Many Thousands Gone', in his *Notes of a Native Son*, p. 32.
24. Ralph Ellison, 'The World and the Jug', in his *Shadow and Act*, p. 114.
25. Richard Wright, *Native Son*, p. 461.
26. Toni Morrison, *Playing in the Dark*, p. xiv.
27. Ibid., pp. 7–8.
28. Toni Morrison, *Beloved*, p. 42. References to the novel will hereafter be cited in the main text, prefixed by the abbreviation *B*.
29. Toni Morrison, 'The Art of Fiction CXXXIV', pp. 103–4.
30. Jean Baudrillard, *Selected Writings*, p. 170.
31. Ibid., p. 172.
32. Ibid.
33. Ibid.
34. Ibid., p. 168.
35. Ibid., p. 149.
36. Ibid., p. 182.
37. Don DeLillo, *Underworld*, pp. 49–50.
38. Fredric Jameson, *Marxism and Form*, p. 37.
39. Don DeLillo, *White Noise*, p. 3. Further references to the text will be to the same edition and will be marked in the main text, prefixed by the abbreviation *WN*.

40. Frank Lentricchia, 'Tales of the Electronic Tribe', in *New Essays on 'White Noise'*, ed. F. Lentricchia, p. 95.
41. Don DeLillo, *Mao II*, p. 19. Further references to the text will be to the same edition and will be marked in the text, prefixed by the abbreviation *MII*.
42. Baudrillard, *Selected Writings*, p. 177.
43. Leonard Wilcox, 'Baudrillard, DeLillo's *White Noise* and the End of Heroic Narrative', pp. 346–7.
44. Don Delillo, *Libra*, p. 141. Further references to this text will be to the same edition and will be marked in the main text, using the prefix *L*.
45. Frank Lentricchia, '*Libra* as Postmodern Critique', in *Introducing Don DeLillo*, ed. Frank Lentricchia, p. 203.
46. Fredric Jameson, 'Reification and Utopia in Mass Culture', in his *Signitures of the Visible*, p. 14.
47. Jameson, *Postmodernism*, p. 9.
48. Ibid., p. 17.
49. Lentricchia, 'Tales of the Electronic Tribe', p. 93.
50. Ibid., p. 97.
51. Jameson, *Postmodernism*, p. 26.
52. John Frow, 'The Last Things before the Last: Notes on *White Noise*', in *Introducing Don DeLillo*, ed. F. Lentricchia, p. 187.
53. Michael Valdez Moses, 'Lust Removed from Nature', in *New Essays*, ed. F. Lentricchia, p. 64.
54. Lentricchia, 'Tales of the Electronic Tribe', p. 102.
55. Wilcox, 'Baudrillard', p. 348.
56. Further examples can be encountered on pp. 96 and 201 of *WN*.
57. Jameson, *Postmodernism*, p. 37; see also McHale, *Constructing Postmodernism*, p. 181.
58. McHale, *Constructing Postmodernism*, p. 182.
59. Ernst Bloch, 'A Philosophical View of the Novel of the Artist', in his *The Utopian Function of Art and Literature*, p. 277.
60. Lentricchia, '*Libra* as Postmodern Critique', p. 213.
61. Ibid., p. 210.
62. Ibid.
63. Tom LeClair, 'An Interview with Don DeLillo', p. 27.
64. Tom LeClair, *In the Loop: Don DeLillo and the Systems Novel*, p. 121.
65. See Don DeLillo, *Ratner's Star*, pp. 243–7.
66. Adorno and Horkheimer, *Dialectic of Enlightenment*, p. 27.
67. Ibid., p. 21.
68. Ibid., p. 22.
69. Ibid., p. 28.
70. Lukács, 'Reification and the Consciousness of the Proletariat', in his *History and Class Consciousness*, p. 83.
71. Adorno and Horkheimer, *Dialectic of Enlightenment*, p. 28.
72. Elias Canetti, *Crowds and Power*, pp. 59–60.

73. Ibid., p. 56.
74. Bruce Bawer, 'Don DeLillo's America', p. 35.
75. Lentricchia, 'Tales of the Electronic Tribe', p. 112.
76. Paul Cantor, 'Adolf, We Hardly Knew You', in *New Essays*, ed. F. Lentricchia, p. 55.
77. Don DeLillo, *Running Dog*, p. 235.
78. Cantor, 'Adolf', p. 60.
79. Ibid., p. 61.
80. Adorno, 'The Schema of Mass Culture', in his *The Culture Industry*, p. 66.
81. Ibid., p. 67.
82. Jameson, *The Political Unconscious*, p. 148.
83. See Raymond Williams, *Marxism and Literature*, pp. 121–7.
84. Jameson, *Postmodernism*, p. 6.
85. Fredric Jameson, *Late Marxism*, p. 192.
86. Adorno, *Aesthetic Theory*, pp. 53–4.
87. Williams, *Marxism and Literature*, p. 122.
88. See Jameson, *Late Marxism*, p. 130. This theme will be discussed more fully, and in more theoretical terms, in the final chapter.
89. Lentricchia, 'Introduction', in his *New Essays*, p. 14.
90. Noel King, 'Reading *White Noise*: Floating Remarks', p. 69.
91. Wilcox, 'Baudrillard', p. 348.
92. Ibid., p. 362.
93. Ibid., p. 363.
94. LeClair, 'An Interview', p. 26.
95. For a discussion of historical transition as a 'contradiction which symbolically preoccupies much of modern historiography', see Fredric Jameson, 'The Existence of Italy', in his *Signatures of the Visible*, pp. 155–229; and, in particular, pp. 225–9.
96. Lentricchia, '*Libra* as Postmodern Critique', pp. 200–1.
97. Ibid., pp. 206–7.
98. Walter Benjamin, 'Theses on the Philosophy of History', in his *Illuminations*, p. 261.

Postmodernity and the Historical Novel

The representation of history in postmodern fiction has long been a source of critical conflict. For Marxists like Jameson and Aijaz Ahmad postmodern fiction, post-Fordist to its self-conscious finger-tips, generally portrays History as little more than narrativised bunk. Even at his most forgiving, his most generously dialectical, Jameson is unwilling to claim any more for the postmodern historical novel than a knowing employment of strategies of historical representation it implicitly acknowledges either as in-adequate or as some form of compensatory fantasy. Postmodern critics influenced by Lyotard, such as Thomas Docherty and Robert Holton, take of course a very different line. They identify as a distinctive feature of postmodern fiction its portrayal of 'the heterodox historical moment', a form of historical representation which destabilises the 'hegemonic hold on historical discourse' and allows 'marginalised people to emerge as equal historical subjects and narrators'.[1] Both critical perspectives, though, pro-ceed from a similar premise, that of postmodern fiction's abandon-ment of some of the principal features of realist and modernist modes of historical representation. Happily, too, the Marxists and postmarxists are in broad agreement over what works of fiction can be identified as postmodern (names such as Pynchon and Rushdie, for example, figure prominently in both definitions).

Jameson describes, somewhat infamously, the abject inability of the postmodern novel to offer a plausible representation of the historical past. 'The historical novel', he writes,

> can no longer set out to represent the historical past; it can only 'represent' our ideas and stereotypes about that past (which thereby at once become 'pop history'). . . . If there is any realism left here, it is a 'realism' that is meant to derive from the shock of grasping that confinement and of slowly becoming aware of a new and original historical situation in which we are

condemned to seek History by way of our own pop images and simulacra of that history, which itself remains forever out of reach.[2]

It seems that what is lacking in the postmodern, for Jameson, is any sense of the recoverability in narrative form of 'authentic' historical experience. Perhaps more accurately, Jameson's position can be described as one which identifies in postmodern culture an abandonment of the longing, however ironic and qualified, for a recoverable 'authenticity' or 'essence', a graspable sense of how things really are or were. Notions of authenticity and narrative authority are of course rigorously questioned in modernist literature too; but Marxist literary criticism has tended to locate in such writing a more ironic and melancholy mood. Adorno's insistence on the significance of art's broken promise of happiness, the dialectical conflict between the realised aesthetic form and the alienating forces of the capitalist marketplace, is predicated on the radical pretence (what Adorno might call 'the necessary lie') that a reconciled aesthetic and social truth is possible. 'Proust', writes Adorno, 'decomposes the unity of the subjective mind by dint of its own introspection: the mind ends by transforming itself into a stage on which the objective realities are made visible.'[3] Or, at least, Proust's novel would do this if we were not reminded in the closing pages that this work of art is about the coming into being of itself, that this stage on which the relationship between subjective and objective realities is made visible to us is, in fact, just that: a stage. This, as we saw earlier with Faulkner, is Adorno's *'promesse du bonheur'*.

The mood of the postmodern is quite different. Ahmad contrasts the 'terrors of High Modernism at the prospect of inner fragmentation and social disconnection' with the 'celebratory' attitude of postmodernism. Postmodern culture, he argues, suggests that 'one is free to choose any and all subject positions . . . because history has no subjects or collective projects in any case'.[4] It is clear that for Marxists the question of individual and collective identity, the identification of individual and collective subjects, is a crucial feature of historical representation. In that context, it is hardly surprising that what is often seen as the dissolution of both these categories in postmodern culture should provoke such alarm. If the subject is understood as a version of what Terry Eagleton calls 'Lyotard's jet-setters' (McDonald's for lunch, local cuisine for dinner, wears French perfume in Tokyo, listens to reggae, etc.) or the simulated selves that we see in Don

DeLillo's fiction, then perhaps the 'pop history' that Jameson associates with the postmodern historical novel is the very best that could be hoped for.

This issue of the representation of subjectivity – which most often becomes an issue of character construction – is one of the key features that both Marxist and postmarxist critics have used to distinguish modernist and postmodern writing. As we shall see, the descriptive terms used are often similar, but the analyses of the effects that the changes in characterisation produce are in direct conflict. '"Moderns" such as Virginia Woolf', writes Thomas Docherty, 'were continuing the struggle for existence, for realization of her characters.'[5] Expanding on this theme in *Alterities*, Docherty states: 'Even in these modernist experiments, however, it is to be stressed that character is still organized around the basic notion of *anagnorisis* or re-cognizability: the individual characters can, at some level, be "known", cognized and recognized.'[6] Marxist critics would have little difficulty in accepting these claims. Likewise, Docherty's reference to the contrasting 'elusiveness of character' in postmodern fiction would produce little dissent. Docherty's understanding of postmodern character is perhaps made most explicit in his comments on Italo Calvino's *If on a Winter's Night a Traveller*. Calvino's novel begins with a direct address to the reader and discusses in its opening pages the act of reading and, more particularly, the act of reading *If on a Winter's Night a Traveller*. The text itself mutates, as different texts, owing to problems at the binders, are interwoven with each other. The reader of *If on a Winter's Night a Traveller* is then placed in the position of constantly having to readjust to the different situations and perspectives of the different texts. "This multiplication of 'the Reader'", writes Docherty, '(and the confusion of the *character* of the Reader with "real" readers of the text) is an analogue of what happens to characterisation in postmodern narrative generally.'[7]

At least part of what Docherty seems to be suggesting is that postmodern narrative both generates and reflects on questions of ontology. In this sense, his argument is not all that far removed from the model of postmodern (or 'postmodern*ist*') fiction that we saw at the very outset sketched out by Brian McHale. McHale's definition of postmodern fiction as a form of writing which foregrounds issues of ontological instability has, as we also saw earlier, been found useful by Marxist (or, at least, Marxian) commentators. David Harvey, of course, suggests that the ontological plurality of these postmodern texts is mimetic of an age of consumer

capitalism. This interpretation would seem to identify the ontological instability that Docherty sees in postmodern characterisation with the reproduction of what Marxists such as Jameson and
Harvey see as the ideological effects of late capitalism. In other
words, Docherty's initial description of postmodern characterisation is generally consistent with the analysis and ideology critique
of Marxist critics. The postmarxist interpretation of that initial
description, though, is completely different.

Both Thomas Docherty and Robert Holton read this disruption
of characters' and readers' identities as profoundly radical and
enabling strategies. 'Postmodern narrative', writes Docherty,
'seeks to circumvent the phenomenological elaboration of a definable spatial relation obtaining between a transcendent ontological
reading subject and an equally fixed and non-historical object of
that reader's perception, the "character"'.[8] It is the very premise
of a static, definable (and defining) relationship between a Self and
Other that, for Docherty, is contested by postmodern characterisation. This, he argues, opens the narrative to the possibility of
change thereby opening it to history itself. The postmodern historical novel, to the postmarxist, is not principally the reproduction of a historical narrative (something which, for Jameson and
Ahmad, it does inadequately) but is more concerned with the
creation of history, the rediscovery of a historical dimension in
the reading process itself.

'To read postmodern characterisation', claims Docherty, 'is to
reintroduce the possibility of politics, and importantly of a
genuinely historical political change, into the act of reading.'[9]
Docherty's justification for this claim is extremely important. He
argues that in a narrative of this sort the reader is forced to
understand herself or himself as Other. Denied the stable perspective of the 'traditional' reader and the fixed identities of equally
'traditional' (or what Docherty calls 'pre-modern') characters, the
reader of postmodern fiction develops an endlessly differing series
of subject positions, grasping a sense of 'dissident' subjectivity, a
subjectivity marginalised from 'a centralized or totalized narrative
of selfhood'.[10] This, for Docherty, is a profoundly ethical and
political manœuvre.

Equally, Holton argues that the dissolution of the individual
subject also involves a radical 'dissolution of certain kinds of
traditional social and narrative authority'.[11] Drawing on the
writings of Hayden White as well as Lyotard, Holton suggests
that 'postmodern historical relativism' can be understood as the
deligitimisation of hegemonic structures of social and cultural

authority. While Marxists such as Jameson and Eagleton bemoan the abandonment of an understanding of history in terms of a narrative of class conflict and exploitation, Holton points to the way in which such an abandonment of grand narratives provides the opportunity for a more genuinely radical critique of those authorative forms by which historical and social narratives are constructed.

The following sections of this chapter will explore two examples of postmodern historical fiction: Thomas Pynchon's *Mason & Dixon* and Martin Amis's *Time's Arrow*. Pynchon is often read as an almost exemplary postmodernist. *Gravity's Rainbow*, for example, constructs a 'Zone' (occupied Germany immediately after the fall of the Nazis) which, for Brian McHale, is 'paradigmatic for the heterotopian spaces of postmodernist writing'. '[A] large number of fragmentary possible worlds', he explains, 'coexist in an impossible space which is associated with occupied Germany, but which is in fact located nowhere but in the written text itself.'[12] McHale reads the ontological instability and playfulness of Pynchon's text as ultimately incompatible with modernist aesthetics of narrative reliability/unreliability. Extending his argument, McHale suggests that *Gravity's Rainbow* is parodic of the modernist interrogation of issues relating to subjectivity/objectivity and appearance/reality. Whilst in *Ulysses*, for example, the use of stream-of-consciousness narration foregrounds, however comically, the serious question of characters' subjective construction of the world around them – and the world views extrapolated from those constructions are shown (as with the Cyclopic Citizen's vision of a 'New Ireland') often to be fanciful illusions (though perhaps, of course, no less significant for that) – *Gravity's Rainbow* is different. *Mason & Dixon*, though, is less overtly disruptive of older literary conventions. Its postmodernity is perhaps more subtle and complex. As we shall see, through an analysis of the novel's modes of characterisation, its representation of historical subjects enacts precisely that sense of anachronism that Thomas Docherty associates with the postmodern.[13]

The discussion of Amis's novel is preceded by some comments on Adorno and post-Auschwitz culture. The necessary self-critique that Adorno associates with art after Auschwitz is shown to be at work in *Time's Arrow*. Amis's novel is located in relation to the Western Marxist interpretation of postmodernism's distortion of historical narratives. However, this reading insists on the text's serious engagement with the complexities and contradictions of a postmodern reworking of the Holocaust, suggesting that *Time's Arrow* demonstrates the possibilities of a self-critical, postmodern, historical novel.

With the Grain: Reading Thomas Pynchon's *Mason & Dixon*

> Here have come to rest a long scarr'd sawbuck table, with two mismatch'd side-benches, from the Lancaster County branch of the family . . . – a few old chairs sent from England before the War, – mostly Pine and Cherry about, nor much Mahogany, excepting a sinister and wonderful Card table which exhibits the cheaper Wave-like Grain known in the Trade as Wand'ring Heart, causing an illusion of Depth into which for years children have gaz'd as into the illustrated Pages of Books . . . along with so many hinges, sliding Mortises, hidden catches, and secret compartments that neither the Twins nor their Sister can say they have been to the end of it.
>
> (Thomas Pynchon, *Mason & Dixon*)

Walter Benjamin wrote that it was the duty of the historical materialist to read culture's barbaric documents 'against the grain', to seek to reawaken our sense of the historical suffering to which culture and art so beautifully anaesthetise us. Much of Thomas Pynchon's work can be seen to read earlier, realist and modernist, modes of representation 'against the grain', implicitly critiquing some of the ideological assumptions upon which such work is based. The reading of *Mason & Dixon* that is to follow will suggest that, in this novel, Pynchon's implicit critique of the realist mode and all its cosy satisfactions for a reader reaches new extremes of perversity. *Mason & Dixon*, inviting us to read 'with the grain', offers us the 'illusion of Depth', the playful yet earnest and moving indulgence of all the pain and pleasures of the realist novel.

Mason & Dixon narrates the almost picaresque adventures of Charles Mason and Jeremiah Dixon, who chart in the 1760s the boundary between Pennsylvania and Maryland later to be known as the Mason–Dixon line. The language of the novel, as should be clear from the extract quoted above, is a painstaking pastiche of eighteenth-century prose. A framing third-person narrative – from which the extract is taken – introduces us to the narrative of Wicks Cherrycoke, centred around the adventures and expeditions of Mason and Dixon; but the Revd Cherrycoke's storytelling is itself interrupted, most notably by the narratives of the Ghastly

Fop, a riveting series of mock-pornographic tales. The narrative complexity of *Mason & Dixon* is of course nothing new in Pynchon's work. In fact, the relative simplicity and accessibility of *Vineland*, his previous novel, was taken by some critics as evidence of real under-achievement. A reader familiar with the juxtaposition and fusion of different narrative worlds in *Gravity's Rainbow* will have little problem with the structure of *Mason & Dixon*. On the contrary, the most surprising aspect of the novel for those who have read Pynchon's earlier work is the fact that, despite its narrative complexities, it sometimes reads more like Dickens than Nabokov. It has been this, rather than the pedantic eighteenth-century prose or the exuberantly pornographic interludes, which has been the focus of critical commentary on the novel thus far.

'You start the book bewildered,' writes Jenny Turner, 'then slowly ease into its curious patternings of order and disorder. . . . By the time you get to the Talking Dog, your face will be cracking into the nicest of new-dawn smiles. "Nice guys," you'll be think-ing of Mason and Dixon.'[14] For Louis Menand:

> [Mason and Dixon] can stand each other's company, but just barely, and their continual bickering becomes one of the leit-motifs of the book, and forms, in the end, the basis for a rather touching friendship of a very inarticulate, very 'guy' sort. This is, in Hollywood terms, a buddy story.[15]

Mason & Dixon is here discussed in terms quite different to those used in criticism of Pynchon's previous work. The relish that many early reviewers of the novel showed for Pynchon's anachro-nistic employment of realist conventions in his construction of character – particularly in the case of his two principal protago-nists – is both striking and significant. Turner contrasts Pynchon's 'usual weakness for lumbering his characters with gross-out names like Tyrone Slothrop or Hubert Stencil' with the status of Mason and Dixon as fully rounded and credible portraits of historical figures.[16]

It is hardly surprising, then, to find that other commentators, more reluctant to be robbed of Pynchon as a postmodern icon, should express some frustration at these celebrations of 'substan-tial' characters, the drawing of sympathetic and sometimes even 'heroic' figures in whose 'humanity' we can perhaps recognise our own. Stefan Mattessich, for example, argues that

What these reviews have in common is an enthusiasm for realist conventions of fiction as they peek through Pynchon's 'absurdities,' reducing these to stylistic traits that function to confirm the very substances they seem to traduce. . . . Unlike in *Gravity's Rainbow*, it is implied, where manipulation by technocratic forces dehumanizes author, text and reader alike, Pynchon in *Mason & Dixon* manages to be a humanized and humanizing producer, one whose agency the reader can discern and identify with in the product itself.[17]

'There seems to be little patience nowadays', laments Mattessich, 'for reflexive textual practices, for double and ironic anti-realist fabulations of the kind associated with Pynchon's early work.'[18] That description of Pynchon sketched out earlier might seem due, in the light of *Mason & Dixon*, for a fairly major revision. In fact, such a revision both is and is not necessary. The postmodern characterisation that, some pages ago, we saw Thomas Docherty analyse is clearly less directly relevant to *Mason & Dixon* than to either *The Crying of Lot 49* or *Gravity's Rainbow*. Nonetheless, it remains important to acknowledge Mason and Dixon both as realist characters and, through that, as vehicles in the critical exploration of modern subjectivity. Subjectivity in *Mason & Dixon* remains a problem – and not just for the novel's critics.

Pynchon's most recent novel depicts the eighteenth-century development of rational, enlightened modernity. Mason and Dixon's ostensible purpose in America is to impose some kind of rational order on time and space; through the application of universal, scientific laws, they standardise the spatial and political boundaries of the New World. *Mason & Dixon* thus depicts an eighteenth-century world newly subject to such universal, scientific truths, a world apparently demystified of fantastic events and explanations of the world. This, though, is a mere starting point for the novel. *Mason & Dixon* can be read as a meditation on the contradictions and insecurities of modernity, at times a lament for all the fantastic and fanciful worlds discarded in the name of scientific truth and the rationalised modern world.

This implicit critique of modernity makes *Mason & Dixon* quite consistent with much of Pynchon's earlier work, particularly *Gravity's Rainbow*. In *The Philosophical Discourse of Modernity*, Jürgen Habermas draws on Hegel to explain the centrality of 'subjectivity' to a concept of modernity. Defining that 'subjectivity', he refers to a number of its principal connotations, among which he cites '*autonomy of action*': 'our responsibility for what we do', he argues, 'is a characteristic of modern times'.[19] *Gravity's Rainbow* represents a negation of the concept of autonomous, subjective agency. This negation extends both to the portrayal of characters' fates as possibly determined by a vast, conspiratorial 'They', and to the self-conscious depiction of those characters as linguistic or literary constructs (for example, consider Tyrone Slothrop's status as an anagram of 'sloth or entropy'). This latter feature is less foregrounded in *Mason & Dixon*, but the sense of conspiracy or the paranoid fears of conspiracy is just as potent as in Pynchon's previous work. '"For a while"', Neville Maskelyne tells Mason, '"I firmly believ'd this Place a conscious Creature, animated by power drawn from beneath the Earth, assembl'd in secret, by the Company, – entirely theirs, – no Action, no Thought nor Dream, that had not the Co. for its Author"' (*M&D, p.* 128).

Caught in a brief, though potentially fatal, naval skirmish before their professional partnership has even properly begun, each trying 'not to be the first to foul his breeches in front of the others', Mason and Dixon reflect on their misfortune:

> It seems not to belong in either of their lives. 'Was there a mistake in the Plan of the Day? Did we get a piece of someone else's History, a fragment spall'd off of some Great Moment, – perhaps the late Engagement at Quiberon Bay, – such as now and then may fly into the ev'ryday paths of lives less drama-tick? And there we are, with our Wigs askew.'
> 'Happen,' Dixon contributes in turn, 'we were never meant at all to go to Bencoolen, – someone needed a couple of Martyrs, and we inconveniently surviv'd . . .?' (*M&D,* p. 44)

These speculations indicate the astronomer's and the surveyor's suspicion that they may be only marginal figures, inadvertently thrust to the centre of historical events. It is a suspicion that would appear to be supported by Cherrycoke's insistence that their efforts in America were 'brave, scientifick beyond my under-standing, and ultimately meaningless': their line is 'but eight years later to be nullified by the War for Independence' (*M&D,* p. 8). Pynchon is here playing on the historical irony that the Mason–Dixon line, made irrelevant by the United States' anti-colonial victory, should become symbolically crucial in the Republic's subsequent history. The marginal, the 'nullified', become impor-tant and profoundly significant as we look back on Cherrycoke looking back on Mason and Dixon's adventures. But to return to

the original point about the adventurers' fears that they are
subject to obscure greater forces, it is worth noting that sugges-
tions of plotting and conspiracies abound throughout the novel.
At times, Mason and Dixon suspect each other of working for
the benefit of other interested parties, principally the Jesuits
and the East India Company. And, of course, we mustn't forget
the Chinese. There is, then, a large degree of overlap between the
negation of autonomous, subjective agency in *Gravity's Rainbow*
and the treatment of that same theme in *Mason & Dixon*. The
singularity of characterisation in Pynchon's most recent novel is a
subject I'll be returning to soon. First, though, it is worth looking
at the text's self-conscious portrayal of an equally self-conscious
Age of Reason, and at the colonial suffering which attends, all too
hauntingly, modernity's heroic projects.

Mason and Dixon's scientifick age is one of demystification and
newly discovered Truth. It insists on the abandonment, though, of
now illegitimate falsehoods and illusions. Pynchon's text focuses
on that experience of loss, the recognition that, in the birth of this
new world, others are lost or nullified:

'"Saint Brendan set out in the fifth century"', says Maskelyne,

'to discover an Island he believ'd was the Paradise of the
Scriptures, – and found it. Some believ'd it Madeira, Columbus
was told by some at Madeira that they had seen it in the West,
Philosophers of our own Day say they have prov'd it but a
Mirage. So will the Reign of Reason cheerfully dispose of any
allegations of Paradise.' (*M&D*, p. 134)

In part, *Mason & Dixon* dramatises the deceptions and self-
deceptions of modern, enlightened rationality. As with the postmodern critique of modernity, Pynchon's portrayal of the Age of
Enlightenment suggests less that scientific rationality has replaced
or superseded all other forms of thought or belief, than that its
status as an autonomous and unsullied mode of thought is an
illusion, an expedient pretence. Irrational superstition is here presented as the negative truth of rational discourse. In the course of
a discussion with Mason, Maskelyne comments conspiratorially:

'Kepler said that Astrology is Astronomy's wanton little sister,
who goes out and sells herself that Astronomy may keep her
Virtue, – surely we have all done the Covent Garden turn. As to
the older Sister, how many Steps may she herself already have
taken into Compromise?' (*M&D*, p. 136)

The novel suggests at times the possibilities glimpsed in those all too fleeting moments of release from the constraints of the enlightened world. The 'notorious Wedge', for example, is the result of 'the failure of the Tangent Point to be exactly at this corner of Maryland, but rather some five miles south, creating a semi-cusp or Thorn of that Length, and doubtful ownership' (M&D, p. 469). The Wedge, we are told, is 'priz'd for its Ambiguity, – occupied by all those whose Wish, hardly uncommon in this Era of fluid Identity, is not to reside anywhere' (M&D, p. 469). The desire to escape a fixed identity and location is a more than understandable reaction to what the novel depicts as one of the most significant consequences of modernity: the globalisation of slaveholding domination and colonial subjugation. Mason and Dixon confront the peculiar institution of slavery in the Cape, Mason subjected to a prolonged seduction by the Vroom girls with the object of having him impregnate the slave-girl Austra. Later, Dixon views the scarred walls of Lancaster Town, the site of a massacre of twenty-six Native Americans. His response to the bloody and chipped walls will be discussed below. For the moment, it is necessary only to note the way in which Mason & Dixon depicts the intimate yet unacknowledged relationship of slavery and colonialism to the enlightened principles of the Age of Reason.

The linguistic, punning playfulness that we would normally associate with Pynchon's writing remains a prominent feature of Mason & Dixon. Those self-reflexive, cartoonish elements of previous novels' characterisation and historical portraits are again stressed in Pynchon's most recent work. The name of the novel's principal storyteller, Cherrycoke (a name also used in Gravity's Rainbow), surely can't be taken seriously. The Reverend is advised that, were he to smoke Indian Hemp, he should on no account inhale. This is another fairly facile joke on Pynchon's part, alluding to President Bill Clinton's explanation in 1992 of the youthful restraint he had shown when practising similar, private pleasures or vices. The reference, too, to a song apparently called 'Philadelphia Girls' reinforces this sense of the novel's play on late twentieth-century cultural references.

Yet for all this postmodern, textual playfulness, there remains the scandal of the novel's depth of characterisation – at least to the extent of the two main protagonists. Mason and Dixon stand apart from Pynchon's previous characters in this respect. As we have already seen both Jenny Turner and Louis Menand comment, these are characters who engage readers on both intellectual and emotional levels, drawing us into precisely the sort of fantasies of

emotional empathy that postmodern fiction was supposed to have
rendered irrelevant, if not ridiculous. Dixon attempts to persuade
Mason to join him in a visit to a particular bar. The description of
Mason's response tells us something about the almost caricatured
roundedness and depth of the characters: 'Mason directs at Dixon
an effortful smile, meaning, "Go ahead, but don't expect me to
ascend wearily out of my Melancholia just so ev'rybody else can
have their own idea of a good time"' (*M&D*, p. 272). Even the
characters' looks and gestures have depth and meaning; every
nuance and shading becomes analysable and interpretable. In a
postmodern mode, supposedly given to surface, superficiality and
'elusiveness of character', the figures of Mason and Dixon seem
profoundly anachronistic. Their characterisation, like Mason's
grief-ridden Melancholia, seems to remain tied to a past whose
loss can never be undone, and whose scarred legacy cannot possibly be ignored. The realist depth and consistency of that characterisation are indicative of both the loss of an older idea of the
subject and subjectivity, and the acceptance that that idea was
always illusory and ideological anyway.

The Revd Wicks Cherrycoke can remain as a guest of the
LeSparks 'for as long as he can keep the children amused'
(*M&D*, p. 6). His fate, like that of Sheherazade, is tied inextricably
to the entertainment and amusement value of his tales. This may
account, at least in part, for his willingness to flesh the narrative
out with detailed speculation and lengthy accounts of stories he
describes at the outset as false: 'Here is what Mason tells Dixon of
how Rebekah and he first met. Not yet understanding the narrative lengths Mason will go to, to avoid betraying her, Dixon
believes ev'ry word' (*M&D*, p. 167). Many of the novel's teaming
narratives are produced in this way. We know that the characters'
histories that are being constructed are false; yet for page after
page we are entertained and seduced by their idiosyncratic tales of
romance and adventure. Here we can recognise the novel's celebration of 'substantial' and 'sympathetic' characters, while
remaining aware that what we are doing is reading ideologically
'with the grain' and experiencing that 'illusion of Depth' which is
so central to *Mason & Dixon*.

To dismiss such modes of characterisation, insisting on the
falsity of their implicit assumptions about 'human nature' or the
'truth' of the subject, is itself to fall into a misleading position of
demystificatory analysis. The postmodern critique of realist characterisation, as summarised by Thomas Docherty in the previous
section, still privileges a particular model of the subject, a model

which is surely just as provisional, contingent and ideologically saturated as any other. Like realist characters, the postmodern critique of realist characterisation is 'substantial', it has 'depth'. In fact, that postmodern critique can be compared to Dixon's response to the aftermath of the massacre at Lancaster Town:

> He sees where blows with Rifle-Butts miss'd their Marks, and chipp'd the Walls. He sees blood in Corners never cleans'd. Thankful he is no longer a Child, else might he curse and weep, scattering his Anger to no Effect, Dixon now must be his own stern Uncle, and smack himself upon that Pate at any sign of unfocusing. What in the Holy Names are these people about? Not even the Dutchmen at the Cape behav'd this way. Is it something in this Wilderness, something ancient, that waited for them, and infected their Souls when they came? (*M&D*, p. 347)

Dixon's reaction to some extent reproduces the deceptions and delusions of those guilty of the murders. The infection of souls sounds all too plausible as a horrific justification of the deaths; the question of whose souls were supposed to have been infected almost seems irrelevant. There is no escape from ideology, from an ideologically infused understanding of ourselves and of others. *Mason & Dixon* teaches us this, suggesting something of how history has affected the forms that those understandings of the subject have taken. The reading experience of Pynchon's novel forces us to engage with those different attempts to grasp, define and represent who we think we are. The historical changes that those attempts represent are an integral part of this postmodern novel, written in an eighteenth-century style and employing nineteenth-century conventions of characterisation.

The acknowledgement of its own play on surface and depth runs throughout *Mason & Dixon*, exemplified in its comments on lamination:

> 'Lamination,' Mason observes.
> 'Lo, Lamination abounding,' contributes Squire Haligast, momentarily visible, 'its purposes how dark, yet have we ever sought to produce these thin Sheets innumerable, to spread a given Volume as close to pure Surface as possible, whilst on route discovering various new forms, the Leyden Pile, decks of Playing-Cards, Contrivances which, like the Lever or Pulley, quite multiply the apparent forces, often unto disproportionate results. . . .' (*M&D*, pp. 389–90)

Both lamination and the grain of the card table stand as metaphors for the book itself, using contrivances to discover new forms in a 'Volume as close to pure Surface as possible'. The disproportionate results of those contrivances produce a novel which reflects on the history of the modern subject, the modern history of racial subjugation, and the pain of losing what was perhaps never really there. Those first two subjects of reflection are probably to be expected from Pynchon's fiction. The final one, though, entailing that anachronistic, realist model of the graspable, recognisable subject, those fantastic worlds discarded in the name of rational enlightenment, and the grief of Mason's sons as they mourn the death of their ever-absent father, is where we can locate what Adorno would call the 'truth content' of Pynchon's novel. *Mason & Dixon* makes us feel how even absent history hurts.

Adorno: The Ageing of the New

'To write poetry after Auschwitz is barbaric', writes Adorno in 'Cultural Criticism and Society';[20] by which, of course, he does not mean that poetry should not be written. Explaining his point perhaps more cogently in *Negative Dialectics*, he insists:

> All post-Auschwitz culture, including its urgent critique, is garbage. In restoring itself after the things that happened without resistance in its own countryside, culture has turned entirely into the ideology it had been potentially. . . . Whoever pleads for the maintenance of this radically culpable and shabby culture becomes its accomplice, *while the man who says no to culture is directly furthering the barbarism which our culture showed itself to be.*[21]

Adorno here stresses the dialectical nature of his critique, implying that, particularly in the aftermath of the Holocaust, the cultural critic must affirm Walter Benjamin's dictum that '[t]here is no document of civilization which is not at the same time a document of barbarism',[22] and simultaneously negate any suggestion that culture is therefore best jettisoned. While it is common to associate this aspect of Adorno's late thought with the critique of culture he identifies in his essay on Beckett's *Endgame*,[23] I intend here to look briefly at the ways in which, particularly in some of his essays on New Music, Adorno applies something like this dialectic to offer his intimations of the irreversible ageing of modernism.

In 'Music and New Music' he writes that '[a]s a concept "new music" seems to share the fate of growing old which has so often been its destiny in the past'.[24] The critical content of New Music is itself in danger of being dissipated, lost in a process of cultural commodification through which emerge the values of the culture industry triumphant:

> Just as traditional music has culminated in the synthetic illit-
> eracy of the culture industry, it may well turn out that the
> extraordinary efforts which the new music makes and which it
> imposes on its audiences will come to grief on the rocks of
> barbarism. Its fate is not wholly in its own hands, but depends
> on whether it is possible to break through the fatedness of
> society, a fatedness before which every bar of its music stands
> as if hypnotized.[25]

We have already seen Adorno's fear that the culture industry will change art irrevocably and the suggestion, by Bernstein, that the ageing of modernism was implicit in Adorno's writing from the very outset; but what we find in the essays on New Music of the 1950s and 1960s is an oppressive recognition that even those forms which had taken negativity into their core – for example, in the jarring dissonance of twelve-tone composition – were now subject to the laws of socio-aesthetic reconciliation:

> The sounds remain the same. But the anxiety that gave shape to
> its great founding works has been repressed. Perhaps that anxiety
> has become so overwhelming in reality that its undisguised image
> would scarcely be bearable: to recognize the aging of the New
> Music does not mean to misjudge this aging as something acci-
> dental. But art that unconsciously obeys such repression and
> makes itself a game, because it has become too weak for serious-
> ness, renounces its claim to truth, which is its only *raison d'être*.[26]

What Adorno fears here is the acceptance of '[t]he detestable ideal of a moderate modernism'. Those very forms which had been developed to shock, to scandalise, to offend have, he sug-gests, lived on into an age in which they are no longer radical, but 'radically empty'.[27] And yet it remains impossible for the significance of that earlier moment of the New Music ('the twen-ties') to be wrested back:

the geological shifts that have taken place since then are such that nobody could step outside of them, no matter how earnestly he wanted to devote himself to a time that already appeared riddled with crises and yet was a paradise compared to what was to come.[28]

The experience which was to follow was, of course, that of the Third Reich. In his essay on Beckett's *Endgame*, Adorno discusses the work's assumption that 'the individual's claim to autonomy and being has lost its credibility'.[29] Here, he argues, such an assumption facilitates the expression of both the historical contingency of the individual subject and, as a consequence, 'the antinomy of contemporary art' – its post-Holocaust depiction of the end of the self, and its acknowledgement that 'in art only what has been rendered subjective, what is commensurable with subjectivity, is valid'.[30] In the New Music of the Federal Republic, though, Adorno refuses to accept a similar expressiveness. In part, this distinction may perhaps be seen as one of personal taste. More significantly, though, it can be understood as a symptom of the force with which Adorno's argument tore him in separate directions. While accepting that the logic of his argument led, in the final instance, to the end of that bourgeois art which the critical theorists of Western Marxism held so dear, he nonetheless felt the need to retain some affiliation to what he perceived as its final remnants:

> the foundation of music, as of every art, the very possibility of taking the aesthetic seriously, has been deeply shaken. Since the European catastrophe culture hangs on like houses in the cities accidentally spared by bombs or indifferently patched together. . . . Even so, the earnestness that would rather renounce art than put it in the service of a debased contemporary reality may itself be only a disguised form of adaptation to an already universal attitude of a praxis: submission to a praxis that aspires to the given without in any way going beyond it.[31]

If Jay Bernstein is right to claim that Adorno's writings on the culture industry and the ageing of modernism can be seen as his 'judgement in advance on postmodernist culture',[32] it may well be possible to suggest a revision of Adorno's most misunderstood sentence: To write poetry after Auschwitz is postmodern.

Martin Amis's *Time's Arrow*: The Art of Justification

Martin Amis's *Time's Arrow* is a novel which exposes, while simultaneously exemplifying, the inadequacy of a postmodern reimagining of history. Amis's novel indulges in apparent celebration of postmodern textual play – for example, modelling its reversal of narrative order on the capabilities of video – while silently implying regret for all that that celebration leaves unacknowledged. The novel tells the story, backwards, of the life of a Nazi doctor, a member of the medical staff in Auschwitz who later (and, therefore, at the novel's outset) practises medicine in the USA. It is this playfulness of form, the narrative mimicry of film or videotape running in reverse, which most obviously marks *Time's Arrow* as a characteristically postmodern text. This postmodern status might be reinforced by the fact that Amis's novel applies such features of textual play to the writing or reimagining of a historical narrative, thereby seeming to identify *Time's Arrow* with Linda Hutcheon's postmodern genre of historiographic metafiction. Furthermore, in common with the work of a number of other postmodern writers (such as, for example, Don DeLillo and E. L. Doctorow), Amis's novel also suggests a certain continuity between the rhetoric of Nazi propaganda and the kitsch melodrama of American tabloid culture. The elderly Tod Friendly sits reading his American tabloid while the narrator inside him reports its contents to the reader: 'Greta Garbo, I read, has been reborn as a cat. All this stuff about *twins*. A Nordic superrace will shortly descend from the cosmic iceclouds; they will rule the earth for a thousand years. All this stuff about *Atlantis*'.[33] Later in the novel, when Odilo (formerly Tod) has reached Auschwitz, Nazi propaganda replays the messages he first read in the USA:

> In the clubroom I am told (I think I've got this right): Jews come from monkeys (from Menschenaffen), as do Slavs and so on. Germans, on the other hand, have been preserved in ice from the beginning of time in the lost continent of Atlantis. This is good to know. A meteorology division in the Ahnenerbe has been looking into it. Officially these scientists are working on long-range weather predictions, in fact, though, they are seeking to prove the cosmic-ice theory once and for all.
>   It sounds familiar. Atlantis . . . twins and dwarfs. (*TA*, p. 140)

The association of Nazi Germany with the trash culture of contemporary America here serves to mock the pseudo-grandiosity of

Nazi rhetoric, bathetically exposing its kitschness. It is also, though, in the spirit of Adorno and Horkheimer's *Dialectic of Enlightenment*, identifying forms of contemporary mass culture with political barbarism. The novel itself seems to suggest that the contemporary culture of postmodernity, in which it is situated, ought to be regarded with a degree of scepticism and suspicion.

This theme of the ambiguous moral and political status of the text is expressed, as in Amis's *London Fields*, through the metaphor of the novel as child. One of Tod's dreams is of a powerful baby who holds the power of life and death over everyone around it. Its 'drastic ascendancy has to do with its voice. Not its fat fists, its useless legs, but its voice, the sound it makes, its capacity to weep' (*TA*, p. 54). 'In here,' says the narrator, 'the baby is more like a bomb' (*TA*, p. 55). Sentimentality and force are unified in the figure of the child; human concern and manipulation are made one. As well as referring to the text itself, the baby is also a reference to the young Odilo Unverdorben. As Frank Kermode writes, the impotent baby to which Tod/Odilo finally regresses 'has a potential of evil so dreadful that one can think of it as a bomb'.[34] Both Odilo and the text are in some way as dangerous as Little Boy. In *London Fields*, Samson Young dreams of telling the expectant Missy Harter that he will give up his 'wicked book', but his book is not so wicked that it transforms Auschwitz into a fantastical site where men, women and children are born from the womb of the gas chambers or reassembled on 'Uncle Pepi's' operating table. It takes *Time's Arrow*, where '[c]reation is easy', to do that.

If we want to see why Amis should associate his text so strongly with forces of destruction, it is necessary to look more closely at the way in which *Time's Arrow* rewrites the history of the Nazis' Final Solution. The texts used to shed further light on this aspect of the novel are, for the most part, those cited by Amis in his 'Afterword' to *Time's Arrow*: *The Nazi Doctors* by Robert Jay Lifton; and *If This is a Man*, *The Truce* and *The Drowned and the Saved* by Primo Levi. I will also refer, though perhaps less frequently, to Hannah Arendt's classic study *The Origins of Totalitarianism*.

The narrative order of *Time's Arrow*, which I have thus far attributed to the text's postmodernity, might also be ascribed to a mimetic impulse, a narrative reflection of the process of remembering. As James Wood, in his excellent review of the novel, writes:

The backwards momentum of the Nazi's life, narrated by a soul who knows what has already happened, is not unlike the way in which a guilty man (say a Nazi war criminal) goes back, again and again, over past crimes. Memory, especially guilty memory, forces us to live our lives backwards.[35]

However, it would be wrong to believe that the narrator, who for Wood is the Nazis' soul, comes to any true understanding of what Odilo has actually done. The backward repetition of the events of Odilo's life, dictated perhaps by guilty memory, here leads only to an obscene distortion of the facts: 'The world, after all, here in Auschwitz, has a new habit', insists the narrator. 'It makes sense' (*TA*, p. 138). Rather than offering a morally informed perspective on the acts committed by Odilo in Auschwitz, the narrative of *Time's Arrow* conforms more closely to the example of how Nazi doctors and camp functionaries have in memoirs sought to excuse or justify their actions. In her preface to the second edition of *The Origins of Totalitarianism*, Hannah Arendt offers the following comments on such 'literature':

> I left out, without regret, the rather voluminous literature of memoirs published by Nazi and other German functionaries after the end of the war. The dishonesty of this kind of apologetics is obvious and embarrassing but understandable, whereas the lack of comprehension they display of what actually happened, as well as of the roles the authors themselves played in the course of events, is truly astonishing.[36]

A more specific model for the absence of moral awareness in *Time's Arrow* is to be found in Robert Jay Lifton's *The Nazi Doctors*, a book without which Amis's novel, as he confesses, 'would not and could not be written' (*TA*, p. 175). Lifton's approach is psychohistorical: he is interested in the psychological states necessitated and formed by specific historical crises. In *The Nazi Doctors* he reports lengthy interviews carried out with those who put into effect the Nazis' genocidal biological programme. From these interviews, Lifton attempts to formulate the general principles of what he calls 'the psychology of genocide'. Early in the book, he reveals one of the most striking features common to all the interviews:

> Some part of these men wished to be heard: they had things to say that most of them had never said before, least of all to

people around them. Yet none of them – not a single former
Nazi doctor I spoke to – arrived at a clear ethical evaluation of
what he had done, and what he had been part of. They could
examine events in considerable detail, even look at feelings and
speak generally with surprising candour – but almost in the
manner of a third person. The narrator, morally speaking, was
not quite present.[37]

Lifton's judgement is similar to Arendt's, but it is these two
concluding sentences, in which he hints at the reason why there
is no 'clear ethical evaluation' of their crimes, that offer one of the
keys to understanding the mode of narration in *Time's Arrow*.

The narrator of Amis's novel is the 'Auschwitz self' created by
Odilo to allow him to carry out his genocidal duties unsullied or,
as his name suggests, unspoilt. Lifton writes of the Nazi doctors'
practice of *doubling*, 'the formation of a second, relatively autonomous self, which enables one to participate in evil' (*ND*, p. 6).
This second self he calls the 'Auschwitz self', explaining that
this in a sense replaces the original self, thereby allowing the
doctor to convince himself of his own innocence. 'In doubling,'
he adds,

> one part of the self 'disavows' another part. What is repudiated
> is not reality itself – the individual doctor was aware of what he
> was doing via the Auschwitz self – but the meaning of that
> reality. The Nazi doctor knew that he selected, but did not
> interpret selection as murder. (*ND*, p. 422)

It is precisely this distortion of the significance of historical acts
and events that the narration of *Time's Arrow* is made to reflect.

The result of Amis's narrative strategy is an intensification of
the novel's reflection of Auschwitz from the Nazi doctor's perspective, at least in as far as that perspective is described by Lifton.
After all, perhaps the principal (and probably the most shocking)
consequence of the narrative's inversion of past and future is the
inversion of healing and killing represented in the text. The
narrator describes seeing 'an old Jew float to the surface of the
deep latrine, how he splashed and struggled into life, and was
hoisted out by jubilant guards, his clothes cleansed by the mire'
(*TA*, p. 132). His world is that of the healing mugger and rapist,
where 'violence is salutary'. The novel thus dramatises a world in
accordance with what Lifton identifies as the '"healing" claim' of
the Nazi regime: the 'reversal of healing and killing', he writes,

'became an organizing principle' of the Nazi doctors' work (*ND*, pp. xii–xiii). The same reversal is so similarly central to *Time's Arrow* that some of Lifton's descriptions look as though they could be summaries of passages from Amis's novel. For example:

> [The Nazi doctor] is a recognized healer with special powers; his killing is legitimated by, and at the same time further legitimates, the regime's overall healing–killing reversals. Thus it became quite natural to use a vehicle marked with a red cross to transport gas, gassing personnel, and sometimes victims, to the gas chambers. (*ND*, 431)

What this reversal achieved was 'the destruction of the boundary between healing and killing' (*ND*, p. 14). The binary opposition is here nullified, as it is in *Time's Arrow*, by the process of inversion. Furthermore, Lifton explicitly states that the destruction of this boundary was dependent upon the medical staff's fictional interpretation of their situation. He writes that those whose job was to kill children in mental hospitals 'proceeded *as if* these children were to receive the blessings of medical science, were to be healed rather than killed' (*ND*, p. 54). To show how this fictional 'as if' operated, he refers to a Dr Heinze, who later excused his actions in court by claiming that a fatal overdose might have to be prescribed in order to ensure that an excitable child would '"avoid endangering itself through its own restlessness"'. Lifton argues that the psychological adoption of this fiction was so effective and so widespread that it

> is quite possible that Dr Heinze not only was consciously lying, but was enabled by the medicalization of the murders partly to deceive himself: to come to believe, at least at moments, that the children were being given some sort of therapy, and that their deaths were due to their own abnormality. (*ND*, p. 54)

Just as the reversal of time's arrow inverts the healing–killing opposition, this inversion naturally extends itself to the roles of the healer and the persecutor. Early in *Time's Arrow* it is Tod and his American colleagues who inflict violence: Tod, we are told, rubs dirt in the prostitutes' wounds 'before the longsuffering pimp shows up and knocks the girls into shape with his jewelled fists' (*TA*, pp. 39–40). Later, as John Young, his violence is more extreme: 'Some guy comes in with a bandage around his head. We don't mess about. We'll soon have that off. He's got a hole in his head. So what do we do. We stick a nail in it' (*TA*, p. 85). When he reaches Auschwitz, however, as Odilo Unverdorben, his role changes to that of healer. The 'patients' he treats are remarkably compliant with all his treatments, though some seem less than grateful afterwards. Even then, though, there are exceptions: 'an old man hugging and kissing my black boots; a child clinging to me after I held her down for "Uncle Pepi"' (*TA*, p. 144).

This depiction of the Jews and Nazis as complicit in the experience of the camp indirectly reflects the way in which, according to Lifton, Nazi doctors would attempt to involve prisoner doctors in the murderous process of selection:

> To the extent that they could succeed in tainting those they ruled over, they felt themselves to be less tainted. In that way they could blur, at least for themselves, distinctions between victimizer and victim, between physician jailer and physician prisoner. (*ND*, p. 218)

It is precisely this distinction that is blurred in Amis's choice of Odilo's surname: Unverdorben. A literal translation would be 'unspoilt' or 'undepraved'. More importantly, however, it alludes to two historical figures, one a Nazi doctor and the other a camp inmate. Eduard Wirths was the chief doctor in Auschwitz who, because of his comparative mildness and compassion, was given the nickname 'Dr. Unblütig' (Dr Unbloody). Primo Levi, on the other hand, writes in *The Truce* of 'a mild touchy little man from Trieste' called Mr Unverdorben who, recalls Levi, 'had survived the Birkenau Lager'.[38] Not only are Odilo Unverdorben's actions in Auschwitz transformed by the novel into those of a miraculous healer, but his very name symbolically undermines the distinction between victim and persecutor. Levi himself, in one of the books Amis cites as an influence on his novel, comments at some length on the blurring of this distinction:

> This mimesis, this identification or imitation, or exchange of roles between oppressor and victim, has provoked much discussion. . . .
>   I am not an expert of the unconscious or the mind's depths, but I do know that few people are experts in this sphere, and that these few are the most cautious; I do not know, and it does not much interest me to know, whether in my depths there lurks a murderer, but I do know that I was a guiltless victim and I was not a murderer. I know that the murderers existed,

not only in Germany, and still exist, retired or on active duty, and that to confuse them with their victims is a moral disease or an aesthetic affectation or a sinister sign of complicity; above all, it is a precious service rendered (intentionally or not) to the negators of truth.[39]

Levi here touches on one of the central elements underpinning *Time's Arrow*: that the means by which we interpret or attempt to represent a historical situation are themselves open to moral and ideological critique.

Before turning to the analytical self-reflexivity of Amis's novel, it is important to acknowledge the extent to which language itself was directly implicated in the Nazi programme. 'A leading scholar of the Holocaust', writes Robert Lifton, 'told of examining "tens of thousands" of Nazi documents without once encountering the word "killing", until after many years he finally did discover the word – in reference to an edict concerning dogs' (*ND*, p. 445). Lifton lists the euphemisms employed in Auschwitz to disguise what was really happening. Doctors there, he claimed, spoke not of executions but of 'ramp duty', 'medical ramp duty', 'prisoners presenting themselves to a doctor', 'evacuation', 'transfer' and 'resettlement'. The psychological effect of this language is clear:

> [it] gave Nazi doctors a discourse in which killing was no longer killing. . . . As they lived increasingly within that language – and they used it with each other – Nazi doctors became imaginatively bound to a psychic realm of derealization, disavowal, and nonfeeling. (*ND*, p. 445)

This is reflected, in *Time's Arrow*, in the naming of the gas chamber and sprinkleroom as '*the central hospital*' (*TA*, p. 133). More significantly, though, the whole novel represents 'a discourse in which killing was no longer killing'. The title of Primo Levi's *The Drowned and the Saved* is a reference to the victims and survivors of the death camps. *Time's Arrow* draws on the description in *The Nazi Doctors* of how language, too, was victimised, taken apart and reassembled for ideological purposes: 'What was she saying, Irene, what was she going on about, in words half saved, half drowned – in gasps and whispers?' (*TA*, p. 44).

The bilingual puns, the cartoon names, the playfulness of form and intertextuality all surely indicate to the reader the text's self-reflexivity. The arbitrariness and ease with which the text resurrects the victims of Auschwitz suggests that here death is merely a textual predicament. At the moment of selection, the narrator describes 'fathers, mothers, children, the old scattered like leaves in the wind. *Die . . . die Auseinandergeschrieben*' (*TA*, p. 141). As well as playing on the English 'die', the last phrase translates literally into 'the written apart' and links with the earlier claim that, when Odilo first arrived at the camp, '[h]uman life was all ripped and torn' (*TA*, p. 124). It is also, however, a more specific reference to Paul Celan's poem 'Engführung' (the following are the first two stanzas only):

Verbracht ins
Gelände
mit der untrüglichen Spur:

Gras, auseinandergeschrieben. Die Steine, weiss,
mit den Schatten der Halme:
Lies nicht mehr − schau!
Schau nicht mehr − geh![40]

Celan describes the landscape here as textual. Those driven into that landscape, then, are also driven into a text; they are textualised. It is the violence of this process of textualisation in *Time's Arrow* that Amis's narrative here acknowledges in its definition of the Jews to be murdered as *die Auseinandergeschrieben*: the written asunder.

The construction of Amis's novel reflects not only the perspective of a Nazi doctor but also the cultural dominant of postmodernism. In this sense, the novel as a whole reinforces that association of a contemporary, late capitalist, tabloid culture with the rhetoric of Nazi propaganda referred to earlier. *Time's Arrow* may be read as a specifically postmodern attempt to rewrite the history of the Holocaust which simultaneously foregrounds the ways in which that rewriting reflects the Nazi justification of the act in the first place. Thus, the backwards order of narration is determined by both its focalisation through Odilo's Auschwitz self and its imitation of a video or film running in reverse (as in Vonnegut's *Slaughterhouse Five*). It would seem, then, that *Time's Arrow* is at least in part offering a critical dramatisation of a specifically postmodern reworking of historical phenomena.

The reader of Amis's novel is made to undergo a process of disorientation that is also to some extent a reflection of the cognitive dislocation of Nazi doctors in the synthetic environment of the camps:

Doctors assigned there, then, had limited contact with anything but Auschwitz reality. They became preoccupied with adapting themselves to that reality, and moral revulsion could be converted into feelings of discomfort, unhappiness, anxiety and despair. Subjective struggles could replace moral questions. They became concerned not with the evil of the environment but with how to come to terms with the place. (*ND*, pp. 198–9)

Hannah Arendt also emphasises this feature of the camps, though with regard to their intended effect on prisoners. She writes that the total domination which could be practised there depended 'on sealing off [the camps] against the world of all others, the world of the living in general'.[41] It would seem no mere coincidence that the main camp of Auschwitz appeared to Primo Levi as 'a boundless metropolis'.[42] *Time's Arrow* reproduces this feature of a sealed-off environment through the inverted temporal order of its narration. The readers' need to locate themselves in the disorientating textual environment of the novel thus creates a literary analogy for the spatial confusion of both the prisoners and personnel of the camps.

But if the novel's reliance on an internal logic sealed off from the outside world associates it with the Lager, it also identifies Amis's text with the creation of what Fredric Jameson calls 'postmodern hyperspace'. In his analysis of postmodern architecture, Jameson discusses the Westin Bonaventure Hotel in Los Angeles. He compares it with a number of other characteristically postmodern buildings (for example, the Beaubourg in Paris; the Eaton Centre in Toronto) and argues that, in common with them, the Bonaventure 'aspires to being a total space, a complete world, a kind of miniature city'.[43] The effect on the individual subject who has entered one of these buildings is, I think, comparable to that experienced on one level by the reader of *Time's Arrow*, who has imaginatively entered an environment in which Auschwitz 'makes sense':

[T]his latest mutation in space – postmodern hyperspace – has finally succeeded in transcending the capacities of the individual human body to locate itself, to organize its immediate surroundings perceptually, and cognitively to map its position in a mappable external world.[44]

Just as for both Arendt and Lifton the concentration camp is designed to overwhelm, or perhaps to short-circuit, the ability of the individual (whether prisoner or functionary) to comprehend the events that take place with any degree of moral or political awareness, 'postmodern hyperspace' effects a similar confusion of the means by which we relate ourselves to the social and cultural forms that surround us.

Time's Arrow does not simply assert a simplistic equation of a Nazi past and the postmodern present, but (like Don DeLillo's *White Noise*) rather exposes, while simultaneously exemplifying, the inadequacy of the postmodern reimagining of history. Like *London Fields*, it indulges in the relief of the postmodern – here, moulding its narrative form to one reminiscent of the capabilities of video – while silently implying regret for all that the celebration of textual play leaves unacknowledged.

Again reasserting the mimetic element of the novel's inversion of narrative order, James Wood writes that '[t]he Nazis first attempted to turn the Holocaust into a Utopian narrative, not Amis'.[45] The reproduction of that narrative is not, though, in Western Marxist terms, the utopian element of Amis's text. 'The ideology in a great work', writes Ernst Bloch, 'reflects and justifies its times, the utopia in it rips open the times.'[46] The irony of *Time's Arrow* lies in its suggestion that it is its utopian reclamation of the history of the Holocaust that is most thoroughly ideological, re-enacting in the cultural forms of the contemporary a rhetoric of past justifications.

In contrast, the utopian aspect of Amis's novel can be situated in the continuously (and guiltily) implied expression of what it can never quite openly acknowledge: namely, the horror of its own aesthetic mutilation of a narrative of others' suffering. *Time's Arrow* relies for its power on the reader's appreciation of how its narrative has distorted the history of the *Endlösung*. 'A dream of reversal, of reconstruction: who has not, in the fifty years since the European devastation, swum off into this dream?' asks Cynthia Ozick. 'As if the reel of history – and who does not see history as tragic cinema? – could be run backward';[47] but *Time's Arrow* suggests that that dream had been dreamt at the outset, had in fact helped to anaesthetise the doctors to the peculiarity of their work. It is in the incidental details – the motif of the deadly child; the words 'half drowned, half saved'; '*die Auseinandergeschrieben*' – that the novel signals some acknowledgement of its guilty ideological complicity, expressing something of the guilt and remorse that has been banished from the narrator's account.

The end of *Time's Arrow* is signalled as a boundary point, a point of disorientation as we move out of the novel's textual world. Keats' final line in 'Ode to a Nightingale' – 'Fled is that

music – Do I wake or sleep?' – conveys the giddy uncertainty of
the speaker's state of consciousness as the poem is brought to a
close. Amis's narrator, too, is confused as the novel finishes, but
his uncertainty is temporal. The arrow of time reverses again as
the text slips away and a new form of reality rushes on to greet us:

> Beyond, before the slope of pine, the lady archers are gathering
> with their targets and bows. Above, a failing-vision kind of
> light, with the sky fighting down its nausea. Its many nuances
> of nausea. When Odilo closes his eyes I see an arrow fly – but
> wrongly. Point-first. Oh no, but then . . . We're away once
> more, over the field. Odilo Unverdorben and his eager heart.
> And I within, who came at the wrong time – either too soon, or
> after it was all too late. (*TA*, p. 173)

The narrator, disorientated and confused, disappears with Odilo,
leaving readers to make their necessary departure from the text.
Amis is aware, though, that his readers have been outside the text
all along, measuring up their knowledge of the history of the
Holocaust to *Time's Arrow*'s distortions.

This suggests the limits to ideological domination, the inability
of a textualised postmodern hyperspace ever to absorb our cognitive faculties totally; in fact, *Time's Arrow* implies the coexistence
in the postmodern of the playful regurgitation of the past and the
retention of some necessary historical memory to which the former
must eventually appeal. As well as retaining, then, in earlier
novels such as *Money* and *London Fields*, some necessary distinction between the values of the aesthetic and the market, Amis's
writing also seems to insist on an identifiable, external reality
which art transforms, thereby disavowing (whether in an act of
critique or evasion) the claims of the postmodern to the dissolution of those very distinctions. A postmodern novel, *Time's Arrow*
implies the necessity of its own ideology critique; but it does so by
making a seemingly unpostmodern assumption, that there is an
external space outwith cultural representation by which those
representations might be judged.

Notes

1. Robert Holton, *Jarring Witnesses: Modern Fiction and the Representation of History*, p. 256.
2. Fredric Jameson, *Postmodernism*, p. 25.

3. Theodor W. Adorno, 'Reconciliation under Duress', in Ernst Bloch et al., *Aesthetics and Politics*, p. 160.

4. Aijaz Ahmad, *In Theory: Classes, Nations, Literatures*, p. 130.

5. Thomas Docherty, *Reading (Absent) Character: Towards a Theory of Characterization in Fiction*, p. 158.

6. Thomas Docherty, *Alterities*, p. 47.

7. Ibid., p. 57.

8. Ibid., p. 58.

9. Ibid., pp. 66–7.

10. Ibid., p. 67.

11. Holton, *Jarring Witnesses*, p. 221.

12. McHale, *Postmodernist Fiction*, p. 45.

13. See Thomas Docherty, *After Theory*, pp. 8–13.

14. Jenny Turner, 'When the Sandwich Was still a New Invention', p. 23.

15. Louis Menand, 'Entropology', accessible online at www.nybooks.com/nyrev/WWWarchdisplay.cgi?19970612022R

16. Turner, 'When the Sandwich . . .', p. 25.

17. Stefan Mattessich, 'Telluric Texts, Implicate Spaces', accessible online at http: //jefferson.village.virginia.edu/pmc/text-only/issue. 997/review-5.997

18. Ibid.

19. Habermas, *The Philosophical Discourse of Modernity*, p. 17.

20. T. W. Adorno, 'Cultural Criticism and Society', in his *Prisms*, p. 34.

21. T. W. Adorno, *Negative Dialectics*, p. 367 (emphasis added).

22. Walter Benjamin, 'Theses on the Philosophy of History', in his *Illuminations*, p. 256.

23. T. W. Adorno, 'Trying to Understand Beckett's *Endgame*', in his *Notes to Literature*, Vol. 1, pp. 241–75. For a comparison of this essay to the above section from *Negative Dialectics*, see Lambert Zuidervaart, *Adorno's Aesthetic Theory: The Redemption of Illusion*, pp. 150–77.

24. T. W. Adorno, 'Music and New Music', in his *Quasi una Fantasia*, p. 250.

25. Ibid., pp. 263–4.

26. T. W. Adorno, 'The Aging of the New Music', pp. 97–8.

27. Ibid., p. 110.

28. Ibid., p. 111.

29. Adorno, 'Trying to Understand Beckett's *Endgame*', p. 249.

30. Ibid., p. 250.

31. Adorno, 'The Aging of the New Music', p. 116.

32. Bernstein, 'Introduction', in T. W. Adorno, *The Culture Industry*, p. 17.

33. Martin Amis, *Time's Arrow*, p. 20. Hereafter, references to the novel will be to the same edition and marked in the main text, prefixed by the abbreviation *TA*.

34. Frank Kermode, 'In Reverse', p. 11.
35. James Wood, 'Slouching towards Auschwitz to be Born again', p. 9.
36. Hannah Arendt, *The Origins of Totalitarianism*, p. xii.
37. Robert Jay Lifton, *The Nazi Doctors*, p. 8. Further references to the text will be to the same edition and will hereafter be marked in the main text by the prefix *ND*.
38. Primo Levi, *If this Is a Man* and *The Truce*, p. 275.
39. Primo Levi, *The Drowned and the Saved*, pp. 32–3.
40. Paul Celan, 'Engführung', in his *Gesammelte Werke*, Vol. 1, pp. 197–204. For an English translation see P. Celan, *Poems of Paul Celan*, pp. 137–49:

> Driven into the
> terrain
> with the unmistakable track:
>
> grass, written asunder. The stones, white
> with the shadows of grassblades:
> Do not read any more – look!
> Do not look any more – go!

41. Arendt, *The Origins of Totalitarianism*, p. 438.
42. Levi, *If this Is a Man*, p. 194.
43. Jameson, *Postmodernism*, p. 40.
44. Ibid., p. 44.
45. Wood, 'Slouching towards Auschwitz', p. 9.
46. Ernst Bloch, 'Art and Society', in his *The Utopian Function of Art and Literature*, p. 39.
47. Cynthia Ozick, *What Henry James Knew*, p. 323.

IV Postmodern Political Fictions

The Fetish of the New: Culture and
Class in Alasdair Gray's *Something Leather*

The culture industry perpetually cheats its consumers of what
it perpetually promises. The promissory note which, with its
plots and staging, it draws on pleasure is endlessly prolonged;
the promise, which is usually all the spectacle consists of, is
illusory: all it actually confirms is that the real point will never
be reached, that the diner must be satisfied with the menu. In
front of the appetite stimulated by all those brilliant names and
images there is finally sat no more than a commendation of the
depressing everyday world it sought to escape.

> (Theodor W. Adorno and Max Horkheimer,
> *Dialectic of Enlightenment*)

Alasdair Gray's *Something Leather* is a sex-and-shopping novel.
Between the two shopping excursions with which her story begins
and ends, June Tain undergoes two simultaneous – sexual and
sartorial – transformations: the 'strikingly good looking' divorcee
who enjoys men's admiration but 'refuses to bring it to a very
ordinary sexual conclusion' experiences a painful but ultimately
enjoyable conversion to the rigours of lesbian S&M; equally, she
leaves behind her favoured clothes styles of the 1930s and 1940s
('which flirt elegantly or luxuriously with the human outline') in
favour of figure-hugging leatherwear and lacy or elaborate lingerie.
Gray tells us, though, in the Epilogue, of a further transformation
with which he had originally flirted. The much-put-upon Senga
and Donalda, whose fastidious work with needles and cuffs makes
possible June's metamorphosis, were then to have been used by
the leather-clad, wasp-tatooed Revenge Angel 'to entangle and
corrupt important legislators, thus provoking a feminist socialist
revolution'.[1]

Of course this does not happen. Instead, June retains her index-linked pension plan and her shares in British Gas and BP. On the Monday morning following her initiation, she is told on the telephone by Harry, the artist for whom Senga and Donalda arrange these S&M sessions, that their £3000 cheque has been stopped. For June this is unimportant; her present needs are sexual rather than financial (and anyway, she already 'has nearly seven thousand pounds in two bank accounts'). She and Harry agree to meet that evening. Later, an envelope is pushed under June's door: Senga has sent her payment of £700 ('all I have except a bit in my purse to tide me over') before the cheque clears – which of course it never will. Sharply pocketing the notes – 'thinking smugly, "A chap should always have money in his pockets"' – June sets out on the shopping spree with which her story ends, finding herself ultimately returning to the leather shop she had visited two hundred and twenty-one pages previously. She approaches the same assistant who had sent her to Senga and the Hideout in the first place, and asks whether she recognises her:

> After a wondering stare the assistant says, 'Yes! . . . Did you find that place you were looking for?'
> 'Oh yes.'
> 'So you're happy now?' asks the assistant, smiling.
> 'Yes,' says June, smiling. (*SL*, p. 231)

This is the novel's concluding moment of resolution. Yet to see it as the true fulfilment of that promise of happiness suspended at the end of chapter 1 – as Donalda kisses June in 'a kiss which is almost a bite,' and June 'enjoys a melting delicious weakness like nothing she has known' – is surely misleading. In a recent article on Gray, Alison Lumsden cites June Tain's final affirmation of contentment and writes:

> Thematically, then, Gray's work seems to suggest that, while the vast economic and political structures which form systems of entrapment . . . may be difficult, if not impossible, to challenge, the individual may nevertheless find some kind of freedom within these frameworks.[2]

Not surprisingly, she goes on to claim that 'the conclusions which Gray's work implies are in fact fairly traditional, classically bourgeois ones'.[3] If we assume that the novel offers only a celebratory affirmation of June's fate, that the reconstruction of

her sexual practices and dress-sense are depicted as in some way
sufficient, then we too shall be led to the association of Gray's
novel with individualistic bourgeois liberalism – a sort of
pseudo-transgressive Pants Down for Paddy. However, such an
interpretation would be ill-advised. Rather than focusing on the
transformation that undoubtedly does occur, then, it will be the
intention of this reading to insist on the paramount significance of
the changes that do not take place: namely, those in the representation of relations of production.

Gray himself points to precisely this feature of the novel in his
Epilogue:

> It was now clear that June was a new woman, and to describe
> how she used her newness would limit it. There was a clear hint
> that having been liberated by the work of Senga and Donalda,
> June (the professional person) and Harry (the inherited wealth
> person) would cut themselves off from the poorer folk and have
> fun together. You need not believe that ending but it is how we
> normally arrange things in Great Britain. It is certainly how
> things were arranged in Glasgow in 1990, when that city was
> the official capital of Europe – culturally speaking. (*SL*, p. 251)

We shall later return to the significance of the final sentence,
which was only added to the novel's second edition. For the
moment, though, it is important to note that, despite the significant changes that have taken place, class relations and class exploitation remain undisturbed. It is, furthermore, the work of the
'poorer folk' which allows both June and Harry to set off on their
path of liberating sexual fantasy. Thus, Harry's insistence that she
and June 'don't need these otha little people' (*SL*, p. 226) relates,
quite predictably, to the sharing of the spoils – sexual and financial – rather than to the bruise and welt-inducing labour into
which the little people – and especially Senga: 'As usual at the
end all the dirty work is left to me so here it comes!' (*SL*, p. 221) –
had put such pitiful effort. A clear class division is hereby signalled among those – Senga, Donalda and Harry – who contribute
to the artistic production of the New June.

Moreover, this acknowledgement of Harry, the artist, as a producer is significant in itself. As we shall see, it is important for
the novel that Harry's artistic production is never subject to
mystificatory claims of aesthetic transcendence or autonomy.
This disavowal of a separate, autonomous aesthetic or cultural
sphere is reflected even in Harry's almost excessively functional

dress-sense, the uniform of 'crumpled army combat trousers, shirt, tunic and boots' which she wears 'because it suits her work (*SL*, p. 185). Harry's work is art, and the novel's identification of artistic production as a functional practice signals a transformation in the relation of the aesthetic or cultural sphere to that of the socio-economic.

Since Kant's *Critique of Judgement* (1790), the cultural or aesthetic sphere has traditionally been characterised in philosophical aesthetics as an autonomous realm. The critique of this claim, as it is formulated by Georg Lukács, focuses on the extent to which it masks the economic and class interests which cultural forms serve, thereby displacing critique and analysis of those interests themselves. However, Theodor Adorno, in *Aesthetic Theory*, testifies to the critical power of art which holds fast to the necessary lie of autonomy (while remaining, in fact, only semi-autonomous) in his claim that 'by their presence art works signal the possibility of the non-existent; their reality testifies to the feasibility of the unreal, the possible'.[4] They do this, he writes, through their disavowal of social utility: 'If any social function can be ascribed to art at all, it is the function to have no function.'[5] Thus, art offers, above all, in the estrangement of its subject-matter by aesthetic form itself, the vision of an alternative to actuality; 'Art', writes Adorno, 'is the negative knowledge of the actual world.'[6] Once the aesthetic no longer claims that autonomy for itself, however, its element of critique is lost and instead, as a proper culture industry, it can effectively express only a form of flight: 'not, as is asserted, flight from a wretched reality, but from the last remaining thought of resistance'.[7] It is precisely this semi-autonomy, whose political import Adorno seeks to redeem, which is discarded by the cultural sphere in which Harry operates. Instead, it openly proclaims itself as a culture industry, fully and harmlessly integrated into daily economic life. The critique of the culture industry, now to be grasped as the historico-cultural moment of the postmodern, is most effectively, then, the critique of a cultural sphere which has renounced in that semi-autonomy a past critical distance from that same network of class conflict and domination in which it is itself produced. It is important, therefore, to acknowledge the unabashed complicity of that cultural realm in which Harry works with the maintenance and reproduction of those class relations – or relations of production – that we find dramatised so starkly in the novel's conclusion.

Harry is of course questioned on the status of her art in the course of the novel. 'Aren't you sick of being a Post-Modernist' –

asks an obviously unpleasant journalist (*SL*, p. 145). He continues
to pester her by asking whether she is envious of past generations
of 'truly creative artists'. Her reply – 'No.' – does little to dissuade
him. The annoyance goes on:

> 'But to most people nowadays the new things in the galleries
> look like doodling! They add very little beauty or intelligence to
> the places wha they appia, none at all to those who see them.
> Does it occur to you that yaw art may be a game played for
> nobody's plesha but yaw own? Like doodling. Or mastabation.'
>   'Yes.'
>   'Does it occur to you often, or only when yaw depressed?'
>   Harry says slowly, 'It occurred to me when you asked me
> about it.'
>   'But it still strikes you as true?'
>   'I don't know. Ask Harvey about that.'
>   Harvey is her dealer. (*SL*, p. 146)

If there is some truth in the musings of the dislikeable questioner,
as I think there is, then it is surely grasped more acutely, if rather
more unwittingly, through Harry's own invocation of Harvey, her
dealer, than in any discussion of the high seriousness or otherwise
of her work. Again according to Lukács, 'the objective forms of all
social phenomena change constantly in the course of their ceaseless dialectical interactions with each other'.[8] It is, then, the
change in the relation of culture to the market, discussed earlier
and here signalled in Harry's overt and stated dependence on
Harvey (who is also responsible, a footnote tells us, for the titles
of each of Harry's works), that justifies the identification of a
transformation in the status and function of art such as Harry's,
that is a modification in the processes through which artistic
meaning and signification are constructed.

The loss of autonomy and outright formal assent to the values of
the market that are necessary for this distinction to be made are
further displayed in the chapter 'Culture Capitalism', where Harry's
dealer considers the feasibility of building and exhibiting an all-
new bum garden:

> He sees that if Harry now makes a lavish indoor sculpture park
> representing her eerily horrid schooldays (and with right help
> Harry can make anything) then Harry's work will be profitably
> sold by the London art market to the end of the century. So
> much can be said about it! – this tragically feminist remake of

Pooh Corner, Never Never Land, the Secret Garden; this shrine to a dead millionairess who was loved by Marc Bolan, Jimi Hendrix and Sid Vicious, if only for a few minutes. Get the show an explanatory catalogue written by a brainier than usual popular writer (William Golding too old and grand perhaps but try him and Muriel Spark Iris Murdoch Fay Weldon Germaine Greer George Melly Angela Carter David Lodge or whoever wrote *The History Man* Adam Mars-Jones or whoever wrote *The Cement Garden* Roald Dahl, Martin Amis, *Tom Stoppard? Harold Pinter?* Whoever springs to mind seems suitable) it could be a small bestseller, a cult book if televised why not a feature film? Bill Forsyth directing? But first, the exhibition. (*SL*, p. 177)

Perhaps the key phrase here is that late comment: 'Whoever springs to mind seems suitable'. Harvey's thoughts tell us something not about the specific authors he cites, but about the general sphere of culture itself, a sphere which no longer even pretends to be autonomous from economic life and which we have seen Fredric Jameson define as postmodernism.

If *Something Leather* is itself to escape outright complicity with the social forces it depicts, then it can do so only through a form of self-critique. 'Ostensibly working on works of art,' writes Adorno, 'the artist also works on art – proof again of the fact that art and works of art are not coterminous.'[9] The work of art is itself engaged in a dialectical and thoroughly mediated relationship with the aesthetic or cultural sphere in which it is produced. The critical distance that art had previously retained, but to which the culture industry has lost all pretension, might then be relocated in that still conflictual relation of the individual text – in this case, *Something Leather* – to the cultural dominant of postmodernism. We need not, therefore, speculate with Jameson on 'some as yet unimaginable new mode' of cultural representation; rather, we should analyse the extent to which texts such as *Something Leather* already offer both representation and critique of the complicity of that cultural realm to which they owe their production with the social exploitation and domination that they take as their subject. This is a complicity in which the individual text shares, but with which it cannot wholly be identified.

The extent to which *Something Leather* is successful in associating itself with, and simultaneously distancing itself from, that 'Culture Capitalism' it portrays depends, as we shall see, primarily on how well it can unmask its own function as that of the illusory

mystification of class relations. These relations, from whose maintenance and reproduction attention is ultimately diverted by the
creation of the New June are nonetheless lengthily dramatised not
only in chapter 12's 'Class Party', but also in the precocious
power-play of Hjordis and her peers in the teacher-free shrubbery
of Harry's boarding school. The young Linda, whose Cockney
accent survives its RP surroundings with the aid of continual
replayings of her nouveau-riche pop-star father's record, is condemned to remain an eternal 'Applicant' to Hjordis' gang, perpetually denied entry to the elusive Fortress: 'I'll allwise allwise be
an applicant', she sobs (*SL*, p. 29). For her part, Hjordis invokes
class solidarity in her failed attempt to convince Harry to join her
in opposition to the Headmistress. Accepting her failure, she
reflects bitterly that '"[t]he descendant of Teutonic warlords is
now spying fo the liberals"' (*SL*, p. 35).

The behaviour of Harry in the shrubbery is a significant pointer
to her later role as an artist. Rather than intervening directly in
the class-based power-games of her fellow pupils, Harry appears
willing quite literally to transcend such matters by retreating to
the safe, lofty heights of a tree. But the imaginative play in which
she indulges proves to be less transcendence of power relations
than their aestheticisation in the form of sado-masochistic fantasy.
Witness her first words in the shrubbery, directed to the poor
outsider Linda:

> We have no time for interlopas be they German, Greek, black,
> brown or Irish. We do not speak fo the lost cause of racial
> purity, we speak against boredom. Please direct your attention
> to this paw little horrid gel who does not deserve ha great
> advantages. How will we punish ha? Smacking and nipping a
> the usual thing. (*SL*, p. 36)

When Linda's accent finally fades, replaced by the RP for which
her father is paying, she is no longer of interest to the future
artist, who 'cannot be friendly with someone whose voice does not
strike her as comically coarse and ill-bred' (*SL*, p. 46). The very
next sentence – 'Twenty seven years pass before she meets Senga'
– directs us immediately, then, to an acknowledgement of the
significance of class relations to those S&M get-togethers that
Harvey pays Senga and Donalda (the 'little people') to arrange.

Chapters 3 and 4 – 'The Proposal' and 'The Man who Knew
about Electricity' – introduce us, respectively, to Senga and
Donalda at their youngest. Senga is 15 when Tom proposes to

her; she is thrilled, but eventually refuses. To Tom's parents, his youthful fancy for Senga is a mistake. They are keen for their son to better himself, to leave behind 'this wee dolly bird' and go to university: 'You'll meet girls of your own sort there', says his father (*SL*, p. 54). Above all, though, they fear that he will discard the possibility of social mobility in which they place such faith: 'And don't get entangled, Tom' is their usual refrain. Escaping both entanglement and university (the former through no fault of his own), Tom becomes a prosperous small-businessman but remains besotted with Senga. His second proposal to her is even less successful than the previous attempt; they go their separate ways: 'She marries the cranedriver, a man with many friends who talks a lot about politics. Two months later Tom marries a woman who looks like Senga but was bred in a wealthier home and wants to be kept in another one' (*SL*, p. 63). Tom, then, is an 'interlopa' like Linda, although on a significantly smaller scale and into a class necessarily more predisposed to successful aspirants. It might be tempting to see here an example of that individual who, as Alison Lumsden has put it, 'find[s] some kind of freedom *within* these [economic and political] frameworks'. In fact, we see Tom, two chapters later, running his own firm and employing the as-yet-fairly-staid June Tain. Having accepted those 'systems of entrapment' and started to prosper within them, he does not, however, go on to live in a way that Gray can plausibly be accused of recommending:

> Tom, with the assistance of an expert accountant goes profitably bankrupt. He moves to London where his ability to deal with buyers and suppliers is found useful by a subsidiary of a gigantic company whose directors will never know his name or face. (*SL*, p. 99)

The freedom that Tom finds within the capitalist system is really a form of absorption, his transformation into yet another poor faceless functionary. His early contradiction of his father is proved wrong: Tom is dependable. Thus, he betters himself; Senga – crucially – does not.

The episodes describing Donalda's life before her meeting with June show, like those centring on Senga, her perpetual interpellation, to borrow Louis Althusser's term, as a working-class female subject. The daily exploitation of which this process consists appears most overtly in those scenes where her economic vulnerability collides with the shiny-beaded lure of prostitution. She tells the story of her first proper foray into that particular job market to Mrs Liddel, her landlady, in chapter 7; however, an earlier incident is perhaps even more revealing. The Irishman's attempt to rent her sexual services to the young student who knows about electricity provides an ironic subtext to Donalda's later lesbian grapplings in the service of Harry:

> 'Don't be put off by her rough tongue, sir. That is a temporary consequence of superficial economic tensions – she's afraid of bein chucked out into the street. Solve these tensions and you'll find her the most docile creature imaginable. You'll be able,' he whispers, 'to do anything you like with her.' (*SL*, p. 79)

The Irishman's promise is hardly misleading, as Senga – who later 'seek[s] relief from misery by pulling with both hands Donalda's pleasuring head harder into her crotch' – might well attest; the rough tongue is clearly no longer a problem.

It is in her relations with these two women that Harry is able to find a substitute for her class-inflected schoolgirl fantasies. The imaginative world which her work constructs is a monument to the power-games of Harry, Hjordis and the others. With news of Hjordis' death, however, that dream world (and all its exciting cruelties) cannot survive. Harry's response – to plan a new, bigger, better bum garden renders unnecessary Linda's plea that, as part of the Year of Culture, she '*let them bring the bums to Glasgow*' (*SL*, p. 150). Glasgow, instead, is to have its own bums. Although the novel appears to end before the work is constructed, there is, nonetheless, a sense in which Harry does indeed make of Glasgow's bums a fitting tribute to her dead friend's memory. Senga and Donalda are extremely versatile.

The work of art which Harry can be said to complete is the New June. Like Harry, June is shaven bald; more distinctive and particular to her, though, are the tatoos to whose painful application she drowsily succumbs:

> While sleeping she feels things being done to her body which are partly real. A wasp is stinging her shoulder repeatedly as it crawls around a spot on it. The stinging throb is also ticklish, but June is sure waking will not cure it. She sleeps until Senga shakes her awake saying, 'Look! Isn't it real-looking?'
>
> She touches June's throbbing shoulder and June, looking there, sees a small black-and-yellow trembling wasp. (*SL*, pp. 217–18)

The New June is thus marked from the start as a member of a particular class – that of Wasps – just as Senga and Donalda cannot escape their roles as skivvies, 'little people', or bums.

Although *Something Leather* invites these class associations, it also colludes in their mystification. The book which Linda gives Harry is by a Glasgow writer; it reminds her, she says, of games they used to play with Hjordis. Initially excited, Harry soon becomes frustrated with it:

> Each chapter contains a dialogue between women trying to trap each other but seem otherwise self-contained, with no male characters, no plot, no climaxes: nothing but furtive movements toward something sexy and sinister which never happens. Is this supposed to be funny? thinks Harry, exasperated. (*SL*, p. 180)

A correspondence between this novel and *Something Leather* itself is certainly suggested. The promise of sexual pleasure and fulfil-ment which is suspended at the end of chapter 1 has not yet been redeemed; June might stay tied up but unmolested for a very long time. However, this does not happen. The exasperation with which Harry reacts to *Another Part of the Forest* is unlikely to be repeated for the reader of *Something Leather*. Resolution – and this is important – is finally reached.

The quotation with which this section begins comes from Adorno and Horkheimer's chapter on the culture industry in *Dialectic of Enlightenment*. 'Art', writes Adorno in *Aesthetic Theory*, 'is the promise of happiness, a promise which is constantly being broken.'[10] The culture industry's own promise of pleasure is not broken, however; rather, it insists that it is its own fulfilment, that the aesthetic act is fully sufficient in itself. If art, for Adorno, tells the diner that some of the dishes on the menu are at present denied to him or her, the culture industry, in contrast, insists that the menu is all that is necessary, tasty and nutritious in its easy-wipe plastic coating: 'Not Italy is offered, but proof that it exists.'

Something Leather concludes with precisely the false but neces-sary resolution that the culture industry demands. June Tain's concluding contentment is doubtless heart-warming, but it does nothing to challenge the power-structures of class domination that can be seen to pervade the entire novel. Instead, it functions much as one of Mr Geikie's strategies for dealing with the public, as described in the Epilogue: 'Our main job is to defuse potentially painful confrontations by arranging alternative procedures' (*SL*, p. 236). The necessity of such action is clear to Geikie:

'The fact is that Her Majesty's Government is cutting back the social services so vigorously that it is detaching itself from a big class of people it is supposed to govern. All I and Bleloch and Tannahill do is erect façades to the fact.' (*SL*, p. 240)

The conclusion to *Something Leather* is another of these façades. Thus, the point of the creation of the New June is that it need not involve any transformation in class relations; in fact it is there to mask the absence of change, to divert attention from the continuing reproduction of class domination. Its function, therefore, is principally ideological.

The final sentence of Gray's Epilogue in the second edition, cited earlier, points to the extent to which Glasgow's year as Culture Capital (changed in chapter 10 to 'Culture Capitalism') colluded in the maintenance of class privilege, ditching the likes of Senga and Donalda. Of course *Something Leather* itself cannot fail to be implicated in this. As the sort of Glasgow novel to which Linda draws Harry's attention (*SL*, p. 174), it cannot fully deny its status as part of Glasgow's official culture. Moreover, its own resolution, in the form of the New June, serves precisely those interests with which Gray associates the Year of Culture. Yet, as I suggested some pages ago, the politics of *Something Leather* are rather more complicated than that.

In 'A Letter on Art in Reply to André Daspre' Louis Althusser writes the following:

> What art makes us *see* . . . is the *ideology* from which it is born, in which it bathes, from which it detaches itself as art, and to which it *alludes* . . . . Balzac and Solzhenitsyn give us a 'view' of the ideology to which their work alludes and with which it is constantly fed, a view which presupposes a *retreat*, an *internal distantiation* from the very ideology from which their novels emerged. They make us 'perceive' (but not know) in some sense *from the inside*, by an *internal distance*, the very ideology in which they are held.[11]

This is exactly what *Something Leather* does, offering social, cultural and self-critique. The novel confronts the complicity of culture with social exploitation. The ideological function of art is thus shared by the work of art that is *Something Leather*, but it is also portrayed and dissected there before our very eyes.

The final image to face the reader – before Gray's ubiquitous 'GOODBYE' – is a St Andrew's cross of wasps. Like the reference in the Epilogue to Glasgow's year as Culture Capital, it was only later added to the second, paperback edition. Symbolising Scottish nationhood and – probably – aspirations for Scottish independence, the cross is extremely ambivalent. A hint of this is given in the Epilogue, where Lucy, the politician, describes to June CIA plans to deal with an independent Scotland:

> 'Do you know June Tain that the Yanks were going to be quite kind to an independent Scotland? A lot kinder than to Guatemala, Nicaragua, etcetera. They were NOT afraid of us becoming a socialist republic because they felt we'd be even easier to manipulate than England – fewer chiefs to bribe was how my friend put it.' (SL, pp. 246–7)

In the absence of any radical transformation in relations of production, Scottish independence might well, then, turn out to be yet another cruel sting in the service of Wasps. The novel itself, adorned throughout (like June) with black-and-white reproductions of the foul beasties, must also fulfil this ideological role – although it does so while simultaneously exposing to us readers culture's own complicity in the maintenance of class structures. Thus, the specificity of the novel's references to Scotland and to Glasgow provide a means of insisting on the importance of class in any consideration of real social and cultural change, rather than, as Alison Lumsden argues, offering 'a form of containment' and 'pulling the tropic impulses in his [Gray's] own work back towards a specific and limited field of hectoring reference'.[12]

Something Leather must be read carefully, with close attention paid to its contradictions and its silences. Apparently a novel of transformation, it is more about the absence of transformation; ostensibly a sex-and-shopping novel, its primary concerns are with bums and Wasps.

Salman Rushdie

'If books and films could be made and consumed in the belly of the whale,' wrote Salman Rushdie in 1984,

> it might be possible to consider them merely as entertainment, or even, on occasion, as art. But in our whaleless world, in this world without quiet corners, there can be no easy escapes from history, from hullabaloo, from terrible, unquiet fuss.[13]

The concluding paragraph of *Midnight's Children*, with its image of the individual subject's inescapable and destructive engagement with history 'sucked into the annihilating whirlpool of the multitudes' – suggests a similar acceptance of the implausibility of social or aesthetic transcendence, though here with a quite different, melancholy inflection. The status of his texts as a form of public discourse is implicitly acknowledged by Rushdie, a point made perhaps even more readily apparent by those texts' own ideology critique of a European literary tradition, generated (as we shall see) through a pattern of intertextual allusion.

The following reading of Rushdie's work traces the analytical self-consciousness in those texts of their own ideological location(s). As before, the argument engages with the Western Marxist understanding of postmodernism. In this particular case, though, it is worth pointing out that Rushdie's writing has already been the subject of a well-known Marxist confrontation with postmodern aesthetics: Aijaz Ahmad's *In Theory: Classes, Nations, Literatures*. This section will, then, extend the discussion of a theoretical approach to postmodern fiction not only with specific reference to Salman Rushdie's work, but initially through a brief engagement with Ahmad's own reading of Rushdie, an engagement whose critical points will be developed throughout the course of the argument.

Aijaz Ahmad on Rushdie and the Postmodern

Ahmad writes principally about Rushdie's novel *Shame*, but uses a number of the conclusions to which his analysis leads on which to base a more general critique of Rushdie's fiction. In order to follow Ahmad's reading of Rushdie, though, it is helpful first to identify the literary and political contexts in which he situates the novels' production and reception.

According to Ahmad, the crucial contextual factor for Rushdie's writing is the Three Worlds Theory. As a politico-geographical concept, the Third World is, he argues, hazy and ill-defined at best; at worst, at its most nakedly ideological, it is a recognisably postmodern child of capitalist imperialism. The result of the propagation of the Three Worlds Theory is, for Ahmad, the absence of any recognition of the need to promote the social liberation of those oppressed within today's post-colonial states. He argues that the principal ideological force of the Theory lies in its pretences to radicalism. This pseudo-radicalism accounts for its institutional popularity, particularly in those countries where decolonisation has already taken place. Thus the Three Worlds Theory offers no concrete social transformation towards which praxis might still be directed; yet it tantalisingly seems to promise something else as compensation: the surface glamour of radical chic. It is this promise that Ahmad identifies as the siren call to so many intellectuals. This is, in fact, to be at the heart of Ahmad's criticisms of Rushdie. In the postmodern and post-colonial era, he argues, intellectuals in the capitalist, developed nations of the West have all too readily embraced a pseudo-radicalism, the faded reflection of a past struggle that can now be used to avoid facing the necessity of new struggles.

Ahmad identifies the chief manifestation of this process as the development and growth of the academic study of Third World Literature. He argues that, for example, this development meant that the teaching of Black and African literatures in American universities that had been the achievement of the Civil Rights movements of the 1960s could later be assimilated into the teaching of a new, homogenous 'Third World Literature', 'pushing the focus of thought not into the future but into the past'.[14]

It is as a prominent part of this newly canonised and homogenised 'Third World Literature' that Ahmad insists on situating Rushdie's texts. If the creation of this particular area of study is itself to be seen as a post-colonial, late capitalist ideological manoeuvre, as Ahmad indicates, then it should come as no surprise to find that the ideology critique that he offers of Rushdie's *Shame* should take the form of 'a *symptomatic* reading of an ideological location which makes it possible for Rushdie to partake, equally, of the postmodernist moment and the counter-canon of "Third World Literature"' (*IT*, p. 125). For Ahmad, the two are inextricably entwined, so that no matter how focused on 'Third World' matters and the experience of (de)colonisation such newly canonised texts might be, they remain abundantly complicit with the forms of reading currently favoured by what Ahmad calls 'the metropolitan critical avant-garde'. 'Third World Literature' here takes on the appearance of another form of cultural colonisation, though one that is more overtly bourgeois capitalist than nationalist in origin.

Rushdie's prominence within this canon is, for Ahmad, a result of the extent to which his texts are appropriable to a bourgeois, predominantly Western intelligentsia. As Ahmad sees it, this ideological complicity is betrayed through Rushdie's texts' own postmodernist qualities. The emphasis Rushdie places on ideas of cultural eclecticism and the experience of migrancy, in particular, is thus to be interpreted as the celebration of a postmodern cultural condition, a further reflection of the reification of culture into so many consumerist choices. In his essay 'The Location of *Brazil*' Rushdie describes the effect of migrancy on the construction of the individual subject in terms that might, from Ahmad's perspective, be interpreted as a form of escapism from the complexities and political intensities of specific historical and cultural experiences:

> The effect of mass migrations has been the creation of radically new types of human being: people who root themselves in ideas rather than places, in memories as much as in material things; people who have been obliged to define themselves – because they are so defined by others – by their otherness; people in whose deepest selves strange fusions occur, unprecedented unions between what they were and where they find themselves. The migrant suspects reality: having experienced several ways of being, he understands their illusory nature. To see things plainly, you have to cross a frontier.[15]

This notion of migrancy and the simultaneous elevation of the status of the migrant himself are central to Rushdie's writing. But in the centrality of these themes and in the wide-ranging cultural eclecticism by which they are given formal expression Ahmad sees echoes, intentional or not, of some of Rushdie's Anglo-American literary predecessors. These echoes incite perhaps his most caustic remarks:

> How very enchanting, I have often thought, Rushdie's kind of imagination must be for that whole range of readers who have been brought up on the peculiar 'universalism' of *The Waste Land* (the 'Hindu' tradition appropriated by an Anglo-American consciousness on its way to Anglican conversion, through the agency of Orientalist scholarship) and the 'world culture' of Pound's *Cantos* (the sages of Ancient China jostling with the princely notables of Renaissance Italy, with Homer and Cavalcanti in between, all in the service of a political vision framed by Mussolini's fascism). One did not have to belong, one could simply float, effortlessly, through a supermarket of packaged and commodified cultures, ready to be consumed. (*IT*, p. 128)

Market ideology is here explicitly associated with the imperial, colonising mentality. In the era of High Modernism, however, this 'sense of cultural excess' is accompanied by the artist's sense of alienation, itself the result of capitalist reification. 'In none of the major modernists', writes Ahmad, 'was the idea of a fragmented self, or the accompanying sense of unbelonging, ever a source of great comfort; it came, usually, with a sense of recoiling, even some terror' (*IT*, p. 129). For Ahmad, it is this second aspect that is conspicuously absent in postmodernism:

> The terrors of High Modernism at the prospect of inner frag-
> mentation and social disconnection have now been stripped, in
> . . . post-modernism, of their tragic edge, pushing that experi-
> ence of loss, instead, in a celebratory direction; the idea of
> belonging is itself seen now as a bad faith, a mere '*myth* of
> origins', a truth effect produced by the Enlightenment's 'meta-
> physics of presence'. (*IT*, p. 129)

It seems to me that this description of postmodernism cannot realistically be applied to Rushdie's fiction (for reasons to be discussed later). But for now we need only note that Ahmad suggests the similarity of this intellectual migrancy to the supposed '*excess* of belongings' of multinational or transnational firms, whose countries of origin, whither the profits are speedily transported, are depicted as entirely irrelevant. Ahmad is here, of course, employing a rather crude reflectionist model of the relation of literary form to economic forces in order to identify this feature of Rushdie's writing principally as an ideological expression of late capitalism.

It is not only in the celebration of 'migrancy' that Ahmad depicts Rushdie's work as ideologically saturated. Ahmad claims that the social world dramatised in *Shame* is one in which political resistance is impossible; such, he continues, is the prevalent political temper of all Rushdie's writing. Using an argument similar to that which Rushdie himself applies to George Orwell's *1984* in 'Outside the Whale', he insists that the severity of the limitations of Rushdie's political vision in *Shame* is such that it bespeaks of a fundamental flaw in the novelist's understanding and portrayal of social relations, and that this has implications for Rushdie's work way beyond the specific instance of *Shame*.

Ahmad confronts *Shame* with two accusations: first, the drama of the ruling classes is accorded an undue and misleading representative function; and secondly, the sole members of an oppressed or socially excluded group to be portrayed in the novel – the women – are shown to be incapable of ever transforming their social status. As we shall see, these two principal complaints are complemented by a number of additional points – in particular, the choice of metaphors with which Rushdie represents the effect on the women of their subjugation at the hands of patriarchal society – but it is on the basis of these two criticisms that Ahmad's case against *Shame* must stand or fall.

Though distinct in themselves, these two points of criticism outlined above are of course intimately related to the earlier critique of 'migrancy'. Ahmad refers to the passages in *Shame* in which Rushdie appears to be directly assuming the narrative voice in order both to describe and to justify his narrative and structural techniques. In one of these passages Rushdie writes:

> Although I have known Pakistan for a long time, I have never lived there for longer than six months at a stretch . . . I have learned Pakistan by slices . . . however I choose to write about over there, I am forced to reflect that in fragments of broken mirrors . . . I must reconcile myself to the inevitability of the missing bits.[16]

The fact that Rushdie can have only a migrant's eye-view is used to justify the limited scope of the society to be depicted in the novel; it is, as it were, the defining feature of Rushdie's own 'geometry', by which he draws, in a Jamesian sense, the enclosed circle of relations that the novel is to include. It is with the nature of the political vision that is to result from Rushdie's 'geometry', from his migrant's perspective, that Ahmad takes issue.

The problem for him is really the ease with which the novel's 'missing bits' can be ignored:

> If one has 'known Pakistan for a long time' and yet, because of circumstance, 'learned' it only 'by slices', the question naturally arises: *which* slices has one chosen to 'learn'? For, if we do not *choose* our own 'bits' of reality, those 'bits' will then be chosen for us by our class origin, our jobs, the circuits of our friendships and desires, our ways of spending our leisure time, our literary predilections, our political affiliations – or lack of them. There are no neutral 'bits', not even of not-knowing. (*IT*, p. 138)

Rushdie, claims Ahmad, is one whose class origin has allowed him tremendous insight into 'the history of the corruptions and criminalities of Pakistani rulers', but little else. To this limited spectrum of familiarity is added the postmodernist celebration of the migrant's perspective, the untroubled learning 'by slices' that leads to what for Ahmad is an unacceptable and unearned elevation of the experiences of one segment of society to representative status.

In his search for some centre of resistance to this enclosed state apparatus, Ahmad turns to Rushdie's representation of female characters. The absence of any male figures who might represent 'the oppressed and oppositional strata' is so complete, he writes, that it is only in the female characters, and quite particularly in the person of Sufiya Zinobia, that we might realistically hope to find 'some determinate energies of an emancipatory project'. Ahmad's quest is a forlorn and ultimately embittering one. It is not that the novel's women are passive victims, quietly accepting their allotted social roles. Rather, Ahmad identifies what is perhaps a more sinister tendency: at no point is such resistance shown to be capable of effecting a productive transformation; instead, it breeds only a savage and destructive violence. Women are depicted as grotesque victims who come to resemble more and more a series of misogynist stereotypes. The sexless Arjumand, known as the 'Virgin Ironpants', is joined in this way to her opposite, Sufiya Zinobia, who has become, for Ahmad, 'the oldest of the misogynist myths: the virgin who is really a vampire, the irresistible temptress who seduces men in order to kill them, not an object of male manipulation but a devourer of hapless men' (*IT*, p. 148). This is too much for Ahmad to take; here, he suspects, is to be found a disregard – even, intellectual contempt – for the basic longing to create a better life. Rushdie's is, he states, an Orwellian vision, complete with all the lovelessness, 'permanence and pervasiveness of betrayal' and conviction that resistance can only exacerbate one's torments that, for many Marxist critics, is the hallmark of postmodernist, anti-utopian ideology.

It seems to me that criticisms of the Three Worlds Theory and of the unambivalent celebration of 'migrancy' are both apposite and necessary. Likewise, the way in which Ahmad demonstrates how these features lead logically, in *Shame*, to the abandonment of faith in the very possibility of an 'emancipatory project' offers a fairly impressive example of how the hidden ideological threads of a text can be teased out for analysis and critique. But when Ahmad attempts to broaden the relevance of his critique – which adopts a consistent Lukácsian perspective – to all Rushdie's writing, up to and including *The Satanic Verses*, the limitations of his analysis become more and more apparent.

Rushdie and Orientalism

There is one other crucial point to be made in terms of the ideological elements of Rushdie's work (and perhaps of *The Satanic Verses* in particular). It is important to identify the extent to which Rushdie's writing seems unable to escape the discourse of Orientalism. Ahmad draws attention to the claim made by the narrator of *Shame* that his novel is to be his 'last words on the East',[17] a claim that assumes, as the Orientalists of the Western Imperialist powers have always done, that there is a homogenous entity called the East (or 'the Orient') about which it might be possible to say a few 'last words'. In Saleem Sinai's introduction of his 'grandfather', too, we find something of a flirtation with Orientalist discourses:

> One Kashmiri morning in the early spring of 1915, my grand-father Aadam Aziz hit his nose against a frost-hardened tussock of earth while attempting to pray. Three drops of blood plopped out of his left nostril, hardened instantly in the brittle air and lay before his eyes on the prayer-mat, transformed into rubies. Lurching back until he knelt with his head once more upright, he found that the tears which had sprung to his eyes had solidified, too; and at that moment, as he brushed diamonds contemptuously from his lashes, he resolved never again to kiss earth for any god or man. This decision, however, made a hole in him, a vacancy in a vital inner chamber, leaving him vulner-able to women and history. Unaware of this at first, despite his recently completed medical training, he stood up, rolled the prayer-mat into a thick cheroot, and holding it under his right arm surveyed the valley through clear, diamond-free eyes.[18]

It is important to note the way in which this family history – which is to run parallel to a national history – begins with a loss of faith. However, the expression of this preference for doubt remains itself in some sense ambivalent. The 'grandfather' who loses his faith is called Dr Aziz, a name borrowed from E. M. Forster's *A Passage to India* (1924). In fact, Rushdie's representa-tions lean quite heavily on the literature of Imperialism, on Western, Imperial representations of India.[19] The religious doubt that Aadam Aziz experiences is, then, also associated with the forces of Empire and European Enlightenment. (For example, much is made of his scientific training, his stay in Europe and his European friends.) The problematic notion of migrancy, noted above in relation to Ahmad's critique, is thus connected to a further problem of ideological representation.

It is precisely the question of the reflection in *The Satanic Verses* of Orientalist attitudes towards Islamic culture and history that Edward Said identifies as the principal objection to the novel in Muslim circles:

> Why must a Moslem, who could be defending and sympathetically interpreting us, now represent us so roughly, so expertly and so disrespectfully to an audience already primed to excoriate our traditions, reality, history, religion, language, and origin? Why, in other words, must a member of our culture join the legions of Orientalists in Orientalizing Islam so radically and unfairly?[20]

Probably no one has written as extensively and perceptively on questions of Orientalist ideology as has Said. However, when we look at how he has defined Orientalism, it is clear how ill-suited to *The Satanic Verses* such descriptions are; it is as though (to borrow a metaphor from *Shame*) *The Satanic Verses* were to exist at a slight angle to Orientalist practice, neither quite fitting in nor fully divorced. Take, for example, Said's insistence on the Orientalist's exteriority to 'the Orient'. The Orientalist, he writes, 'is never concerned with the Orient except as the first cause of what he says'. He continues: 'What he says and writes, by virtue of the fact that it is said or written, is meant to indicate that the Orientalist is outside the Orient, both as an existential and as a moral fact.'[21] Such exteriority clearly does not apply to Rushdie himself who, as a migrant, can be confidently defined neither as outside nor as within; the basic categories on which Said's definition of Orientalism depends do not somehow seem appropriate to Rushdie's situation. In fact, the relation of *The Satanic Verses* to Orientalist ideology can better be understood in terms of the novel's exploration, through the dramatised predicaments of its characters, of what Said identifies as 'the main intellectual issue raised by orientalism': 'Can one divide human reality, as indeed human reality seems to be genuinely divided, into clearly different cultures, histories, traditions, societies, even races, and survive the consequences humanly?'[22]

In the context of situating these novels as narrative 'explorations', it might also be useful to view Rushdie's fiction (and particularly *Midnight's Children*) in relation to the genre of the 'Historical Novel', first fully developed by Sir Walter Scott in the early nineteenth century. Georg Lukács, in his study *The Histor-ical Novel*, argues that this is a form of writing that can appear only when a 'rational' (that is, historical) understanding of society, society seen as the product of human agency, has displaced the 'irrational' view of society as Divinely ordered. In Lukács's read-ing, the historians of the mid to late eighteenth century laid the ideological groundwork for the French Revolution; and the experi-ence of the French Revolution in turn helped pave the way for the historical novels of Scott.[23] Rushdie's fiction, though, attempts to absorb that genre, to offer – simultaneously – a critique and a reworked expression of it. Thus, *Midnight's Children* might be seen as quite a good example of Hutcheon's genre of 'historiographic metafiction'. These are novels which *are* historical novels and yet make quite overt their differences from the more traditional (and, quite crucially, European) examples of the genre; particularly in terms of their representation of the irrational, the magical. In the same way that the secular rationalism of Aadam Aziz is held slightly suspect, the fantastical elements of Rushdie's fiction allow it both to associate itself with, and maintain a form of critical distance from, the 'Historical Novel' of nineteenth-century European, imperial cultures. Thus, it is as critical explorations rather than as mere reflections that both *Midnight's Children* and *The Satanic Verses* demand to be read. It is important to acknowl-edge the existence in these novels of elements that are perhaps oppositional to those ideological aspects that we have thus far noted (with reference to both Ahmad and Said).

The sort of oppositional, anti-ideological (and, yes, even post-modern) reading of the novel that I am suggesting is one that involves an acceptance that *The Satanic Verses* offers representa-tions of not only Islamic but also of Western, late capitalist society. Sara Suleri's essay 'Contraband Histories: Salman Rushdie and the Embodiment of Blasphemy' is of particular interest in this regard, as it proposes a dialectical reversal of the arguments of those who have attacked the novel as a blasphemous and deeply offensive attack on the Islamic faith launched by the culture industry of a decadent, faithless West. Suleri reads the novel, instead, in terms of its opposition to postmodernist rather than Islamic culture. 'The author well knows that faith is obsolete to its discourse', she writes, 'but must struggle to explain why the betrayal of faith should be so necessary to an unbelieving, postmodern narra-tive.'[24] Rather than a disavowal or mockery of religious belief, a narrative demonstration of postmodern incredulity towards meta-narratives, *The Satanic Verses* is, she claims, 'a deeply Islamic book' about the nature and even possibility of blasphemy in the postmodernist, late capitalist West. Such a reading, of course, turns upside down the usual assumptions made about the book:

> If one of the integral concerns of the text is the question of how blasphemy can be articulated in a secular world, the term *blasphemy* itself must be reread as a gesture of reconciliation toward the idea of belief rather than as the insult that it is commonly deemed to be.[25]

We are here offered *The Satanic Verses* as betrayer of the postmodernist anti-faith, as an act of apostasy from contemporary secularism.

Suleri's interpretation seems to me misleading only in its lack of appreciation of the extent to which Rushdie's text is undoubtedly ideologically complicit. The reading of the novel that she provides is a welcome and necessary rejoinder that posits the text as other or more than mere ideology and yet takes some account of the cultural and historical forces at work in the production of the text. Nevertheless, this is ultimately as limited an understanding of the novel as that implicit in Aijaz Ahmad's more general criticisms of Rushdie's writing. What is needed instead, is an exploration of both the ideological and the utopian elements of the text, and a historicising analysis of their dialectical conflict. The following reflections on *The Satanic Verses* are an attempt to do precisely that.

'No Place like Home': Postmodern Politics and The Satanic Verses

In 1992 Rushdie published a little book on *The Wizard of Oz*. Though clearly a fan of the film, he is critical of what he sees as a contrived and politically conservative conclusion, a conclusion which, he claims, is 'untrue to the film's anarchic spirit'.[26] The ending, of course, is Dorothy's final realisation that it's a mistake to want to go 'over the rainbow', that the grass is never greener, that there is 'no place like home' (even if home happens to be Kansas in black-and-white). Rushdie asks:

> How does it come about, at the close of this radical and enabling film, which teaches us in the least didactic way possible to build on what we have, to make the best of ourselves, that we are given this conservative little homily? Are we to believe that

Dorothy has learned no more on her journey than that she
didn't need to make such a journey in the first place? Must
we accept that she now accepts the limitations of her home life,
and agrees that the things she doesn't have there are no loss to
her? *'Is that right?'* Well, excuse *me*, Glinda, but is it hell. (*WO*,
pp. 56–7)

The abandonment of a determinate and fixed social and cultural
location – and, in particular, a point of social and cultural origin –
is also in Rushdie's work the abandonment of those collective
parameters of judgement, the inherited and fixed set of cultural
contexts, which such locations define for us.

What I want to explore is Rushdie's expression, in *The Satanic
Verses*, of a postmodern anti-foundationalism, the novel's renun-
ciation of *a priori* criteria for judgement. In particular, I'll be
arguing that *The Satanic Verses* represents – both on the page
and in its political significance – a crisis in legitimation.

The Satanic Verses is a novel about authority. Infamously, it is a
novel which questions, or asks us to rethink, aspects of religious
authority. The incident of the 'satanic verses' is only one example
of the novel's critique of the authenticity of religious revelation –
and therefore, of course, the legitimation of those judgements
reached in the name of a Divine or absolute authority. Similarly,
Rushdie satirises British state authority in his representations of
police violence and the desperate narratives concocted to legitimise it. Critics such as the Ayatollah Khomeini of Iran and Norman
Tebbit of Chingford proved equally attentive to these aspects of
Rushdie's work.

But the novel's principal site of authority is its narrator, the
voice that leads us through the teeming tales of political scepticism, religious doubt and suspicions of romantic infidelity. What
I'm about to argue is that, while *The Satanic Verses* dramatises
narratives which question forms of social and cultural authority,
Rushdie adopts a narrative perspective which integrates this thematic concern with the construction of authority into the novel's
structure itself.

It is this single narrative voice on whom we must rely, whose
intentions and motives we have to take into account; above all, it
is this voice whose origin we must first attempt to identify. 'Who
am I?' he asks us almost immediately, having described only the
start of Saladin and Gibreel's miraculous fall. It is a fairly pre-
sumptive question, suggesting a measure of self-importance, but
perhaps also hinting that his identity might affect our interpreta-

tion of the story to be told. 'Who else is there?' is not the most helpful of answers.

Hints of the narrator's identity are scattered throughout the text. The two questions I've just quoted indicate the possibility that the words we read are divine words, that the narrator is God. The novel's title, though, points towards a less exalted narrative authority: the Father of Lies himself, Satan or Shaitan. It is these two opposed possibilities with which the narrator continually teases us. Once Saladin and Gibreel have finally floated down to England, having fallen from heaven or been reborn of a big bang, the narrator pauses to comment on the event and on himself:

> I know the truth, obviously. I watched the whole thing. As to omnipresence and -potence, I'm making no claims at present, but I can manage this much, I hope. Chamcha willed it and Farishta did what was willed.
>   Which was the miracle worker?
>   Of what type – angelic, satanic – was Farishta's song?
>   Who am I?
>   Let's put it this way: who has the best tunes?[27]

A miracle, we are told, has taken place; but it is one that seems to have been produced by a song, unrecognised by its singer, whose 'type' – angelic or satanic – is uncertain. This miracle itself therefore becomes questionable, not as a narrated fact, but rather in terms of how we ought to react to it – with reverence? or with horror?

The situation becomes more complicated still when the narrator returns to his initial question about his identity. His answer this time is a clear pointer to his diabolic status, yet falls far short of outright confirmation. If he is Shaitan, as he seems to be hinting, we can presume that his purpose is one of mischief, that he intends to deceive us. Are the doubts that he plants in the reader's mind concerning the miracle and Gibreel's song an example of his mischief making? He may be trying to make us suspicious or doubtful of clear evidence of Divine power and compassion. The possibility that the narrator is the devil raises yet another question in relation to this first scene: is the entire account – the fall and the miracle, life lost and regain'd – a complete lie? As he reminds us himself, he is our only authority concerning this fantastic event.

If, though, the narrator is not Shaitan, what then? If he is God – he claims, after all, to be omniscient; he might not confirm his 'omnipresence and -potence', but he doesn't deny them – then perhaps his teasing questions can be seen either as tests of faith or as holy proddings to be wary of the wiles of the Deceitful One. The implications of either of these possible identities are open to analysis only when we presume, for the sake of hypothesis, that one of the two – first Shaitan, then God – can definitely be attributed to the narrator. But outwith the realms of hypothesis these elaborations tell us very little. It is the fate of the reader of *The Satanic Verses* to be never quite certain on the basis of which identity to hypothesise. Later in the novel, the narrator deigns to join the action himself. 'Gibreel Farishta saw God', we are told. '"Who are you?"' asks Gibreel. Thankfully, he isn't forced to suffer the hints and teases thrown our way with regard to precisely this same question: '"Ooparvala,"' he is told, '"The Fellow Upstairs."' At this stage, we can't yet be certain that Gibreel's apparition and the novel's narrator are indeed one and the same, but we are likely to harbour suspicions. '"How do I know you're not the other One"' answers the film star, '"Neechayvala, the guy from Underneath?"' Gibreel seems to have reached the same state of confusion as has the reader.

But has he? The story of Gibreel's encounter with the Fellow Upstairs (Who might, he suspects, be the Guy from Underneath) not only reflects our complicated encounter with the narrator, but is itself contained within it. Likewise, the narrator's claim to be the subject of Gibreel's interrogation might also be doubted. There are, then, the initial complications and ambiguities of the meeting with the apparition; added to these is the uncertainty over whether the narrator of the scene (who could be either God or Shaitan) really is the same figure who claims in that meeting to be God (but whom Gibreel suspects to be Shaitan); and encompassing all of these features of indeterminacy is the reader's abject inability to be confident of the narrator's degree of reliability or nature of intention concerning any point at all in his narration.

Gibreel Farishta loses his faith and blasphemes. The dreams that follow Gibreel's blasphemy have, we are told, a specific function: 'after he ate the pigs the retributions began, a nocturnal retribution, a punishment of dreams' (*SV*, p. 32). It is Gibreel's religious doubts that are to be dramatised in his dreaming mind and on the page. To be haunted by such dreams is, the narrator implies, the fate of those who turn away from God. Clearly, though, the dreams also serve another purpose: they suggest to the reader certain alternative and unorthodox reinterpretations of history.

The blasphemous stories recounted in Gibreel's dreams of

Jahilia can be seen as, at once, the psychological manifestations of
the actor's lack of faith (these concern both religious and romantic
attachments) *and*, if we presume for a moment that the narrator is
Shaitan, a deceptive misrepresentation of the origins of Islam,
intended to mislead the reader and tempt him or her to doubt,
like Gibreel, the absolute truth of religious faith. The contradictoriness of these two functions should come as no great surprise.
In either case, our interpretation of how we are to account for the
dreams' blasphemy must presuppose a stable, identifiable authority responsible for the dreams (whose motives and interests are
clearly definable) of precisely the type that is so markedly absent
in this novel. In other words, *The Satanic Verses* is supported by a
narrative structure that appears to lead the reader to make moral
or political evaluations of both narrated acts and those acts'
narration that are based on *a priori* assumptions about the nature
of the authority invoked as their justification (for example, if the
narrator is God, the dreams are a punishment; if Shaitan, they are
a blasphemous temptation). But that same narrative structure
simultaneously thwarts the reader's attempt to reach conclusions
on the basis of such assumptions by constructing the aporia of two
possible identities of the source of narrative authority that the
reader has been conditioned to accept as contradictory.

The fact that the dreams themselves, as well as the main
narrative which they punctuate, are explicitly concerned with
questions of how cultures or societies establish authoritative conventions of reverence and demonisation confronts readers with
yet another challenge to their understanding of, and reliance
upon, voices of authority. The mental contortions required of
any reader who, first struggling with the indeterminate theological
status (and, therefore, reliability) of the narrator, must then consider the political construction of the whole notion of the holy and
the blasphemous (and, therefore, the very validity of her or his
struggles at narratorial identification) are only to be imagined.

This impossibility of deciding conclusively whether the narrator is Shaitan or whether he is God, or even anything in between,
forces the reader of *The Satanic Verses*, I would argue, to give up
on the whole idea of making moral and political evaluations on the
basis of given or *a priori* responses to an identifiably responsible
authority – an idea that the novel itself provokes. The excessive
complexity of the construction of the identity and degree of
reliability of the novel's narrator leads to the futility and irrele-
vance of any attempt to interpret or analyse that narrative authority. We have to abandon the belief that by interrogating the

narrator's status and discovering the precise extent of his narrative manipulations we can reveal the true, hidden, unsullied
narrative. Thus the novel offers, it seems to me, a narrative
demonstration of postmodern anti-foundationalism.

This, though, leads to tremendous problems in terms of discussing the political significance of *The Satanic Verses*. Zygmunt
Bauman writes the following:

> It is perhaps debatable whether the philosophers of the modern
> era ever articulated to everybody's satisfaction the foundations
> of the objective superiority of Western rationality, logic, mor-
> ality, aesthetics, cultural precepts, rules of civilized life, etc. The
> fact is, however, that they never stopped looking for such an
> articulation and hardly ever ceased to believe that the search
> would bring – must bring – success. The postmodern period is
> distinguished by abandoning the search itself, having con-
> vinced itself of its futility. Instead, it tries to reconcile itself
> to a life under conditions of permanent and incurable uncer-
> tainty; a life in the presence of an unlimited quantity of com-
> peting forms of life, unable to prove their claims to be grounded
> in anything more solid and binding than their own historically
> shaped conventions.[28]

Rushdie's novel appears to enact precisely such a critique; and
would therefore seem to deny its readers ready recourse to a
legitimating narrative of Enlightenment rationality with which
to defend the novel from its fundamentalist, monotheistic critics.
The novel itself already suggests that such narratives, presuppos-
ing a liberal, democratic model of cultural expression, cannot be
assumed as universal criteria for judgement. Thomas Docherty
associates, I think astutely, this aspect of the novel's political
reception with Jean-François Lyotard's description of what he calls
a 'differand', 'a conflict between (at least) two parties, that cannot
be equitably resolved for lack of a rule of judgement applicable to
both arguments'.[29] In the case of *The Satanic Verses*, Docherty
argues:

> one side wishes to argue that the text contravenes one Islamic
> law, while the other side does not see that the text is to be
> judged by such law or only by such law. In [this example] we
> appear to lack a terrain on which to reach a consensus whose
> foundations are regarded as equally legitimate by both sides in
> the case.[30]

An enabling postmodern political defence of *The Satanic Verses,* a defence compatible with the politics of the novel itself, can neither define Rushdie's work as a totem of some abstract and automatically legitimating principle of 'free speech', nor, of course, accept its definition as a blasphemous tract (however it is then to be judged). Instead, it seems to me crucial to insist on the very *particularity* both of the novel itself and of the political circumstances during which the bans and the *fatwa* were announced. These are not reducible to those postures of general principle I've just described. The need for forms of 'human rights' and 'free speech' is created *in* the political situation itself, not accepted as an *a priori* rhetorical position since that rhetorical position is shown to have been historically complicit with a lack of adherence to precisely such values. *The Satanic Verses* creates a political world, both on and off the page, which can rely on no given criteria, no inherited legitimation, but whose values must be newly formulated, newly constructed in the light of particular and specific circumstances. *The Satanic Verses* is, after all, a novel about how newness enters the world. In his book on *The Wizard of Oz,* Rushdie turns finally to the series of sequels that Frank L. Baum wrote to the children's book from which the film was adapted. He notes that in the sixth book Auntie Em, Uncle Henry and Dorothy, despite those ties to the familiar and comforting world of Kansas, all eventually move to the Land of Oz:

> So Oz finally *became* home; the imagined world became the actual world, as it does for us all, because the truth is that once we have left our childhood places and started out to make up our lives, armed only with what we have and are, we understand that the real secret of the ruby slippers is not that 'there's no place like home', but rather that there is no longer any such place *as* home: except, of course, for the home we make, or the homes that are made for us, in Oz: which is anywhere, and everywhere, except the place from which we began.[31]

In conclusion, *The Satanic Verses* seems to me simultaneously to accept the postmodern fulfilment of Marx's description of capitalism's liberating and destructive power 'All that is solid melts into air; all that is holy is profaned' while insisting on the inescapable and endlessly repeated demand for the creation of political judgement and political solidarity, but judgement and solidarity here understood as within history and not as transcendent, transhistorical or reified concepts.

The Satanic Verses *and the New*

In an essay called 'Is Nothing Sacred?' Rushdie describes the role of literature in terms which explicitly identify it with some form of religious longing:

> What appears plain is that it will be a very long time before the peoples of Europe will accept any ideology that claims to have a complete, totalized explanation of the world. Religious faith, profound as it is, must surely remain a private matter. This rejection of totalized explanations is the modern condition. And this is where the novel, the form created to discuss the fragmentation of truth, comes in. . . . The elevation of the quest for the Grail over the Grail itself, the acceptance that all that is solid *has* melted into air, that reality and morality are not givens but imperfect human constructs, is the point from which fiction begins. This is what J.-F. Lyotard called, in 1979, *La Condition Postmoderne*. The challenge of literature is to start from this point, and still find a way of fulfilling our unaltered spiritual requirements.[32]

The desire to represent imaginatively something which might challenge a postmodern incredulity towards grand narratives seems to be one of the prime features of Rushdie's writing. We have just seen how, in *The Satanic Verses*, a narrative technique can be made to mimic the anti-foundationalist stance of the postmodern condition, short-circuiting the application of more conventional assumptions of narrative (un)reliability. I now want to look at some of the ways in which Rushdie's novel attempts to compensate for this by the depiction of characters coming to terms with a residual faith in utopian grand narratives, a desire to reconstruct some notion of the New.

The New, in *The Satanic Verses*, is asked two specific questions: 'What kind of idea are you?' and 'What kind of idea are you at the moment of triumph?' For the most part, the critical focus on Rushdie's interrogation of the New has been principally directed at his depiction of the origins of 'Submission', the fictional shadow of Islam. There are, though, at least two other exemplars of the New included in *The Satanic Verses*: Thatcherism and Marxism (though the latter is present not in its east European or Chinese variants – what Rushdie calls 'Actually Existing Socialism' – but in the form of the Communist Party of India (Marxist) which, as Aijaz Ahmad reminds us, was the first Communist Party to come

to power through democratic elections). 'Islam is, after all, one of
the greatest ideas that ever came into the world', says Rushdie. 'I
suppose that the next idea of that size would have been Marxism.'[33]
The claims of Thatcherism to the status of the New are not made
by Rushdie himself, as with the other two, but by one of the
characters of *The Satanic Verses*: Hal Valance, the 'personification
of philistine triumphalism'. 'What she wants', he tells Saladin
Chamcha, 'What she thinks she can fucking *achieve* – is literally
to invent a whole goddamn new middle class in this country. . . .
It's a bloody revolution. Newness coming into this country that's
stuffed full of fucking old *corpses*' (*SV*, p. 270). The novel, though,
is more concerned with the violence that Thatcherism brings – in
particular, the racially motivated violence of the security forces.
Valence is right: Thatcher's is 'a bloody revolution'; and if the
death of Dr Uhuru Simba is anything but the 'million-to-one shot'
that the police insist (and let's face it . . .), the prison cells at least,
if not the country itself, may well be 'stuffed full of fucking old
corpses'. The terms of Valance's description of Thatcherism provide unwitting hints of the carnage that its neo-imperialist delusions eventually unleash.

But if Thatcherism, with its repressiveness and its violence, is
an example of the New, what does this say of the novel's social
and political vision? It might be tempting to see this as a continuation into *The Satanic Verses* of that postmodern despair, the
ideological insistence on the inescapability of violence and
repression, that Ahmad points to in *Shame*. But to do so would
be wrong. Just as Saladin's manipulation of Gibreel is only 'the
echo of tragedy', a pale and distorted imitation of Iago's manipulation of Othello, Thatcherism is a version of the New that is
perfectly attuned to 'our degraded, imitative times' (*SV*, p. 424).
In fact, it is only a pseudo-Novum, an appropriation by conservative and reactionary forces of the rhetoric of the New for
ideological purposes. What *The Satanic Verses* offers in response
to this is the embodiment of a vision of the possibility of the
New in the novel itself.

Rushdie writes:

> *The Satanic Verses* celebrates hybridity, impurity, intermin-
> gling, the transformation that comes of new and unexpected
> combinations of human beings, cultures, ideas, politics, movies,
> songs. It rejoices in mongrelization and fears the absolutism of
> the Pure. *Melange*, hotchpotch, a bit of this and a bit of that is
> *how newness enters the world*, and I have tried to embrace it. *The*

Satanic Verses is for change-by-fusion, change-by-conjoining. It is a love-song to our mongrel selves.[34]

Of course, this vision of transformation remains open to the charge made by Aijaz Ahmad that such faith in cultural mutation and hybridisation is merely a symptom of the assimilation into late capitalist culture of the post-colonial bourgeoisie, in which he squarely situates Rushdie. Yet there is surely something here beyond the purely ideological. Edward Said writes that

> there is no pure, unsullied essence to which some of us can return, whether that essence is pure Islam, pure Christianity, pure Judaism or Easternism, Americanism, Westernism. Rushdie's work is not just *about* the mixture, it *is* that mixture itself.[35]

Said, too, can be identified as part of that bourgeoisie for which Ahmad demonstrates such distaste, but the point that he and Rushdie are making here cannot be so easily dismissed. It would be ridiculous to pretend that the mass migrations to which Rushdie refers above did not take place. Moreover, this is not a phenomenon that exclusively affected the upper-middle class; the young people who, in *The Satanic Verses*, visit the Hot Wax nightclub represent a generation of young British blacks and Asians who actually exist. But the novel's celebration of mutation refers also to Indian society, at least insofar as it is expressed through the views of Zeeny Vakil: 'for was not the entire national culture based on the principle of borrowing whatever clothes seemed to fit, Aryan, Mughal, British, take-the-best-and-leave-the-rest?' (*SV*, p. 52). Here, too, a valid point is being made, which does not seek to elevate to representative status the experiences of a privileged, cosmopolitan intelligentsia.

The New, though, cannot be portrayed in terms of its actual, concrete realisation. Instead, as Adorno explains, it can only be properly depicted as a longing for that which is absent:

> the new is the longing for the new, not the new itself. This is the curse of everything new. Being a negative of the old, the new is subservient to the old while considering itself to be Utopian. One of the crucial antinomies of art today is that it wants to be and must be squarely Utopian, as social reality increasingly impedes Utopia, while at the same time it should not be Utopian so as not to be found guilty of administering comfort and illusion.[36]

So the aesthetic of the New is discovered not in the New itself but in its anticipation. For that reason, *The Satanic Verses* must unmask its utopian or transcendent moments as illusory, while simultaneously insisting on the urge to which such illusions are a response. The emphasis in the novel is not, then, so much on the achievements and rewards of the New as on the struggle that 'the longing for the new' entails. More specifically, *The Satanic Verses* investigates and, as Said notes, itself embodies the struggle even to envisage or to anticipate a New, a utopian possibility, that is not merely a late capitalist ideological appropriation of a utopian discourse.

As a number of critics have noted, and as Rushdie himself has repeatedly insisted, *The Satanic Verses* is a novel preoccupied by questions of race and gender.[37] The treatment of Saladin Chamcha at the hands of the police and immigration authorities is only one of the novel's more overt examples of the racist abuse which, it suggests, is a common feature of the experiences of Britain's non-white population. Rushdie's novel concentrates perhaps less on the physical and verbal abuse to which the characters are inter-mittently subjected than on the psychological effect of such abuse, a point to which we shall later return. It is enough for the moment, though, simply to acknowledge the fact that *The Satanic Verses* attempts to offer some indication of the sense of continual conflict, both psychological and physical, that Rushdie identifies with the predicament or situation of Asians and blacks in Britain.

The treatment of questions of gender in the novel is a little more unusual. Much of the novel's engagement with these issues has hitherto been obscured by attacks on two of the chapters in which they are explored most persistently – 'Mahound' and 'Return to Jahilia' – as either Orientalist or 'blasphemous'. The reimagining of early Islamic history through the dreams of Gibreel Farishta deliberately foregrounds the position allocated to women in Islamic culture. Rushdie is well aware of the constructedness of authority, and it is the conspicuousness of that awareness which makes some scenes appear so shocking. Stripped of the glow of a natural, God-given authority, some of the actions of the most esteemed figures in religious history appear rather less admirable:

In ancient time the patriarch Ibrahim came into this valley with Hagar and Ismail, their son. Here, in this waterless wilderness, he abandoned her. She asked him, can this be God's will? He replied, it is. And left, the bastard. From the beginning men used God to justify the unjustifiable. (*SV,* p. 95)

Likewise, Mahound's eventual retraction of 'the satanic verses' is based, at least in part, on the gender of the deities in question: '"Shall He have daughters and you sons?" Mahound recites. "That would be a fine division!"' (SV, p. 124). From this thinking, suggests Rushdie, sprout those Islamic laws which allow a widow to inherit only an eighth of her husband's estate, which give to sons twice as much inheritance as to daughters, and which, in legal matters, allocate to the evidence of female witnesses only half the worth of male witnesses.[38] To deny the validity of such a critique by dismissing those chapters as merely Orientalist is to construct a hierarchy of ideological repression that is interesting in itself.

It is not necessary to chronicle here the further examples of this sort to be found in Gibreel's dreams of Jahilia – Rushdie's own 'In Good Faith' does this – but it is worth insisting equally on the critique that *The Satanic Verses* offers of the permeation of British culture by similarly patriarchal values and assumptions. In this respect, both Pamela Lovelace and Allie Cone assume almost representative roles. The name of Chamcha's wife, with its echoes of Richardsonian assumptions of female sexuality, indicates the complicity of the British literary and cultural tradition in the male colonisation of female sexuality and the male definition of a woman's 'place' in society.[39] The Orientalist mentality that Edward Said identifies in Marx's comment, 'They cannot represent themselves; they must be represented', might here be seen in parallel with the cultural structures of sexism that allow women, too, to be represented and defined.

The power of these culturally enforced gender assumptions is demonstrated in the predicament of Allie Cone, who must painfully guard the secret of her fallen arches because such a disclosure would tarnish her 'ice-queen' image. The most difficult and significant part of her ascent of Mount Everest, the fact that she did it while suffering excruciating pain, must therefore remain hidden, while the fact that she did it *as a woman* (and a good-looking one at that!) is the source of her celebrity and fortune. Her gender rather than her achievement remains her most defining feature. Perhaps even more extreme, though, is the case of Baby, Hal Valance's wife. This 'wasted child', we are told, is 'maybe one third' Valance's age; her 'spectral look' is the perfect visual contrast to the body of her husband, which, he confesses, is '"in training to be Orson Welles"'. As she has been stripped of any possible sense of worth or identity, it should come as no surprise that Chamcha 'couldn't remember the infant's name'.

The struggle against dominant social forces is also key to the tale of Mahound and the establishment of *Submission*. In this respect, the wrestling bouts in which Mahound and Gibreel engage on the mountain assume a symbolic significance – though this is equally as true for Gibreel as it is for Mahound. It is the intensity of the struggle that the prophet must undergo, the constant mockery and vilification, that tempts him to reach a compromise: '"Sometimes I think I must make it easier for the people to believe"', he says (*SV*, p. 106). The point, though, is that he doesn't. Like the Christ of Dostoevsky's 'The Grand Inquisitor', Mahound ultimately refuses to cut the deals that might make his creed seem more attractive. His revolution remains one 'of water-carriers, immigrants and slaves' because he is unwilling to reach a business-like compromise with the leader of Jahilia's conservatives, the Grandee. Mahound's project, then, shares certain affinities with that of Rushdie in *The Satanic Verses*: both remain tied to ideological forms (Mahound, after all, is a businessman, and one who is less than attuned to notions of gender equality); but both are also sincerely attempting to offer an alternative vision to the values and conditions of the present, and are therefore potentially radical or utopian.

It should not be forgotten, though, that the struggles of Mahound are framed within, and are part of, the psychological turmoil experienced by Gibreel Farishta. Without necessarily ascribing to the dreams some form of didactic, moral (or immoral) intent, which would have to rely on a clear understanding of the intentions of the narrator, it nonetheless remains important to acknowledge them as Gibreel's unconscious attempt to discover a reconstituted religious or transcendent sense, to fill up the god-shaped void. As such, the struggle of Gibreel's that is manifested in these dreams is, even more than is the struggle of Mahound, a reflection of Rushdie's own wrestlings with ideological entrapment and the utopian urge. What Gibreel's dreams demonstrate, perhaps above all else, is the difficulty of grasping a vision of the transcendent that is unsullied by predominant social forces.

The tales of the two prophets, Mahound and Ayesha, of whom Gibreel dreams are clearly inspired by a combination of social forces and more private experiences and traumas. Early in the novel, we are told that '[f]rom his mother Naima Najmuddin he [Gibreel] heard a great many stories of the Prophet, and if inaccuracies had crept into her version he wasn't interested in knowing what they were' (*SV*, p. 22). At the start of his career, before fame had chosen to alight upon him, Gibreel would sit in his room and study tales of metamorphosis, the alleged incident of the satanic verses, 'and the surrealism of the newspapers, in which butterflies could fly into young girls' mouths, asking to be consumed' (*SV*, p. 24). All of these experiences are to play their part in the dreamy torment that the novel describes. Gibreel's amatory anxieties regarding the fidelity of Allie also have a formative influence. Malise Ruthven, in *A Satanic Affair*, points to the significance of the name of the mountain on which Mahound receives his revelations: Mount Cone, he writes:

> The place of revelation bears the name of the beloved. The collapse of religious certainty symbolised by the affair of the Satanic Verses mirrors the betrayal experiences by Gibreel in his waking life, as he becomes increasingly, obsessively jealous.[40]

Perhaps most of all, though, Gibreel's religious dreams are shaped by the movies. In *Midnight's Children*, Saleem Sinai tells of Mary Pereira's account to a young priest of the violent exploits of Joe D'Costa. He begins to speculate on the priest's reactions:

> Will he, in fact, ask Mary for Joseph's address, and then reveal . . . In short, would this bishop-ridden, stomach-churned young father have behaved like, or unlike, Montgomery Clift in *I Confess*? (Watching it some years ago at the New Empire Cinema, I couldn't decide.) (*MC*, p. 105)

Gibreel, the film star, has reached a significantly more advanced state than Saleem; he even *dreams* cinematically. It is perhaps strange that the films into which the dreams are later developed turn out to be so unsuccessful, considering that they were essentially films to begin with. The experience of dreaming is described as similar to that of watching or making a film. Sometimes, we are told, Gibreel's point of view is 'that of the camera and at other moments, spectator':

> mostly he sits up on Mount Cone like a paying customer in the dress circle, and Jahilia is his silver screen. He watches and weighs up the action like any movie fan, enjoys the fights infidelities moral crises, but there aren't enough girls for a real hit, man, and where are the goddamn songs? (*SV*, p. 108)

The manifestations of Gibreel's crisis of faith take on their very form from the culture industry that has contributed to that crisis. It is not particularly surprising that Gibreel's religious visions are so degraded, even trashy or that he should be taken over so completely by delusions of grandeur, given the nature of the environment in which his religious sense and his sense of self have been shaped: Greta Garbo and Grace Kelly ('Gracekali') are described as goddesses; Gibreel's own fame gains him the social status of the mock-divine; he wins that fame by impersonating gods in 'the theological movies'.

What Rushdie expresses through the plight of Gibreel is the tragic struggle to discover a vision of the New that is not entirely formed by the predominant social forces of the present – in the case of Gibreel, this being the pervasiveness in his immediate environment of 'Bollywood' kitsch. Here, as I have said, is a reflection of Rushdie's own artistic struggle in *The Satanic Verses*. Gore Vidal's novel *Live from Golgotha* replays the scene of Christ's crucifixion as though it were a television 'event'. This, suggests Vidal, is what TV evangelists have done to the Christian myths; taken over and repackaged by the culture industry, this is what those myths have become. The dream sequences of *The Satanic Verses* tell us something similar with regard to the Indian movie industry and the origins of Islam.

Were Aijaz Ahmad rather more consistent, he might well have acknowledged precisely this point. Defending Dante from the onslaughts of Edward Said, he insists on the need to interpret the *Inferno* with an awareness of the historical conditions at work in the production of the text. 'The literary-critical point I am making', he writes, 'is that one cannot read the passage about Muhammad outside this whole range of enormous complexity' (*IT*, p. 189). Yet, referring to *The Satanic Verses*, Ahmad writes of 'the book's heresy and its direct representation of the Prophet of Islam and his family in the most vulgar fashion possible' (*IT*, p. 214) while almost completely ignoring those literary and historical complexities on which he has previously placed such emphasis. Rushdie's novel is pictured in relation to its historical moment only to the extent that it can be shown to collude with the Orientalizing tendency in the British cultural sphere. This is inadequate. The ideological location from which Rushdie writes, and the extent to which it forms and limits imaginative possibilities, gradually becomes the subject of his writing.

Imagining Utopia: The Land of Oz

Ernst Bloch, pursuing the subject of art's utopian function,[41] writes of art and literature as the 'not-yet-conscious', by which he means that art is able to embody a 'productive presentiment' that is 'openly aware of itself, particularly as something not-yet-conscious'.[42] As Bloch continues his explication of art as the not-yet-conscious, his terms of description come more and more to resemble the terms that I have been using to analyse the coming to self-consciousness of the longing for the New in *The Satanic Verses*:

> The look forward becomes even more powerful the brighter it becomes aware of itself. . . . The not-yet-conscious itself has to become *conscious* of its own doings; it must come to *know* its contents as restraint and revelation. And thus the point is reached where hope, in particular, the true effect of expectation in the dream forward, not only occurs as an emotion that merely exists by itself, but is *conscious and known* as the *utopian function*.[43]

The 'not-yet-conscious' becomes conscious of itself, then, not as something which can presently be realised, but as what Bloch calls the 'anticipatory illumination' (*Vor-Schein*), the imaginative force that might reform consciousness in such a way that the existing facts of the present can be carried 'toward their future potentiality of the otherness, of their better condition in an anticipatory way'.[44]

This 'anticipatory illumination', offered by art, that might foreshadow a form of cultural and political praxis is at the very heart of what Rushdie attempts to achieve as an artist. In a sense, the god-shaped hole that permeates Rushdie's fiction, both thematically and structurally, can be properly filled only by those same works of fiction themselves, and then only as the anticipatory illumination of a liberating potentiality. When Rushdie asks,

> Can art be the third principle that mediates between the material and spiritual worlds; might it, by 'swallowing' both worlds, offer us something new – something that might even be called a secular definition of transcendence?[45]

it seems to me that he is groping towards a definition of the possibilities of art that is similar to Bloch's, and that seeks to situate in the place now vacated by faith in an Absolute an imaginative demonstration of the future potentiality of radical, social transformation. That it is the tragic misfortune, yet dialectical necessity, of such a demonstration that it must nonetheless remain tied in some way to the ideological needs of the present is a point that we also have to bear in mind.

The creation of an independent India, as accounted for by Saleem Sinai in *Midnight's Children*, is a result of just such a transformation of reality by the powers of the imagination. India, he tells us, is 'a mythical land, a country which would never exist except by the efforts of a phenomenal collective will – except in a dream we all agreed to dream' (*MC*, p. 112). In this respect, the example of Günter Grass is quite crucial. Aijaz Ahmad points to Rushdie's essay on Grass as evidence of his lack of faith in the possibility of a utopian transformation. Here is Rushdie on Grass's novel *The Meeting at Telgte*:

> Grass's subject is how German writers responded to ruination; how, after Hitler, German pens re-wrote Genesis to read: After the end was the word. How they tore their language down and rebuilt it anew; how they used words to assault, excoriate, accept, encompass and regenerate; how the phoenix poked its beak out of the fire.[46]

Surely, what this tells us of Rushdie's response to Grass's writing is that it is primarily a response to the regenerative powers of art, to its capacity to make reality anew. When Ahmad writes of the despair that is evident in the phrase 'night is drawing in', he forgets to temper his judgement with the acknowledgement that Rushdie sees Grass's great achievement in somehow transforming that gloomy darkness into something that is luminous and, above all, hopeful. In fact, he forgets the very first sentence of *The Satanic Verses* itself: '"To be born again," sang Gibreel Farishta tumbling from the heavens, "first you have to die"' (*SV*, p. 3).

The Satanic Verses, like the novels of Grass, reflects not only its author's desire to see a transformed social realm, but also his belief that the powers of the imagination, as exercised through the novel's creation and through its interaction with its readers, have a necessary and significant part to play in that process of transformation and liberation. Rushdie has acknowledged the influence on the novel of Mikhail Bulgakov's *The Master and Margarita*, in which, he says, 'the Devil descends upon Moscow and wreaks havoc upon the corrupt, materialist, decadent inhabitants and turns out, by the end, not to be such a bad chap after all'.[47] Bulgakov's novel is also significant, and clearly influential, in another way. As the book draws to an end, the demonic Woland points out to the Master, who is a writer, that Pontius Pilate, a character in the Master's book, is seated forlornly in his garden, hoping to see a path of moonlight that he might climb in order to meet again the prisoner Ha-Nozri, the novel's Christ-figure. The text continues:

> Woland turned once more to the Master and said: 'Well, now you can finish your novel with a single phrase!'
> The Master seemed to have waited for this as he stood motionless and looked at the sitting Procurator, He folded his hands at his mouth and shouted so that the echoe leapt up and down the deserted treeless cliffs:
> 'You are free! You are free! He waits for you!'
> The mountains transformed the Master's voice into thunder, and the thunder destroyed the mountains. The accursed rocky walls collapsed, leaving only the mountaintop with the stone chair. On the black abyss that swallowed the walls there gleamed a vast city crowned with glittering idole above a garden grown to wild luxuriance during thousands of moons. The moonlit path so awaited by the Procurator stretched directly into his garden, and the first to run out on it was the sharp-eared dog.[48]

It is art that is here depicted as an emancipatory force, a force that is able to make material reality conform to the wishes of men and women (rather than to the fickle whims of market forces). Rushdie's digestion of Bulgakov's masterpiece involves both an appropria-tion of that basic affirmation of art's liberationary potential and a provisional rejection of the relative ease and automatic success with which that potential is seen to be fulfilled.

Instead, Rushdie acknowledges the difficulty of the struggle in which he is engaged. Sara Suleri, whose emphasis on *The Satanic Verses* as 'a deeply Islamic book' is entirely commendable, moves close to the crux of the matter when she remarks of the need to understand the novel in terms of its cultural background that '[h]ere, the crucial context of Islamic secularism requires close attention'.[49] For the attempt to create a new way of understanding that so profoundly problematic relation of the migrant to her or his cultural origins becomes simultaneously, for Rushdie, the attempt to establish a worthwhile and valid notion of Islamic

secularism. In an interview published in the German newspaper
Die Zeit, Rushdie says:

> What I am trying to make a case for is the development of a
> secular tradition within Islam similar to that which Judaism, for
> example, has developed. There are a lot of people who would
> call themselves secular Jews, who would say that Jewish cul-
> ture, Jewish history and Jewish tradition are very important to
> them but that they do not accept the theology.[50]

Where Rushdie sees hope for ideas such as his is in the
largely ignored heterogeneity of Islam. As early as 1981, Rushdie
was chastising V. S. Naipaul for the misleading picture he portrays in *Among the Believers* of a unified, homogenous 'Islamic
world'.[51] More recently he has pointed to Fouad Zakariya's
Laïcité ou Islamisme as an example of the modern *and modernis-
ing* currents of contemporary Islamic thought in which he has
tried to play a part.[52] The fact that Islamic groups in Saudi
Arabia took the opportunity, in the wake of the political furore
over *The Satanic Verses*, to announce a *jihad* or holy war on
literary and philosophical modernism is only one of the more
overt signs that what has happened to Rushdie since the pub-
lication of *The Satanic Verses* may have had little, in fact, to do
with the specific case of that one novel and, rather, been the
manifestation of a political conflict that is taking place within
Islamic culture itself.

When Fadia A. Faqir writes that '[m]ost of the sixty-six Arab
intellectuals blacklisted recently by a Saudi Islamic group who
announced the holy jihad on Modernism live either in London or
Paris', and ends by asking, 'Is exile the only answer to the
resurgence of Islam?',[53] he is perhaps illuminating the issue without quite grasping it fully. Rushdie and other migrants with
Islamic cultural origins have attempted, and are attempting, to
discover a new form of discourse, a new set of self-descriptive
terms, that might embody the fusion of an Islamic cultural inheritance with a doubt-ridden, modernist, demystifying consciousness. Exile (or migrancy) may well be as much a cause as an
effect of the bitter struggle which the *jihad* against modernism
indicates, and in which Rushdie and others have long been
engaged. The Anglo-Saxon 'Right' has, of course, like the Islamic
fundamentalists, been quick to recognise the danger of such a
struggle. 'Why do *you* think', asks Christopher Hitchens, 'that
Peregrine Worsthorne, Paul Johnson and Auberon Waugh are,

pro-tem, in favour of the mosque against secular, brown activists of the Rushdie type?'[54]

In conclusion, I want to look at how this particular struggle finds expression in *The Satanic Verses* as the longing to envisage the New. There are, essentially, two utopian conclusions to the novel. The first is the moment of religious epiphany, dreamt by Gibreel Farishta, in which the prophetess Ayesha finally converts Mirza Saeed Akhtar:

> He was a fortress with clanging gates. – He was drowning. – She was drowning, too. He saw the water fill her mouth, heard it begin to gurgle into her lungs. Then something within him refused that, made a different choice, and at the instant that his heart broke, he opened.
>
> His body split apart from his adam's-apple to his groin, so that she could reach deep within him, and now she was open, they all were, and at the moment of their opening the waters parted, and they walked to Mecca across the bed of the Arabian Sea. (*SV*, p. 507)

The conversion of Mirza Saeed takes a form similar to that of the torture of Muhammad in Dante's *Inferno*. He is cleft in two like Muhammad in a passage that serves to reaffirm Islamic faith rather than to attack it, thereby transforming, once again, a form of abuse into a symbol of affirmation. The parting of the Arabian Sea and the crossing to Mecca are a return to the pilgrims' spiritual homeland. The racism and sexism that the novel portrays are here dissolved in a singularly Islamic utopian vision to which the faithful have been led by a female prophet. Doubt is overwhelmed by the powers of religious belief; the temptations of secular consumerism are discarded in favour of submission to a God-sent authority. It is a vision, though, that exists only in the form of a dream or a film.

'The Parting of the Arabian Sea' is ultimately too reactionary a vision to be properly utopian. Implicit in *The Satanic Verses* is the suggestion that a true utopian yearning must do more than merely point nostalgically to the past, denying the onward rush of History in the manner of a Khomenei[55] or a Thatcher.[56] Instead, as we have already seen Ernst Bloch insist, it must 'carry on the existing facts toward their future potentiality of their otherness, of their better condition in an anticipatory way'. A renewal of religious piety would hardly offer migrants such as Rushdie a new means of comprehending their cultural formation. At the novel's conclusion, Saladin Chamcha (who is, by then, Salahuddin Chamchawala) sees through the false utopia that such a renewal would offer:

> He stood at the window of his childhood and looked out at the Arabian Sea. The moon was almost full; moonlight stretching from the rocks of Scandal Point out to the far horizon, created the illusion of a silver pathway, like a parting of the water's shining hair, like a road to miraculous lands. He shook his head; could no longer believe in fairy-tales. Childhood was over, and the view from this window was no more than an old and sentimental echo. To the devil with it! Let the bulldozers come. If the old refused to die, the new could not be born. (SV, pp. 546–7)

The echoes of Bulgakov's novel seem deliberate. But the path of moonlight must be rejected; easy answers that fail to take into account the complexities and contradictions of the present can no longer be trusted.

The Satanic Verses ends with the homecoming of Saladin Chamcha and his discovery that he is really Salahuddin Chamchawala. This is the novel's true utopian conclusion and its true spiritual homecoming. In his conclusion to *The Principle of Hope*, Ernst Bloch offers a description of the New in terms which would seem to validate the authenticity of the utopian longing in Rushdie's novel:

> *True genesis is not at the beginning but at the end*, and it starts to begin only when society and existence become radical, i.e. grasp their roots. But the root of history is the working, creating human being who reshapes and overhauls the given facts. Once he has grasped himself and established what is his, without expropriation and alienation, in real democracy, there arises in the world something which shines into the childhood of all and in which no one has yet been: *Heimat*.[57]

Bloch's reappropriation of the Nazi term 'Heimat' (homeland), with which to represent the basic utopian goal, is clearly comparable to the strategy of narrative reclamation that is at the heart of Rushdie's novel.[58] But it is the longing for that homeland itself – the homeland that is new; in which the distinction between self and other has begun to lose its sharpness, its capacity to govern thought – that *The Satanic Verses* so thoughtfully, so movingly expresses.

By pointing to the resettlement of Dorothy and her family in the Land of Oz, Rushdie identifies home (or 'Heimat') as that which we make anew; and that is why, at the end of *The Satanic Verses*, though Salahuddin has come home, he is not yet *home*. Rushdie's novel depicts no realisation of the New. Instead it remains faithful to Adorno's dictum that it is only 'the longing for the new' that art can plausibly offer.

What is left, and what represents that longing for the New that is the artistic New itself, is the continuing necessity of political struggle. Having returned to Bombay to see his father die, Salahuddin Chamchawala takes part in a demonstration organised by the Communist Party of India (Marxist). 'CPI (M) observers', we are told,

> reported an unbroken chain of men and women linking hands from top to bottom of the city, and Salahuddin, standing between Zeeny and Bhupen on Muhammad Ali Road, could not deny the power of the image. Many people in the chain were in tears. (*SV*, p. 541)

Later, Salahuddin discovers that the demonstration is to be almost completely ignored by the media: '"It's a Communist show,"' Zeeny tells him. '"So officially, it's a non-event"' (*SV*, p. 542). Here, in Bombay, it is the Communist Party that is demonised.

In his 'Theses on the Philosophy of History' Walter Benjamin writes, 'Like every generation that preceded us, we have been endowed with a *weak* Messianic power, a power to which the past has a claim. That claim cannot be settled cheaply.'[59] The fusion of an Islamic cultural heritage and a modern, socialist political vision does not come easily. In Rushdie's depiction there is a home to be found, but it is one for which we must be prepared to struggle, 'to turn insults into strengths', to envisage 'in an anticipatory way' that which we have learned does not exist. With neither a path of moonlight to follow nor a dry sea-bed on which to walk, the trek homeward can be hazardous. That *The Satanic Verses* should nonetheless insist that that journey is worth while, that no easier option can be trusted, is a sign of its profoundly radical and utopian political perspective. This is a perspective from which the legacy of a cultural past or the limitations of a postmodern present might seem less immutable. *The Satanic Verses* asks us to accept the transience of the present state of things, suggesting the possibility of a time and place in which existing truths might be swept away – in which we might accept

that 'the Orient' and 'the Occident' were man-made, not God-
given, and that the devil might not be quite so bad after all.
'And we', as Rilke wrote,

> who always think
>   of happiness *rising*
> would feel the emotion
>   that almost startles us
>   when a happy thing *falls*.[60]

Notes

1. Alasdair Gray, *Something Leather*, p. 247. Further references are to
   the same edition and will be marked in the main text, prefixed by
   the abbreviation *SL*.
2. Alison Lumsden, 'Innovation and Reaction in Alasdair Gray', p. 118.
3. Ibid.
4. Adorno, *Aesthetic Theory*, p. 192. Adorno also remains aware, however, of the affirmative character (to borrow Herbert Marcuse's
   helpful phrase) of such art. The distinction he draws between autonomous art and the culture industry is that the former, while complicit
   in social domination, can also be critical, thereby expressing an
   unresolved internal dialectic (already present in the false but necessary claim to autonomy) which is itself expressive of the irresolvable
   internal contradictions of the capitalist mode of production. The
   culture industry, for Adorno, is unable to accept conflict in any form.
5. Ibid., p. 322.
6. Adorno, 'Reconciliation under Duress', in Ernst Bloch et al. *Aesthetics
   and Politics*, p. 160.
7. Adorno and Horkheimer, *Dialectic of Enlightenment*, p. 144.
8. Lukács, 'What is Orthodox Marxism?', in his *History and Class
   Consciousness*, p. 13.
9. Adorno, *Aesthetic Theory*, p. 261.
10. Ibid., p. 196.
11. Louis Althusser, 'A Letter on Art in Reply to André Daspre', in his
    Essays on Ideology, pp. 174–5.
12. Lumsden, 'Innovation and Reaction', p. 123.
13. Salman Rushdie, 'Outside the Whale', in his *Imaginary Homelands*,
    p. 101.
14. Aijaz Ahmad, *In Theory*, p. 68. Further references will be to the same
    edition and will be cited in the main text, prefixed by the abbrevia-
    tion *IT*.
15. Salman Rushdie, 'The Location of *Brazil*', in his *Imaginary Home-
    lands*, pp. 124–5.

16. Salman Rushdie, *Shame*, p. 69; cited in Ahmad, *In Theory*, p. 133.

17. Rushdie, *Shame*, p. 28; cited in Ahmad, *In Theory*, p. 133.

18. Salman Rushdie, *Midnight's Children*, p. 10. Further references will be to the same edition and will be cited in the main text, prefixed by the abbreviation *MC*.

19. For a discussion of these elements of Rushdie's fiction see Timothy Brennan, *Salman Rushdie and the Third World: Myths of the Nation*, pp. 79–117.

20. Edward W. Said, in Lisa Appignanesi and Sara Maitland (eds), *The Rushdie File*, p. 176.

21. Edward Said, *Orientalism*, p. 21.

22. Ibid., p. 45.

23. See Lukács, *The Historical Novel*, pp. 19–63.

24. Sara Suleri, 'Contraband Histories: Salman Rushdie and the Embodiment of Blasphemy', p. 607.

25. Ibid.

26. Salman Rushdie, *The Wizard of Oz*, p. 10.

27. Salman Rushdie, *The Satanic Verses*, p. 10. Further references to the text are to the same edition and will be marked in the main text, prefixed by the abbreviation *SV*.

28. Zygmunt Bauman, 'The Fall of the Legislator', in *Postmodernism: A Reader*, ed. Thomas Docherty, p. 135.

29. Jean-François Lyotard, *The Differand*, p. xi.

30. Thomas Docherty, *Alterities*, p. 199.

31. Rushdie, *The Wizard of Oz*, p. 57.

32. Salman Rushdie, 'Is Nothing Sacred?', in his *Imaginary Homelands*, p. 422.

33. Salman Rushdie, 'Bonfire of the Certainties', in Appignanesi and Maitland, *The Rushdie File*, p. 28.

34. Rushdie, 'In Good Faith', in his *Imaginary Homelands*, p. 394.

35. Said, in Appignanesi and Maitland, *The Rushdie File*, p. 177.

36. Adorno, *Aesthetic Theory*, p. 47.

37. See, for example, Brennan, *Salman Rushdie*, pp. 143–66.

38. See Rushdie, 'In Good Faith', p. 400.

39. Pamela's name, as James Harrison suggests, is also a coded reference to Rushdie's first wife: Clarissa Luard. See Harrison, *Salman Rushdie*, pp. 6–7.

40. Malise Ruthven, *A Satanic Affair*, p. 25.

41. Ernst Bloch, 'Art and Utopia', in his *The Utopian Function of Art and Literature*, pp. 78–155.

42. Ibid., p. 104.

43. Ibid., p. 105.

44. Ibid.

45. Rushdie, 'Is Nothing Sacred?', p. 420.

46. Rushdie, 'Günter Grass', in his *Imaginary Homelands*, p. 273.

47. Rushdie, 'In Good Faith', p. 403.

48. Mikhail Bulgakov, *The Master and Margarita*, p. 387.
49. Suleri, 'Contraband Histories', p. 605.
50. Salman Rushdie, Interview in *Die Zeit*, p. 69. Translation by Andrea Heilmann.
51. Salman Rushdie, 'Naipaul among the Believers', in his *Imaginary Homelands*, pp. 373–5.
52. Salman Rushdie, 'One Thousand Days in a Balloon', in his *Imaginary Homelands*, p. 436.
53. Fadia A. Faqir, 'Islam and Literature', in Appignanesi and Maitland, *The Rushdie File*, p. 238.
54. Christopher Hitchens, 'Siding with Rushdie', in his *For the Sake of Argument*, p. 296.
55. See Rushdie, 'In God We Trust', in his *Imaginary Homelands*, pp. 383–4.
56. See Rushdie, 'Outside the Whale', p. 92.
57. Ernst Bloch, *The Principle of Hope*, Vol. 3, pp. 1375–6.
58. For Rushdie's own comments on the literary reappropriation of 'Heimat', see Salman Rushdie, 'Siegfried Lenz', in his *Imaginary Homelands*, pp. 285–7.
59. Walter Benjamin, 'Theses on the Philosophy of History', in his *Illuminations*, p. 254.
60. Rainer Maria Rilke, 'Tenth Elegy', in *Duino Elegies*, p. 94.

V Postmodern Inadequacies: Adorno contra Jameson

A conceptual understanding of postmodernism is, by the logic of a post-Adorno Western Marxism, inherently inadequate. The critique of conceptual reason that Adorno develops in *Dialectic of Enlightenment* (with Horkheimer) and later in *Negative Dialectics* must also be applied to his own conceptual construction of the culture industry, and to Fredric Jameson's lengthy discussions of 'the concept of the postmodern'.

This final chapter will re-examine some of the theoretical points first discussed in Chapter 1, focusing particularly on the extent to which the Marxist theoretical model of postmodernism proposed by Jameson might be revised in light of the preceding literary and theoretical analyses of Chapters 2–4. The logic of Jameson's position, at least in theoretical terms, suggests the impossibility of a critical postmodern culture; and yet, in contrast to Eagleton, Jameson has nonetheless stressed the necessity for Marxist critique to attempt to identify precisely such a moment in postmodernism. The inconsistencies into which these dual arguments have led Jameson will be sketched out briefly below, while the implications that the persistence of some form of critique in postmodern fiction might have for his theoretical model is taken as the basis for a reworking of that model. Since the preceding theoretical and literary-critical analyses have shown at work in postmodern fiction precisely the internal dialectic that Jameson, too, perceives in texts such as E. L. Doctorow's, but can never quite reconcile with his theoretical or conceptual understanding of the postmodern, this chapter will argue that such a reconciliation is unnecessary and that Jameson's continuing vexation with regard to the problem is rather the product of his inconsistent characterisation of individual texts' relation to a cultural sphere grasped in theoretical or conceptual terms.

In *Dialectic of Enlightenment*, Adorno and Horkheimer address the relation of Enlightenment's conceptual rationality to the historical extension of capitalist reification and rationalisation.[1] 'Just as the first categories', they write,

> represented the organised tribe and its power over the individual, so the whole logical order, dependency, connection, progression, and union of concepts is grounded in the corresponding conditions of social reality – that is, of the division of labor.[2]

What is being suggested here, then, is a form of reproduction, whereby conceptual reason cognitively reproduces some of the features of the capitalist mode of production. Adorno and Horkheimer claim of course, quite infamously, that the specific feature of capitalist production to be reproduced by Enlightenment rationality is that of *domination*. They do this by suggesting that instrumental reason, the 'means–ends rationality' of which Peter Bürger depicts the art of the avant-garde as so critical, has been taken as reason *per se*. The development of a concept allows for the absorption of a whole host of particulars into a general definition or category, thereby re-enacting, for Adorno and Horkheimer, the domination under monetary, exchange value of objects' intrinsic and heterogeneous use-values in the process of capitalist commodification.[3]

It is this that Adorno terms 'identity thinking', the suggestion that particulars can be held to be identical by the imposition of a general, abstract concept. In contrast to this, Adorno suggests that dialectical thinking must attempt to grasp the 'non-identical', that which escapes the identity, the homogenising domination, of the concept. As Fredric Jameson writes in *Late Marxism: Adorno, or, the Persistence of the Dialectic*:

> If the concept is grasped as 'the same', as what makes things the same as well as inscribing a sameness – a return of recognizable entities – on the psyche, then the struggle of thought (at least at a certain moment of its history) has to undermine that logic of recurrence and of sameness in order to break through to everything sameness excludes: I put it this way in order to be able to describe this last – the 'non-identical' – both in terms of otherness and of novelty.[4]

Only, for Adorno, the determinate negation of negative dialectics, through the simultaneous critique and application of conceptual thought, can give expression to that which the concept would

dominate. It is necessary, therefore, to bear in mind that whenever
Adorno would seem to have defined phenomena conceptually, as
he does the culture industry, there is already an implicit acknowledgement of guilty inadequacy. In other words, Adorno's thought
is predicated upon its very failure ever to grasp its object wholly,
a failure which it both laments and simultaneously acknowledges
as a critical force:

> If negative dialectics calls for the self-reflection of thinking, the
> tangible implication is that if thinking is to be true – if it is to
> be true today, in any case – it must also be a thinking against
> itself. If thought is not measured by the extremity that eludes
> the concept, it is from the outset in the nature of the musical
> accompaniment with which the SS liked to drown out the
> screams of its victims.[5]

Without this attempt to identify the non-identical, that which
'eludes the concept', thought becomes, for Adorno, a mere ideological tool of the marketplace. However, it would be equally
inaccurate to suggest that Adorno attempts to evade that fate
completely: 'No theory today', he writes, 'escapes the marketplace.'[6] Adorno is primarily interested, as is apparent from the
opening essay of Prisms, in the force of immanent critique – a
critique which operates, to a large extent, from within the boundaries and limitations of its object. In this way, Adorno hopes to
mimic in his thought what he interprets as the historical truthfulness (the 'truth-content') of modernist artworks (see above,
Chapter 1). As Jürgen Habermas writes, Adorno does not give
up entirely on Enlightenment thinking, but rather develops, in
the spirit of a performative contradiction, the critique of reason
from the critical, rational structures of Enlightenment thought
itself. This contradiction then becomes 'the organizational form
of indirect communication': 'Identity thinking turned against
itself becomes pressed into continual self-denial and allows the
wounds it inflicts on itself and its objects to be seen.'[7]

The attempt to grasp social or cultural phenomena conceptually
may also be seen as the attempt to grasp them in their totality. It is
here that that strand of postmodern, anti-Enlightenment thought
which is most obviously predicated on an aversion to the category
of totality – a position perhaps most easily recognisable in
Lyotard's 'war on totality' – must be distinguished from the
more ambivalent structures of Adorno's negative dialectics. For
although Adorno is clearly suspicious of the expression of dom-

ination which he associates with Enlightenment thinking – witness, for example, his famous inversion of Hegel: 'The whole is the
false' – he nonetheless refuses to abandon the notion of a totality.
Thus, Jameson points to the significance of the following passage
from *Negative Dialectics*:

> What is differentiated will appear divergent, dissonant, nega-
> tive just as long as consciousness is driven by its own formation
> towards unity; just as long as it measures what is not identical
> with itself against its own claim for totality. It is this which
> dialectics exhibits to consciousness as a contradiction.[8]

Here, argues Jameson, Adorno's dialectical thinking challenges us
to retain some necessary sense of totality as an acknowledgement
of the desire to grasp and to understand a whole, while also
suggesting

> that the drive towards totality (Lukács's *Totalitätsintention*) may
> have something illicit about it, expressing the idealism and the
> imperialism of the concept, which seeks voraciously to draw
> everything into its own field of domination and security.[9]

Both concept and totality must therefore be subjected to a rigorous
critique, while nonetheless remaining necessary and invaluable
analytic tools. Despite, then, exerting a clear influence on the
work of postmodern philosophers such as Lyotard,[10] this aspect
of Western Marxist thought, as it develops in the writings of
Adorno and is reinterpreted in Jameson's work, does not lead to
the writing of what the latter has characterised as the 'provisional,
fragmentary, self-consuming conceptual performances celebrated
by properly postmodern philosophy'.[11] The logic of Adorno's
position in *Negative Dialectics* does not sanction philosophical
free play. It does, however, suggest the need both to revise what
have hitherto been seen as Adorno's definitive critical judgements
on the culture industry, and to re-examine some of the inconsistencies of Jameson's analyses of postmodernism.

   Here, then, it is worth returning to one of the questions left
open at the conclusion of Chapter 1: namely, why does Jameson
insist on denying the historicity of the postmodern when he is
happy to identify some remnant of historical memory in certain
examples of postmodern culture (such as the novels of Doctorow)?
In part, of course, this question has already been answered:
Jameson is quite explicit that what he intends to delineate is

the contours of a postmodernism which is to be understood as a cultural dominant, a cultural situation to which specific texts (or 'cultural commodities') are a response (see above, Chapter 1). However, the discrepancies between the features of Jameson's 'concept of the postmodern' and the analyses he offers of various cultural texts have, as he recognises, interesting implications for the validity and adequacy of that conceptual construction. In 'The Existence of Italy', an essay whose title is an explicit allusion to Adorno and Horkheimer's critique of the culture industry, he acknowledges that there is a notable degree of incompatibility between his theoretical description of the postmodern and his interpretations of examples of postmodern culture. This leads him to the following speculations:

> Is this then to say that even within the extraordinary eclipse of historicity in the postmodern period some deeper memory of history still deeply stirs? Or does this persistence – nostalgia for that ultimate moment of historical time in which difference was still present – rather betoken the incompleteness of the post-modern process, the survival within it of remnants of the past, which have not yet, as in some unimaginable fully realized postmodernism, been dissolved without a trace?[12]

Significantly, Jameson seems here at some pains to reconcile his theoretical understanding of the postmodern with his analyses of specific cultural commodities. It is precisely this need to reconcile the two which seems to me both unneccessary and responsible for the most glaring inconsistencies of his account.

The difficulty that Jameson has in accepting that postmodern culture might be capable of adopting a critical stance in relation to late capitalism is a product of what he, following Adorno's critique of the culture industry, posits as the dissolution in postmodernism of the critical distance of the aesthetic to the socio-economic. This (as we saw in Chapter 1) is among the principal distinctions that Jameson draws between modernism and postmodernism; more-over, it seems to block off completely any possibility of the con-dition of postmodernity being subject to cultural critique:

> No theory of cultural politics current on the Left today has been able to do without one notion or another of a certain minimal aesthetic distance, of the possibility of the positioning of the cultural act outside the massive Being of capital, which then serves as an Archimedean point from which to assault this last.

What the burden of our preceding demonstration suggests, however, is that distance in general (including 'critical distance' in particular) has very precisely been abolished in the new space of postmodernism.[13]

It would appear from this characterisation that a critical postmodernism is, by definition, impossible. The loss of art's autonomy, outlined in Chapter 1, has also meant the dissolution of its critical distance from the socio-economic. This leaves the aesthetic sphere (and, it would seem, all contemporary cultural production) fully complicit with the economic forces of late capitalism. Yet, still Jameson insists on the critical potential of certain texts.

Discussing Adorno's denunciation of the culture industry, Andreas Huyssen points to the dangers which might result from the wholesale adoption of Adorno's critical perspective: 'I am not denying', he writes,

that the increasing commodification of culture and its effects *in* all cultural products are pervasive. What I would deny is the implied notion that function and use are totally determined by corporate intentions, and that exchange value has totally supplanted use value. The double danger of Adorno's theory is that the specificity of cultural products is wiped out and that the consumer is imagined in a state of passive regression.[14]

Jameson seems continually aware of these problems; his theory, after all, is an explicit response to the Frankfurt School's writings on the culture industry.[15] Nonetheless, he appears, time and again (and despite the frequent, perhaps repetitive, invocations of Doctorow), to hedge his bets, to prefer speculations on 'some as yet unimaginable' new form of political postmodernism to the identification of its present critical potential. As we have already seen, he is even willing to suggest that such a potential might betoken less the persistence of the cultural expression of dialectical conflict than the present incompleteness of the postmodern process itself. What, though, if this process, as Jameson describes it, can never be complete?

Huyssen takes something like this possibility as the basis for his critique of Adorno:

While Adorno recognized that there were limitations to the reification of human subjects through the culture industry which made resistance thinkable at the level of the subject, he never asked himself whether perhaps such limitations could be located in the mass cultural commodities themselves. Such limits do indeed become evident when one begins to analyze in detail the signifying strategies of specific cultural commodities and the mesh of gratification, displacement and production of desires which are invariably put in play in their production and consumption.[16]

What I would like to stress here is Huyssen's identification of the need to analyse *specific* cultural commodities. It is the particularity of the individual postmodern text when viewed in relation to the theoretical model of postmodernism that principally interests me. Moreover, it is perhaps here that the critical distance, whose necessity and absence Jameson notes in his discussion of the postmodern, might be situated.

'Ostensibly working on art works,' writes Adorno, 'the artist also works on art – proof again of the fact that art and works of art are not coterminous.'[17] The 'art' to which Adorno here refers can only be grasped conceptually, as an aeshetic sphere in which works of art are produced. The need to identify the non-identical in conceptual thought, which we have already seen Adorno stress in *Negative Dialectics*, might, then, be seen to suggest a similar requirement to identify those points of conflict between an 'art' or aeshetic sphere thought theoretically and specific works of art – that is to say, the identification of those features of individual texts which elude the domination of the cultural dominant. It is worth acknowledging that the work of art is itself engaged in a dialectical and thoroughly mediated relationship with the aesthetic or cultural sphere in which it is produced. The critical distance that modernist art had previously retained, but which has been renounced by the culture of postmodernity, might then be relocated in that same conflictual relation of the individual text to the cultural dominant of postmodernism. This would allow the force of Jameson's critique of postmodernism's ideological function to remain undiminished, while accounting for texts' retention of critical potential in a manner consistent with the critical theory of Western Marxism. We need not, therefore, speculate with Jameson on 'some as yet unimaginable new mode' of cultural representation; rather, we should analyse the extent to which texts such as *White Noise* or *The Satanic Verses* already offer both representation and critique of the complicity of that cultural realm to which they owe their production with the social exploitation and domination that they take as their subject. This is a complicity in which the individual text of course shares, but with which it cannot wholly be identified.

Again, it is possible to see in Jameson's writings the suggestion of a similar method of recuperation – for example, in his discussions of what he calls Doctorow's 'homeopathic' treatment of postmodernism. In *Late Marxism* he even goes as far as to address directly the distinction Adorno draws between art and artworks, claiming that what is implicit in Adorno's formulation is the self-consciousness of art's ideological function:

> the sheer guilt of Art itself in a class society, art as luxury or class privilege, a ground bass that resonates throughout all of Adorno's aesthetic reflections without a break, even where its vibration has become a virtual second nature in our sensorium, so that from time to time we no longer hear it consciously. This culpability irreparably associated with all artistic activity is, then, the deeper motive for the radical separation, in Adorno, between Art in general and the individual works: for what these last do, what they 'work on' in the artistic process, is to engage this universal sense of guilt, to address it with lacerating acuity, to bring it to consciousness in the form of an unresolvable contradiction. The individual works of art can never resolve that contradiction, but they can recover a certain authenticity by including it as content and raw material, as what the individual work of art must always confront anew, in all its virulence.[18]

If postmodernism, as the cultural logic of late capitalism, cannot be held to maintain a critical distance from the social and economic formations of the latter, a contemporary critical distance of the aesthetic can perhaps only be situated between the individual postmodern text and the cultural condition of postmodernity. The interpenetration of the economic and the aesthetic in postmodernity means that when an individual text 'works on' the situation of art, it is working on the situation of late capitalism too.

Jay Bernstein argues that it was by virtue of its mutilation, by its separation from ethics (religion) and truth (science), that the art of modernity was able to express a 'second-order truth' about the alienation both of itself and of those other, newly autonomous spheres:

> Because only art 'suffers' its alienation, because art discovers its autonomous vocation to be unstable and incapable of being sustained, because art must continually conceive of its auton-

omy as a burden it must both embrace and escape from, in all this art comes to speak the truth – in a 'language' that is not that of truth-only cognition – about the fate of truth and art in modernity. Art's exclusion from first-order cognition and moral judgement is, then, a condition of its ability to register (in a speaking silence) a second-order truth about first-order truth.[19]

For the culture of postmodernity, though, alienation is a thing of the past, perhaps to be invoked nostalgically by images of Parisian cafés and a painting by Edvard Munch. The aesthetic need no longer mourn its historical mutilation, since the wholesome state of its youth has been restored with a little cosmetic surgery. Perhaps, though, those artworks which offer critical reflection on what Jameson calls the cultural dominant of postmodernism, and what Lyotard refers to as the contemporary, eclectic realism of money, can express a similar historical truth-content, reflecting a critical self-consciousness grasped only in the nick of time, in the final instance, in wilful defiance of the condition of postmodernity – as if Hansel and Gretel were to insist that, although gingerbread houses are all very well and good, this particular one at this particular time just isn't for them.

Notes

1. We can see, therefore, the continuity of this strand of Western Marxist critique from Lukács's *History and Class Consciousness*, where he asserts: 'Modern critical philosophy springs from the reified structure of consciousness' (pp. 110–11).
2. Adorno and Horkheimer, *Dialectic of Enlightenment*, p. 21.
3. For a lengthier and more thorough discussion of this aspect of Adorno's thought, see Fredric Jameson, *Late Marxism*, pp. 22–4.
4. Ibid., p. 17.
5. Adorno, *Negative Dialectics*, p. 365.
6. Ibid, p. 4.
7. Habermas, *The Philosophical Discourse of Modernity*, pp. 185–6.
8. This translation, which I found more fluent than the standard one by E. B. Ashton, is Jameson's, to be found in *Late Marxism*, p. 26; a less attractive version is in Adorno's *Negative Dialectics*, pp. 5–6.
9. Jameson, *Late Marxism*, p. 26.
10. For a discussion of the indebtedness of Lyotard to the Frankfurt School's Critical Theory, see Thomas Docherty, 'Postmodernism: An Introduction', in Thomas Docherty (ed.), *Postmodernism: A Reader*, pp. 5–14.

11. Ibid, p. 27.
12. Fredric Jameson, 'The Existence of Italy', in his *Signatures of the Visible*, p. 229.
13. Jameson, *Postmodernism*, p. 48.
14. Huyssen, *After the Great Divide*, p. 22.
15. Note, in this respect, the continuity of Jameson's thought from the essay 'Reification and Utopia in Mass Culture' (1979) to the book-length study *Postmodernism* (1991). See also Douglas Kellner, 'Jameson, Marxism, and Postmodernism', in Douglas Kellner (ed.), *Postmodernism/Jameson/Critique*, pp. 1–42.
16. Huyssen, p. 28.
17. Adorno, *Aesthetic Theory*, p. 261.
18. Jameson, *Late Marxism*, p. 130.
19. Bernstein, *The Fate of Art*, p. 5.

Bibliography

Adorno, T. W. (1967), *Prisms*, trans. Samuel and Shierry Weber, London: Spearman.

Adorno, T. W. (1984), *Aesthetic Theory*, ed. Gretel Adorno and Rolf Tiedemann, trans. C. Lenhardt, London: Routledge & Kegan Paul.

Adorno, T. W. (1987), *Philosophy of Modern Music*, trans. Anne G. Mitchell and Wesley V. Blomster, London: Sheed & Ward.

Adorno, T. W. (1988), 'The Aging of the New Music', *Telos*, 77, 95–116.

Adorno, T. W. (1990), *Negative Dialectics*, trans. E. B. Ashton, London: Routledge.

Adorno, T. W. (1991), *In Search of Wagner*, trans. Rodney Livingstone, London: Verso.

Adorno, T. W. (1991), *Notes to Literature*, Vol. 1, ed. Rolf Tiedemann, trans. Shierry Weber Nicholsen, New York: Columbia University Press.

Adorno, T. W. (1992), *The Culture Industry: Selected Essays*, ed. J. M. Bernstein, London: Routledge.

Adorno, T. W. (1992), *Notes to Literature*, Vol. 2, trans. Shierry Weber Nicholsen, New York: Columbia University Press.

Adorno, T. W. (1992), *Quasi una Fantasia*, trans. Rodney Livingstone, London: Verso.

Adorno, T. W. and M. Horkheimer (1992), *Dialectic of Enlightenment*, trans. John Cumming, London: Verso.

Ahmad, Aijaz (1992), *In Theory: Classes, Nations, Literatures*, London: Verso.

Ali, Tariq (1991), *The Nehrus and the Gandhis: An Indian Dynasty*, 2nd edn, London: Picador.

Ali, Tariq and Howard Brenton (1989), *Iranian Nights*, London: Hern.

Alter, Robert (1984), *Motives for Fiction*, London: Harvard University Press.

Althusser, Louis (1993), *Essays on Ideology*, London: Verso.

Amis, Martin (1991), *Time's Arrow*, London: Cape.

Appignanesi, Lisa and Sara Maitland (eds) (1989), *The Rushdie File*, London: Fourth Estate.

Aravamudan, Srinivas (1989), '"'Being God's Postman is no Fun, Yaar"': Salman Rushdie's *The Satanic Verses*', *Diacritics: A Review of Contemporary Criticism*, 19:2, 3–20.

Arendt, Hannah (1958), *The Origins of Totalitarianism*, trans. Therese Pol, 2nd edn, London: Allen & Unwin.

Auerbach, Erich (1974), *Mimesis: The Representation of Reality in Western Literature*, trans. Willard R. Trask, New Jersey: Princeton University Press.

Baldwin, James (1968), 'Many Thousands Gone', in his *Notes of a Native Son*, New York: Bantam, pp. 18–36.

Barth, John (1980), 'The Literature of Replenishment: Postmodernist Fiction', *Atlantic Monthly*, 245:1, 65–71.

Barth, John (1990), 'The Literature of Exhaustion', in Malcolm Bradbury (ed.), *The Novel Today*, London: Fontana, pp. 71–85.

Baudrillard, Jean (1988), *Selected Writings*, ed. Mark Poster, Cambridge: Polity.

Bawer, Bruce (1985), 'Don DeLillo's America', *The New Criterion*, 3:8, 34–42.

Beddow, Michael (1994), *Thomas Mann: 'Doctor Faustus'*, Cambridge: Cambridge University Press.

Benjamin, Andrew (ed.) (1989), *The Problems of Modernity: Adorno and Benjamin*, London: Routledge.

Benjamin, Walter (1969), *Illuminations*, ed. Hannah Arendt, trans. Harry Zohn, New York: Schocken.

Berman, Marshall (1982), *All that Is Solid Melts into Air*, London: Verso.

Bernstein, J. M. (1984), *The Philosophy of the Novel: Lukács, Marxism and the Dialectics of Form*, Brighton: Harvester.

Bernstein, J. M. (1993), *The Fate of Art: Aesthetic Alienation from Kant to Derrida and Adorno*, Cambridge: Polity.

Bhabha, Homi K. (1994), *The Location of Culture*, London: Routledge.

Bloch, Ernst (1986), *The Principle of Hope*, Vol. 3, trans. Neville Plaice, Stephen Plaice and Paul Knight, Oxford: Blackwell.

Bloch, Ernst (1989), *The Utopian Function of Art and Literature: Selected Essays*, trans. Jack Zipes and Frank Mecklenburg, London: MIT.

Bloch, Ernst et al. (1990), *Aesthetics and Politics*, London: Verso.

Booker, M. Keith (1990), 'Beauty and the Beast: Dualism as Despotism in the Fiction of Salman Rushdie', *ELH*, 57, 977–97.

Booth, Wayne C. (1987), *The Rhetoric of Fiction*, 2nd edn, Harmondsworth: Peregrine.

Brennan, Timothy (1989), *Salman Rushdie and the Third World: Myths of the Nation*, London: Macmillan.

Broch, Hermann (1977), *The Death of Virgil*, trans. Jean Starr Untermeyer, London: Routledge.

Brodhead, Richard H. (ed.) (1983), *Faulkner: New Perspectives*, New Jersey: Prentice-Hall.

Bryant, John (1986), 'Allegory and Breakdown in *The Confidence-Man*: Melville's Comedy of Doubt', *Philological Quarterly*, 65, 113–30.

Buck-Morss, Susan (1977), *The Origin of Negative Dialectics*, Sussex: Harvester.

Bulgakov, Mikhail (1989), *The Master and Margarita*, trans. Mirra Ginsburg, London: Picador.

Bürger, Peter (1984), *Theory of the Avant-Garde*, trans. M. Shaw, Manchester: Manchester University Press.

Bürger, Peter (1992), *The Decline of the New*, trans. Nicholas Walker, Cambridge: Polity.

Callinicos, Alex (1990), *Against Postmodernism*, London: Macmillan.

Canetti, Elias (1981), *Crowds and Power*, trans. Carol Stewart, Harmondsworth: Penguin.

Carey, John (1992), *The Intellectuals and the Masses: Pride and Prejudice among the Literary Intelligentsia, 1880–1939*, London: Faber.

Carnegy, Patrick (1973), *Faust as Musician: A Study of Thomas Mann's Novel 'Doctor Faustus'*, London: Chatto & Windus.

Celan, Paul (1986), 'Engführung', in his *Gesammelte Werke*, ed. Beda Allemann and Stefan Reichert, Vol. 1, Frankfurt: Suhrkamp, pp. 197–204.

Celan, Paul (1988), *Poems of Paul Celan*, ed. and trans. Michael Hamburger, London: Anvil.

Close, Anthony (1990), 'The Empirical Author: Salman Rushdie's *The Satanic Verses*', *Philosophy and Literature*, 14, 248–67.

Cornwell, Neil (1990), *The Literary Fantastic: From Gothic to Postmodernism*, London: Harvester Wheatsheaf.

DeLillo, Don (1986), *White Noise*, London: Picador.

DeLillo, Don (1987), *The Names*, London: Picador.

DeLillo, Don (1989), *Libra*, Harmondsworth: Penguin.

DeLillo, Don (1991), *Americana*, Harmondsworth: Penguin.

DeLillo, Don (1991), *Ratner's Star*, London: Vintage.

DeLillo, Don (1992), *Great Jones Street*, London: Picador.

DeLillo, Don (1992), *Mao II*, London: Vintage.

DeLillo, Don (1992), *Running Dog*, London: Picador.

DeLillo, Don (1993), 'The Art of Fiction CXXXV', *The Paris Review*, 128, 275–306.

DeLillo, Don (1998), *Underworld*, London: Picador.

Docherty, Thomas (1983), *Reading (Absent) Character: Towards a Theory of Characterization in Fiction*, Oxford: Oxford University Press.

Docherty, Thomas (ed.) (1993), *Postmodernism: A Reader*, Hemel Hempstead: Harvester.

Docherty, Thomas (1996), *After Theory*, Edinburgh: Edinburgh University Press.

Docherty, Thomas (1996), *Alterities: Criticism, History, Representation*, Oxford: Oxford University Press.

Dos Passos, John (1966), *USA*, Harmondsworth: Penguin.

Eagleton, Terry (1976), *Marxism and Literary Criticism*, London: Methuen.

Eagleton, Terry (1986), 'Capitalism, Modernism and Postmodernism', in his *Against the Grain*, London: Verso, pp. 131–47.

Eagleton, Terry (1994), *The Ideology of the Aesthetic*, Oxford: Blackwell.

Eagleton, Terry (1996), *The Illusions of Postmodernism*, Oxford: Blackwell.

Eco, Umberto (1994), *Reflections on 'The Name of the Rose'*, trans. William Weaver, London: Minerva.

Ellison, Ralph (1972), *Shadow and Act*, New York: Vintage.

Ellison, Ralph (1989), *Invisible Man*, Harmondsworth: Penguin.

Fanon, Frantz (1973), *The Wretched of the Earth*, trans. Constance Farrington, Harmondsworth: Penguin.

Faulkner, William (1985), *The Sound and the Fury*, Harmondsworth: Penguin.

Ford, Henry (1923), *My Life and Work*, London: Heinemann.

Foster, Hal (ed.) (1983), *Postmodern Culture*, London: Pluto.

Furst, Lilian R. (ed.) (1992), *Realism*, London: Longman.

Gennette, Gérard (1980), *Narrative Discourse*, trans. Jane E. Lewin, Oxford: Blackwell.

Grass, Günter (1981), *The Meeting at Telgte*, trans. Ralph Manheim, London: Secker & Warburg.

Grass, Günter (1989), *The Tin Drum*, trans. Ralph Manheim, London: Picador.

Gray, Alasdair (1991), *Something Leather*, London: Picador.

Habermas, Jürgen (1992), *The Philosophical Discourse of Modernity: Twelve Lectures*, trans. Frederick Lawrence, Cambridge: Polity.

Haffenden, John (1986), *Novelists in Interview*, London: Methuen.

Harrison, James (1992), *Salman Rushdie*, New York: Twayne.

Harvey, David (1990), *The Condition of Postmodernity: An Enquiry into the Origins of Cultural Change*, Oxford: Blackwell.

Hawking, Stephen W. (1990), *A Brief History of Time: From the Big Bang to Black Holes*, London: Bantam.

Hennessey, Val (1990), 'Martin Amis', in V. Hennessey, *A Little Light Friction*, London: Futura, pp. 229–35.

Hitchens, Christopher (1994), *For the Sake of Argument: Essays and Minority Reports*, London: Verso.

Holton, Robert (1994), *Jarring Witnesses: Modern Fiction and the Representation of History*, London: Harvester.

Howe, Irving (1963), 'Black Boys and Native Sons', accessible online at www.english.upenn.edu/~afilreis/50s/howe-blackboys.html

Hutcheon, Linda (1989), *A Poetics of Postmodernism: History, Theory, Fiction*, London: Routledge.

Hutcheon, Linda (1989), *The Politics of Postmodernism*, London: Routledge.

Huyssen, Andreas (1988), *After the Great Divide: Modernism, Mass Culture, Postmodernism*, London: Macmillan.

Jameson, Fredric (1974), *Marxism and Form: Twentieth-Century Dialectical Theories of Literature*, New Jersey: Princeton University Press.

Jameson, Fredric (1984), 'Review of *The Names* and *Richard A.*', *The Minesota Review*, 22, 116–22.

Jameson, Fredric (1988), '*History and Class Consciousness* as an "Unfinished Project"', *Rethinking Marxism*, 1:1, 49–72.

Jameson, Fredric (1988), 'The Ideology of the Text', in his *The Ideologies of Theory: Essays 1971–1986*, Vol. 1, London: Routledge, pp. 17–71.

Jameson, Fredric (1988), 'The Politics of Theory: Ideological Positions in the Postmodernism Debate', in his *The Ideologies of Theory: Essays 1971–1986*, Vol. 2, London: Routledge, pp. 103–13.

Jameson, Fredric (1989), *The Political Unconscious: Narrative as a Socially Symbolic Act*, London: Routledge.

Jameson, Fredric (1990), *Late Marxism: Adorno, or, the Persistence of the Dialectic*, London: Verso.

Jameson, Fredric (1992), *Postmodernism, or, the Cultural Logic of Late Capitalism*, London: Verso.

Jameson, Fredric (1992), *Signatures of the Visible*, London: Routledge.

Jameson, Fredric (1994), *The Seeds of Time*, New York: Columbia University Press.

Kant, Immanuel (1992), *The Critique of Judgement*, trans. James Creed Meredith, Oxford: Oxford University Press.

Kaplan, E. A. (ed) (1988), *Postmodernism and its Discontents*, London: Verso.

Karl, Frederick R. (1989), *William Faulkner: American Writer*, New York: Weidenfeld & Nicolson.

Kazin, Alfred (1988), 'Dos Passos and the Lost Generation', in Barry Maine (ed.), *Dos Passos: The Critical Heritage*, London: Routledge, pp. 223–35.

Keating, Peter (1991), *The Haunted Study: A Social History of the English Novel, 1875–1914*, London: Fontana.

Keesey, Douglas (1993), *Don DeLillo*, New York: Twayne.

Kellner, Douglas (ed.) (1989), *Postmodernism/Jameson/Critique*, Washington: Maisonneuve Press.

Kermode, Frank (1991), 'In Reverse', *London Review of Books*, 12 September, p. 11.

King, Noel (1991), 'Reading *White Noise*: Floating Remarks', *Critical Quarterly*, 33, 66–83.

Kundera, Milan (1995), *Testaments Betrayed*, trans. Linda Asher, London: Faber.

LeClair, Tom (1982), 'An Interview with Don DeLillo', *Contemporary Literature*, 23, 19–31.

LeClair, Tom (1987), *In the Loop: Don DeLillo and the Systems Novel*, Urbana: University of Illinois Press.

Lee, Alison (1989), *Realism and Power: Postmodern British Fiction*, London: Routledge.

Lentricchia, Frank (ed.) (1991), *Introducing Don DeLillo*, London: Duke University Press.

Lentricchia, Frank (ed.) (1991), *New Essays on 'White Noise'*, Cambridge: Cambridge University Press.

Levi, Primo (1987), *If This Is a Man* and *The Truce*, trans. Stuart Woolf, London: Abacus.

Levi, Primo (1989), *The Drowned and the Saved*, trans. Raymond Rosenthal, London: Abacus.

Lifton, Robert Jay (1971), *Death in Life: The Survivors of Hiroshima*, Harmondsworth: Penguin.

Lifton, Robert Jay (1987), *The Nazi Doctors: Medical Killing and the Psychology of Genocide*, London: Papermac.

Lodge, David (1990), *After Bakhtin: Essays on Fiction and Criticism*, London: Routledge.

Lovell, Terry (1987), *Consuming Fiction*, London: Verso.

Ludington, Townsend (ed.) (1974), *The Fourteenth Chronicle: Letters and Diaries of John Dos Passos*, London: Deutsch.

Lukács, Georg (1962), *The Historical Novel*, trans. Hannah and Stanley Mitchell, London: Merlin.

Lukács, Georg (1972), *The Meaning of Contemporary Realism*, trans. John and Necke Mander, London: Merlin.

Lukács, Georg (1979), *Essays on Thomas Mann*, trans. Stanley Mitchell, London: Merlin.

Lukács, Georg (1988), *The Theory of the Novel: A Historico-Philosophical Essay on the Forms of Great Epic Literature*, trans. Anna Bostock, London: Merlin.

Lukács, Georg (1990), *History and Class Consciousness: Studies in Marxist Dialectics*, trans. Rodney Livingstone, London: Merlin Press.

Lumsden, Alison (1993), 'Innovation and Reaction in Alasdair Gray', in Gavin Wallace and Randall Stevenson (eds), *The Scottish Novel since the Seventies*, Edinburgh: Edinburgh University Press, pp. 115–26.

Lyotard, Jean-François (1984), *The Postmodern Condition: A Report on Knowledge*, trans. Geoff Bennington and Brian Massumi, Manchester: Manchester University Press.

Lyotard, Jean-François (1988), *The Differand: Phrases in Dispute*, trans. Georges Van Den Abbeele, Mineapolis: University of Minnesota Press.

Lyotard, Jean-François (1991), *The Lyotard Reader*, ed. Andrew Benjamin, Oxford: Blackwell.

Lyotard, Jean-François (1992), *The Postmodern Explained to Children: Correspondence 1982–1985*, trans. Julian Pefanis and Morgan Thomas, London: Turnaround.

Lyotard, Jean-François (1994), *Lessons on the Analytic of the Sublime*, trans. Elizabeth Rottenberg, California: Stanford University Press.

McHale, Brian (1989), *Postmodernist Fiction*, London: Routledge.

McHale, Brian (1992), *Constructing Postmodernism*, London: Routledge.

McHale, Brian (1992), 'Postmodernism, or the Anxiety of Master Narratives', *Diacritics*, 22:1, 17–33.

Mann, Thomas (1968), *Doctor Faustus*, trans. H. T. Lowe Porter, Harmondsworth: Penguin.

Mann, Thomas (1968), *The Genesis of a Novel*, London: Secker & Warburg.

Marcuse, Herbert (1988), 'The Affirmative Character of Culture', in his *Negations: Essays in Critical Theory,* trans. Jeremy J. Shapiro, London: Free Association Books, pp. 88–133.

Marcuse, Herbert (1991), *One-Dimensional Man: Studies in the Ideology of Advanced Industrial Society,* 2nd edn, London: Routledge.

Marx, Karl (1990), *Capital,* Vol. 1, trans. Ben Fowkes, Harmondsworth: Penguin.

Marx, Karl (1992), *Early Writings,* trans. Rodney Livingstone and Gregor Benton, Harmondsworth: Penguin.

Marx, Karl and Friedrich Engels (1985), *The Communist Manifesto,* trans. Samuel Moore, Harmondsworth: Penguin.

Mattessich, Stefan (1997), 'Telluric Texts, Implicate Spaces', *Postmodern Culture,* accessible online at http: //jefferson.village.virginia.edu/pmc/ text-only/issue.997/review-5.997

Menand, Louis (1997), 'Entropology', *The New York Review of Books,* 12 June, accessible online at www.nybooks.com/nyrev/WWWarch display.cgi?19970612022R

Morris, Matthew J. (1989), 'Murdering Words: Language in Action in Don DeLillo's *The Names', Contemporary Literature,* 30, 113–27.

Morrison, Toni (1988), *Beloved,* London: Picador.

Morrison, Toni (1992), *Playing in the Dark: Whiteness and the Literary Imagination,* London: Picador.

Morrison, Toni (1993), 'The Art of Fiction CXXXIV', *The Paris Review,* 128, 83–125.

Mulhern, Francis (ed.) (1992), *Contemporary Marxist Literary Criticism,* London: Longman.

Ozick, Cynthia (1994), *What Henry James Knew,* London: Vintage.

Pynchon, Thomas (1975), *Gravity's Rainbow,* London: Picador.

Pynchon, Thomas (1997), *Mason & Dixon,* London: Cape.

Rilke, Rainer Maria (1978), *Duino Elegies,* trans. David Young, London: Norton.

Rorty, Richard (1989), 'The Barber of Kasbeam: Nabokov on Cruelty', in his *Contingency, Irony, and Solidarity,* Cambridge: Cambridge University Press, pp. 141–68.

Rushdie, Salman (1982), *Midnight's Children,* London: Picador.

Rushdie, Salman (1984), *Shame,* London: Picador.

Rushdie, Salman (1988), *The Satanic Verses,* London: Viking.

Rushdie, Salman (1991), *Haroun and the Sea of Stories,* London: Granta.

Rushdie, Salman (1992), *Imaginary Homelands: Essays & Criticism, 1981– 1991,* London: Granta.

Rushdie, Salman (1992), *The Wizard of Oz,* London: BFI Publishing.

Rushdie, Salman (1992), Interview in *Die Zeit,* 11–16 March, p. 69.

Ruthven, Malise (1990), *A Satanic Affair: Salman Rushdie and the Rage of Islam,* London: Chatto & Windus.

Said, Edward W. (1991), *Orientalism: Western Conceptions of the Orient,* Harmondsworth: Penguin.

Said, Edward W. (1994), *Culture and Imperialism*, London: Vintage.

Sartre, Jean-Paul (1962), *Literary and Philosophical Essays*, trans. Annette Michelson, New York: Collier.

Scholes, Robert (1980), *Fabulation and Metafiction*, London: University of Illinois Press.

Sturrock, John (ed.) (1996), *The Oxford Guide to Contemporary Writing*, Oxford: Oxford University Press.

Suleri, Sara (1989), 'Contraband Histories: Salman Rushdie and the Embodiment of Blasphemy', *The Yale Review*, 78, 604–24.

Turner, Jenny (1997), 'When the Sandwich Was still a New Invention', *London Review of Books*, 17 July, pp. 23–5.

Vidal, Gore (1993), *Live from Galgotha*, London: Abacus.

Vonnegut, Kurt (1970), *Slaughterhouse Five*, London: Cape.

Waugh, Patricia (1984), *Metafiction: The Theory and Practice of Self-Conscious Fiction*, London: Methuen.

Waugh, Patricia (1992), *Practising Postmodernism/Reading Modernism*, London: Edward Arnold.

Wilcox, Leonard (1991), 'Baudrillard, DeLillo's *White Noise*, and the End of Heroic Narrative', *Contemporary Literature*, 32, 346–65.

Wilde, Alan (1981), *Horizons of Assent: Modernism, Post-modernism and the Ironic Imagination*, London: Johns Hopkins University Press.

Williams, Raymond (1977), *Marxism and Literature*, Oxford: Oxford University Press.

Wood, James (1991), 'Slouching towards Auschwitz to be Born again', *Guardian*, 'Review Section', 19 September, p. 9.

Wright, Richard (1972), *Native Son*, Harmondsworth: Penguin.

Zakariya, Fouad (1991), *Laiceté on Islamisme: les Arabes à l'heure du choix*, Paris: Ed. la Découverte.

Zuidervaart, Lambert (1991), *Adorno's Aesthetic Theory: The Redemption of Illusion*, London: MIT.

Index